RIVER CRUISING
IN EUROPE

BY DOUGLAS WARD
THE WORLD'S FOREMOST AUTHORITY ON CRUISING

◉ Walking Eye App

Your Berlitz River Cruising in Europe guide now includes a free Insight Guides app and eBook of the book, all included for the same great price as before. They are available to download from the free Walking Eye container app in the App Store and Google Play. Simply download the Walking Eye container app to access the eBook and app.

Multiple eBooks & apps available

Now that you've bought this book you can download the accompanying app and eBook for free. Inside the Walking Eye container app, you'll also find the whole range of other Insight Guides destination apps and eBooks, all available for purchase.

Events & activities

Free access to information on a range of local guided tours, sightseeing activities and local events in any destination, with the option to book.

Berlitz River Cruising in Europe app

The app has been designed to give you quick and easy access to insightful ship reviews. The app search function makes it easy to find out which ships are best for you. You will be able to highlight your favourite riverships for future reference, and share with friends and family.

Rivership descriptions

The app also includes descriptions of the facilities and cruise experience on every one of the 310 riverships featured.

How to Download The Walking Eye

Available on purchase of this guide only.
1. Visit our website: www.insightguides.com/walkingeye
2. Download the Walking Eye container app to your smartphone (this will give you access to both the destination app and the eBook)
3. Select the scanning module in the Walking Eye container app
4. Scan the QR code on this page – you will be asked to enter a verification word from the book as proof of purchase
5. Download your free destination app* and eBook for travel and rivership information on the go

* Other destination apps and eBooks are available for purchase separately or are free with the purchase of the Insight Guide book

TABLE OF CONTENTS

Barge Cruising

Rivership and their Ratings

Maps

FROM THE AUTHOR

Would you like to tour Europe in comfort, delivered from A to B with no need to change hotels every night, with your meals cooked for you and with fabulous scenery to enjoy as you go along? Take a river cruise. River cruising in Europe is all about visiting destinations and it is very different from cruising aboard large ocean-going cruise ships, where passengers can number in the thousands, and embarking, disembarking and security queues can be an exercise in frustration. On a river cruise, the maximum number of passengers is around 200, so any visits are done in much smaller groups, or individually, and all on a very personal scale.

Rivers were here eons before roads were created and have always been vital to human settlement and survival. Among the many of Europe's great cities that grew up on the banks of the river are London (Thames), Paris (Seine), Cologne (Rhine), Frankfurt (Main), Prague (Elbe/Vltava), Budapest (Danube) and Vienna (Danube). Rivers have long been used as lifelines by which nations conduct commerce and organise the transportation of goods. They are used for drainage, irrigation, water supply and the production of hydroelectric power. But they are also sources of adventure, discovery and romance.

River cruising in Europe has grown dramatically in recent years. In 2005 there were just over 22,000 beds on offer on cruises of this type. By 2010 that number had grown to 28,000, and in 2015 there were over 43,000 beds. Today, around one million people each year (and growing) choose to cruise on riverships (note they are always referred to as 'rivership', rather than 'boat' or plain 'ship'). These vary from the equivalent of a waterbus to what some, amusingly, like to think of as *eau couture*. The hassles of ordinary travel are almost eliminated in one pleasant package, with someone else doing all the cooking and driving. Don't worry about getting motion sickness, either – it's all smooth sailing. Budgeting is easy, too. Because you pay in advance, you know what you will spend on your holiday, without any hidden surprises. It's all quite low-key – there are no casinos, bingo or knobbly knees contests, or other potentially irritating parlour games on board (unlike on an ocean cruise), and any organised events tend to be geared towards a more cultural crowd. And, when your rivership docks, you simply walk off the vessel. You never have to take a tender to go ashore, because most riverships dock close to the centre of a city or town.

A European river cruise is like an upscale bus tour, only far superior and more comfortable, because,

unlike bus tours, where you stay in a different hotel each night, you only have to unpack once. In almost all cases, you will have a river view from your cabin, too, plus you will dine in familiar surroundings for most meals.

It's worth bearing in mind, of course, that rivers are natural entities, and Mother Nature can be unpredictable. Variable conditions mean that nothing – such as the depth, the current or flow of water – is fixed. River cruise operators and passengers alike must, therefore, be flexible in their approach to this type of holiday. But assuming all goes according to plan, a river cruise can be relaxing, educational, inspirational and sociable. The biggest difficulty is deciding which river cruise to take.

I have been travelling the world's oceans, rivers and inland waterways for over 50 years and have endeavoured to appraise some 300 riverships operating in the heart of Europe. I have concentrated on the established river cruise companies, almost all of whose cruises can be purchased through specialist cruise booking agents and tour operators. I also cover the destination highlights visited along Europe's waterways. Also, there is my breakdown of 310 European riverships, with brief summaries for each, plus our Berlitz rating based on amenities, cuisine, service and the overall experience.

Note that a general image has been used when an actual picture of the ship reviewed is not available.

Douglas Ward

Why take a river cruise?

Here, we describe European river cruising and answer some questions that first-timers often ask before taking the metaphoric plunge.

The biggest challenge when considering a river cruise is deciding which river interests you the most, but all river cruises should be welcoming, scenic, comfortable, effortless, small-scale, inclusive, unhurried, organised and memorable.

CHOOSING A RIVER

Rivers/regions and highlights (in alphabetical order)

Bordeaux region (Gironde, Garonne and Dordogne) – for wine and food
Danube – for Budapest, Vienna and the Iron Gate
Douro – for riverbank vineyards and port wine
Elbe – for Prague, Meissen and mountain scenery
Mosel – for quiet and relaxation
Po – for Venice, Padua and Bologna
Rhine – for Cologne, Heidelberg, castles, the Black Forest and the Lorelei
Rhône/Saône – for Lyon and Provence
Seine – for Paris and Normandy

River Countess in Venice.

River cruising provides an antidote to the pressures of life in a fast-paced world, in comfortable, unfussy surroundings, with decent food and enjoyable (often international) company. Riverships provide a harmonious blend of public and private space, and, once aboard, you only have to unpack once. It's a growing area of tourism, now with over 15,000 river cruises from which to choose and close to one million people having taken a river cruise in 2015.

In this chapter, we give you 10 good reasons to take a river cruise and answer some of the basic burning questions potential rivercruisers might like to ask.

10 REASONS TO TAKE A RIVER CRUISE

1. There's so much to see
River cruising is all about sightseeing, from the key highlights en route to villages and the countryside. On a typical seven-night Danube cruise, you could see Budapest, Bratislava, Vienna (Wien), Salzburg, Melk and Dürnstein. On a two-week journey, you might visit major cities including Amsterdam, Budapest (Hungary), Cologne (Köln), Nuremberg (Nürnberg) and Vienna (Wien), and even sail down to the Black Sea.

2. Almost everything is included
Upfront pricing means few additional costs, so budgeting is simple. Accommodation, all meals (usually including wine, although it may be quite basic), snacks, destination talks, some (or all) excursions, light entertainment and perhaps transfers to get to and from your river cruise are all included.

3. They are small, friendly and comfortable
With their size governed by the length and width of the locks that they need to negotiate, most riverships carry no more than 200 passengers. The atmosphere is friendly, and fellow passengers tend to have similar interests.

4. It's so easy
Simply embark, unpack and enjoy the scenery, as your floating inn takes you from one historic destination to the next. There are no tenders to take to go ashore, and no formalities, and you will no doubt learn something new every day.

5. There's always something to see and do
On a river cruise you can enjoy non-stop scenery, whether an urban landscape or the countryside. There will also be talks by guest speakers, and per-

haps wine- or beer-tasting sessions or cooking demonstrations.

6. You'll have a room with a view
Almost all cabins (except on *Primadonna* and *Rossini*) have windows with river views, so you'll be able to admire the scenery. Most new riverships now come with balconies, although this is most likely to be a French balcony (doors or electrically operated windows opening onto a safety railing) due to the size restrictions. (Some do have full balconies that you can sit out on.)

7. You don't have to look like a tourist on tours
River cruise operators provide guides with microphones and passengers with wireless receivers and earphones, so you can hear what is being said without having to crowd around the guide.

8. It should all be smooth sailing
Some first-timers worry about motion sickness, but don't – the gentle waters of rivers are different to those of the ocean, with no waves for a start. Itineraries can, however, be affected by low or high water: not enough water and the riverships can't cruise; too much and they can't get under the bridges (in such cases, comfortable coaches take you to and from the key attractions).

9. Many riverships are surprisingly chic
The newest riverships are very different from those that previously dominated the market. You can have

Pont du Gard excursion in France.

a balcony, various dining options (eg restaurants in different areas of the rivership and possibly on an outdoor deck), Wi-fi (often at no additional charge) and a flat-screen infotainment system.

10. You don't have to cook
It's all done for you, and so is the washing up. You don't have to make the bed either! Or drive!

Taking in the view ahead.

ARE RIVERS CALLED HE OR SHE?

This depends on their behaviour. The River Rhône, for example, is almost always called he because it can be turbulent, bothersome and rough at times, whereas the Saône is a gentler kind of river – more beautiful and tranquil – and is referred to as she, as is the 'beautiful' Blue Danube (although Napoleon described it as the 'king of the rivers of Europe').

The Rhine is a he, as it is always referred to as 'Father Rhine' (although the adjacent Mosell/Mosel is a she – 'Mother Mosel' although supposedly actually the daughter of 'Father Rhine'). The Mighty Mississippi is called the 'granddaddy of all rivers', and the River Volga is always referred to as the 'dear little mother', even though it is the mightiest river in Europe.

Rivers may also be colourful. The Danube is immortalised in music as being famously blue – although the reality is something different – whereas the Mississippi is brown (the 'Big Muddy'), there's a green river in Utah, a red river in Louisiana, a yellow river in China, and a black river in Brazil.

What the brochures don't say

Brochures make river cruises look wonderfully appealing but they can't tell you everything about the experience on board. We cut through the hype to tell you what they don't.

Whether you look at printed brochures or go online and look at the claims made by the river cruise companies, you'd think that all were the best in the world (most of them say they are 'award-winning'). Well, surprise, surprise – they all aren't, of course.

When companies describe their riverships as 'small and attractive' or 'comfortable,' you can rest assured that these will be older vessels, because companies with newer ships always tend to describe them as 'the most luxurious' or 'the most innovative'. Naturally, some companies are probably trying to hide the fact that they are lagging behind in the design stakes.

And when operators talk about having the highest staff to passenger ratio, it should be noted that some riverships have more technical staff than others, while some have more staff on the hospitality side than others, depending on the configuration.

You'll see statements and tag lines such as 'The ultimate in holiday choice' (APT); 'Leading the way in river cruising' (AMA Waterways); 'First River Cruise Line in Europe' (CroisiEurope); 'The Ultimate River Cruise

Experience' (Riviera Travel); 'Europe's most *luxurious* fleet' (Scenic); and 'World's Leading River Cruise Line' (Viking River Cruises). Then there's 'World's Best River Cruise Line' (Tauck) and 'The World's Best River Cruises' (Uniworld). The list goes on, meaning that you should take the hype with a pinch of salt when you're buying. Remember, also, to check the small print to be sure of what is and isn't included in the price.

Of the river cruise companies operating in Europe, AmaWaterways, Uniworld and Viking River Cruises deliver a product that is the closest to what is claimed in the brochures. AmaWaterways and Scenic Waterways hit the spot for their excellent food and service, while Uniworld deliver in terms of opulent cabins. Viking, meanwhile, are good for Scandinavian minimalism and uniformity, and for their large fleet (their 'Longships' have identical layouts, making it easier when low water problems dictate swapping of vessels) and choice of rivers.

To help you distinguish between companies and be better informed when choosing your cruise, here are some of the most commonly asked questions by

Primadonna in Passau.

potential river cruisers, with answers to the queries that the brochures gloss over.

Are river cruises taken aboard ships or boats?

To set the record straight, river cruises are taken aboard riverships. Ships are always ocean-going. Boats are typically owned for pleasure, with the exceptions of lifeboats, of course, and steamboats (or modern-day replicas), which ply the major rivers of North America. Also, there are cruise barges, which navigate canals. For more on this, see the 'What's in a name?' box.

Are there differences between river cruise operators?

Yes, both in terms of hardware and software, in the manner in which river cruises are packaged, and the pre- and post-cruise add-ons. Thus, the quality for which the company is known is provided throughout the product and experience, and is not dependent on third-party operators, drivers and guides. A-ROSA Cruises and Emerald Waterways, for example, offer a greater number of active excursions, such as mountain biking, than most.

Are there different classes aboard riverships?

No, everyone is treated equally. The only difference is in the size of the accommodation you choose.

Are there different cabin categories and prices?

Yes, but not many (unlike on ocean-going cruise ships). Accommodation is priced according to size and location, from the top deck down. Some suites/cabins have balconies or opening windows; cabins on the lowest deck have smaller windows. Cabin sizes can vary from a dimensionally challenged 6 sq m (64 sq ft) to an expansive 45 sq m (484 sq ft).

Are excursions available?

Excursions are often included in the overall cruise price, depending on the operator. Optional excursions, from helicopter 'flightseeing' and hot-air ballooning to wine tasting and horse riding, are also usually available, although at extra cost. Arrangements can also often be made for you to play golf or tennis.

Are meals included?

Yes. Meals include breakfast and lunch (with hot food), afternoon coffee/tea, full waiter-service dinner and late-night snacks. In some cases, the rivership's chef purchases produce in local markets for consumption during the cruise. Some operators include beer, soft drinks and wine as part of the package.

How about dining arrangements?

Breakfast (typically 7am–9am) and lunch are usually buffet-style, with open seating (sit where you want). Dinner, however, is at one seating, at a specific time, either at assigned tables, where you may or may not know the person next to you, or in an open-seating arrangement, so you can sit with anyone you want.

Are there any theme cruises?

Several theme cruises come to mind. In Europe, you can experience theme cruises for classical and jazz music, fine food and wine tasting, shopping, Christmas markets and Christmas/New Year celebrations.

Music lovers might enjoy being aboard Mozart cruises on the Danube, while the green-fingered among you might like to see the gardens of the Rhine, including visits to celebrated botanical gardens, arboretums, herbariums and castles and their grounds.

Are river cruise brochure ratings accurate?

No. Brochures are designed by company marketing departments to attract you to take a cruise. According to cruise brochures, every vessel is the 'best in Europe'. Use the brochures to determine which itinerary and cruise attracts you most but take the ratings with a pinch of salt. As a professional ship tester and evaluation specialist, I go beyond the brochure to bring you accurate, objective and totally independent Berlitz ratings.

What about safety?

There are numerous regulations regarding riverships. In Europe, those built after January 2007 are required to have two compartments, and, in addition to the main propulsion system, they must also be equipped with a second independent propulsion system (located in a separate engine room) to enable the vessel to move.

Since 2010, riverships longer than 110m (360ft) must have a declaration of sufficient strength by one of three recognised classification societies: Bureau Veritas of France; Germanischer Lloyd; or Lloyd's Register of Shipping (London). In addition, the rivership must remain in a floating condition even if two watertight compartments are damaged and flooded. Most riverships have two or three fire zones, and some basic safety and life-saving equipment, although many older (pre-2000) riverships do not have sprinkler systems.

Do riverships have accidents?

Yes, from time to time. For example, in August 2010, A-ROSA Mia struck a pedestrian bridge at one of the locks on the Danube. There were no injuries, but all 192 passengers and crew were taken off the vessel, which had to cancel three cruises in order for repairs to be made. The rivership's navigation bridge (wheelhouse) was virtually demolished during the incident.

In terms of capsizing, in July 2011, the seriously overloaded rivership Bulgaria tragically capsized on a bend of the river in Russia's central region of Tatarstan. Although 79 passengers survived, 119 (many of them children) perished. No rivership has ever capsized in Western Europe.

Do riverships have to comply with any environmental regulations or restrictions?

Environmental regulation is the concern of authorities that control various rivers, or sections of rivers, under the auspices of the United Nations. In Europe, for example, the 'Central Commission for the Navigation of the Rhine' has strict emissions controls in force on the river (many are covered in EU directives).

Do riverships have accidents?

Sometimes little bumps can happen during docking and undocking, and when going into and out of locks. In August 2015 *Arosa Aqua* bumped into a cargo vessel, and 11 passengers were injured, but none seriously.

Who takes a river cruise?

River cruises tend to appeal to the culturally aware and to those wanting to experience the heart of a country and its people, instead of simply travelling through it. They generally appeal to anyone who prefers travelling in a small group environment.

Isn't it all very regimented?

As on any other packaged itinerary-based holiday, there are schedules. You don't have to go on an included tour if you'd prefer instead to have a relaxing day on board. And you can go sightseeing independently rather than in an organised group – just make sure that you're back on your rivership in time for sailing to the next destination.

Is the brochure price firm?

As there are a limited number of cabins in a rivership, they often sell out far in advance, and there's little reason for travel providers to offer discounts. That said, there may be incentives for booking a year in advance

How inclusive is all-inclusive?

Although river cruise companies state that their river cruises are 'all-inclusive', they are actually 'selectively inclusive', based on a packaging price, ie that their selected items (particularly when it comes to wine and other alcoholic drinks) are included, but there may well be exclusions to this. Depending on the country in which the rivership is marketed, there may be differences as to what is or is not included, so check carefully before you book.

WHAT'S IN A NAME?

There is considerable confusion among passengers, rivership operators, cruise/tour packagers and travel journalists regarding the correct name for the different types of vessel, so here is a breakdown, from the largest to the smallest.

Ship

Ocean-going cruise ships can carry boats (lifeboats, search-and-rescue boats and shore tenders). So a ship can carry a boat, but a boat can't carry a ship. Cruise ships sail on oceans and seas, generally have a deep hull and can carry between 50 and over 5,000 passengers.

Rivership

A rivership has a flat bottom and is designed for extremely shallow water. Riverships typically travel at speeds of between 10 and 18kph (6–11mph). On board, there is a captain (the driver) and crew, accommodation, all meals and some light entertainment. Riverships have two, three or four accommodation decks, and public rooms include at least a panoramic lounge/bar and a restaurant.

Cruise barge

A cruise barge (also referred to as a hotel barge) is a flat-bottomed craft that draws a shallow draft. They are typically about 30m (100ft) long and about 5m (16.5ft) wide. Although a handful of them are custom built, most are converted cargo-carrying craft. Cruise barges travel slowly (between 3 and 10kph/1.8–6mph), slower than riverships. They normally have just one deck (a few have two decks), which houses cabins and a combination dining room/lounge, and they carry between 6 and 12 passengers, although a few can carry up to 24. Most cruise barges carry bicycles for you to use along the canal towpaths or for exploring the local towns and villages.

Boats

Boats are typically privately owned or rented for pleasure, with the exception of lifeboats or shore tenders carried by ocean-going cruise ships.

Steamboat

This term designates riverships powered by steam engines that drive huge stern-mounted paddlewheels. They ply the rivers of the US, such as the Mississippi.

Narrowboat

Found in England, France, Holland, Ireland, Scotland and Wales, these vessels are so named because the canals, waterways and locks they navigate are extremely narrow. They are usually only 2m (6.5ft) wide. Although there are exceptions, they are usually for use as charter or self-drive craft.

Lower-priced 'all-inclusive' companies usually provide basic brand spirits for drinks and low-cost wines for lunch and dinner (not to mention miniscule wine glasses). Higher-priced 'all-inclusive' companies usually provide better-quality brand spirits for drinks and higher-cost wines for lunch and dinner.

What about the facilities?
Companies constantly try to outdo each other in terms of facilities and gimmicks to attract ever-more savvy travellers to the advantages of their products. Examples of this include small swimming pools with covers that can be added to convert the pool room into a cinema, 270-degree wrap-around windows on luxury suites or free iPads during the cruise.

Is it difficult to find one's way around a rivership?
No – two minutes should do it. Most riverships have only two or three accommodation decks plus a sun deck, so it's easy.

Who's got the best food?
My top choices would include AmaWaterways, Scenic, Uniworld and Viking River Cruises.

What's the dress code?
Strictly casual – river cruising is all about comfort. That said, although there are no tuxedos or ties needed, you're more than welcome to dress more smartly for dinner if you want to.

Can I access the internet on board?
Yes – in theory. Aboard the newest vessels, rivership-wide Wi-fi will be available, subject to interrupted reception due to locks and bridges. Connections can be dropped when your rivership crosses borders between countries, when different telecom systems take over the transmissions and apply different rates. Some companies provide iPads for passengers to use, but otherwise you should bring your own tablet or computer.

Is music played everywhere on riverships?
Unfortunately, many riverships have music in the lounge, hallways and outside areas – it's difficult to get away from it all (owners and operators seem to think it creates ambience). What annoys many passengers, too, is being tied up alongside another rivership, which also has music on. There are some exceptions, however – ask your cruise provider to find out about this.

Is river cruising for solo travellers?
River cruising is really designed for couples. Solo travellers are an expensive afterthought, and only a few riverships have solo-occupancy cabins (examples include *Ariana, Emerald Sky, Emerald Star, Heidelberg, Statendam* and *Swiss Pearl*). Although you can occupy a double cabin on your own, the fare will

A *Queen Isabel* junior suite.

usually be higher. However, when river cruises are not sold out, opportunities can arise for solo travellers. The best advice is to keep checking.

Are river cruises for honeymooners?
Why not? Most arrangements will have been taken care of before your cruise, so all you have to do is show up. Some riverships have double-, queen-, or king-sized beds, although you'll find that, in general, the cabins (and particularly the bathrooms) are compact, and the beds are short!

Are river cruises suitable for children?
Although a river cruise is educational, in general, river cruises in Europe are taken by the over 50s. A handful of riverships have cabins with three beds, which are in theory suitable for small families, although cramped.

Are river cruises suitable for disabled passengers?
Not really, although some riverships do have lifts (elevators), typically between the main deck and the restaurant deck and/or stairlifts from the main to the upper (outside) deck. Some have lifts between all decks, and a few riverships have wheelchair-accessible cabins.

Enjoying the sun and scenery.

Many landing stages are linked to steps leading up to a city or town. In some locations, riverships berth side by side (this may also obscure the view from your cabin), and you may have to cross several of them to get to land.

And it's on land where most problems arise, with many historic continental European cities having cobbled streets, steps with no ramps and few facilities aimed at those with disabilities.

Are there laundry facilities?

Not usually, although a handful of riverships do offer some laundry facilities. If your river cruise is part of a longer holiday, take some washing powder or liquid to clean small, personal clothing items in your cabin. Note that most suite/cabin bathrooms are dimensionally challenged and have little space to hang anything. Most do not have a retractable washing line.

Few riverships currently have ironing facilities.

Will I experience motion sickness?

You shouldn't, with the possible exception of cruises around the islands in the open sea at the mouth of the River Elbe in North Germany.

Are there medical facilities on board?

Although riverships carry first-aid kits, they do not generally have a doctor or nurse employed on board (unlike on an ocean cruise ship). However, riverships are always close to land, so any emergency medical arrangements can be made quickly, if necessary.

I'm pregnant – can I still cruise?

River cruise companies don't allow mothers-to-be aboard past their 28th week of pregnancy. Pregnant women may need to produce a doctor's certificate, saying that they are ok to travel. Fortunately, you'll never be far from shore, so medical help can be summoned quickly. If you are taking any river cruise, make sure you have adequate medical insurance.

Is smoking allowed?

Most riverships are totally no-smoking inside (exceptions include the cigar lounge aboard *Premicon Queen*), but allow smoking on the open deck.

Won't I get bored?

No chance. There is always something to see on the river.

What if I don't like it?

I am almost certain that you will enjoy your river cruise and the abundant scenic opportunities. If you really don't like it, or if things go horribly wrong, let your river cruise company or travel provider know at the earliest opportunity.

Do river cruise companies have frequent passenger (loyalty) clubs?

Some river cruise operators have a frequent cruisers club, where you collect points for discounts, upgrades or other benefits. Examples include: Avalon Waterways (Journeys Club), Scenic (Scenic Club), Transocean Tours (Columbus Club), Uniworld (River Heritage Club), Vantage Deluxe World Travel (Platinum Circle and Viking River Cruises (Viking Explorer Society).

Where are riverships registered?

Most riverships are registered in France, Germany, Malta, The Netherlands, or Switzerland. A few (those owned/operated by non-EU companies) are registered in Bulgaria, Poland, Romania or the Ukraine.

What happens when riverships age?

A number of owners of older riverships modernise or convert their vessels during the long winter months and rename them for new operators/charterers. One example of this is Tauck's *Esprit*, introduced in 2015, but actually is the 'modernised' 2010-built *VistaPrima*. CroisiEurope is another example. Its *Camargue* was nicely reconstructed from the same vessel, with the same name, but originally built in 1995. I expect additional modernisations will be made due to the lack of building space and the increasing cost of new riverships.

What happens to old riverships?

Some riverships are sold for use as 'floatels' (permanently moored former riverships that have been converted into hotels). This might be because the owner no longer wants to operate the vessel, because the engines are inefficient or damaged, or for other reasons (dissolved partnerships, for example). Other riverships simply sit and rust away.

Can I eat when I want to?

For breakfast and lunch, there is usually some flexibility on when you can eat, within the restrictions of a 90- to 120-minute time span when the restaurant is open. Generally, you can have your breakfast or lunch at any time within that time slot. Dinner, on the other hand, is always at a set time, typically around 7pm, depending on the itinerary.

Do riverships have room service?

It's not standard, as there simply aren't enough crew members on a rivership to be able to provide it. A handful of vessels do offer this to occupants of suites for breakfast, however. You may also be offered it if you can't leave your cabin due to illness, for example.

Can I bring my own drinks on board?

Most river cruise companies allow you to bring your own drinks on board, but only for in-cabin consumption.

Are tips included?

Gratuities may or may not be included, depending on the river cruise company or tour operator or packager. Some companies have exclusive charters of vessels and may include gratuities in the package price. If the same company offers cruises on 'partner' company riverships, tips may not be included. It's important to read the fine print.

What about rubbish (garbage)?

Rubbish is offloaded in various ports along the way, depending on the port's regulations.

Breakfast in the cabin aboard *Scenic Jasper.*

Pros and cons

Dream getaway or a claustrophobic holiday nightmare? Here is a list of key pros and cons to help you decide whether messing about on the river is right for you.

River cruises don't come cheap, so it's wise to weigh up the pros and cons beforehand. We believe that the advantages far outweigh the disadvantages – most types of holiday have minuses as well as pluses, after all – but here's our frank breakdown to enable you to make your mind up for yourself.

The advantages of a river cruise

Riverships provide a unique way of seeing the interior of a country. They give a new take on a destination from the one you would get on a wholly land-based tour and totally different, too, from the coastal approach of an ocean cruise.

Riverships allow you to enjoy the ever-changing scenery ('riverscape') at eye level and up close.

With this kind of holiday, there is always the anticipation of waking up in a different place each day, usually in the heart of a city or town.

The atmosphere on board is friendly and informal, never stuffy or pretentious.

Good food and service are essential elements of any river cruise, with some food sourced from local markets as you travel.

Riverships lined up in Budapest.

All meals and snacks are provided, and basic table wines may also be included for lunch and dinner.

Open dining is standard (a few low-cost riverships may have assigned tables), so you sit where you want and with whom you wish.

The dress code is completely casual.

It's a single currency world on board.

There's no taking tenders ashore – you simply step off your rivership as soon as it is tied up to a pier.

While ocean-going cruise ships have interior (no-view) cabins, almost all riverships in Europe feature only outside-view cabins – nearly all of which have large picture windows. Exceptions include *Primadonna* (eight interior cabins) and *Rossini* (11 interior cabins).

Most excursions are included in the upfront package price, which is good if you want tight control over your budget from the outset.

The entertainment is geared towards the more cultured customer, so if the casinos and games that are more typical of ocean cruises fill you with dread, a river cruise may well appeal more.

River cruising provides a sense of continuity that is more difficult to achieve on a bus or coach tour, where constant changing of hotels or lodgings each night means greater disruption. This also saves time in terms of packing and unpacking.

Some riverships are marketed in several countries, which means that there's an attractive, cosmopolitan mix of travellers on board.

The disadvantages of a river cruise

The flow of water in almost all rivers cannot always be controlled by man, so there will be times when the water level is so low that even a specially constructed rivership, with its shallow draft, cannot travel. Occasionally, the water level can become so low (a depth of only a few centimetres) that it is impossible for riverships to move at all.

Conversely, the water level can be so high (after much rain) that riverships cannot fit under bridges. Sometimes, multi-rivership companies may be able to transfer you from one side of the blocked waterway to an identical rivership on the other side, thus providing minimum interruption to your cruise.

Being part of an organised group tour means that you have less control over the pace of your holiday. Whether too fast or too slow, it can be equally frustrating. It can also mean that you don't get as long as you might like to spend with local people.

If you are tall, note that the beds on board most riverships are usually less than 1.8m (5ft 11ins) long.

There is generally no room service (except in a few examples; breakfast may be available to occupants of the largest suites), as there aren't enough crew members to cope with this.

If your cabin is towards the aft (rear), there may well be the constant humming of a generator, which supplies power for air conditioning, heating, lighting and cooking, etc.

Cabin insulation may be poor, so you may hear noisy neighbours clearly, whether you want to or not.

Mealtimes are strictly followed (all passengers typically eat at one sitting), so there's no choice of dining times, as there is in the ocean-going cruise industry.

In some popular destinations such as Budapest, Bratislava and Passau, several riverships are often tied alongside each other. Passengers on the outermost vessel(s) must cross the others in order to disembark and embark, which is challenging for anyone with poor ambulatory skills. Also, if your cabin is on the side that is tied up alongside another rivership, not only will you not have a view, but you will need to draw your curtains if you want privacy.

Sailing along the Rhine.

Non-smokers should note that on the open deck, you may find that smokers are right next to you. The only way to avoid this is to move.

RIVER CRUISING VERSUS OCEAN CRUISING

So how does river cruising compare with its more established cousin, ocean cruising? River cruising and ocean cruising can provide very different experiences – this list intends to help you to work out which style of holidaying might be more appropriate for you.

River cruises provide the kind of up-close inland cruising impossible aboard large ocean-going cruise ships.

The ride aboard riverships is typically silky smooth – there's no rolling about as there is on many ocean-going cruise ships.

On riverships, land is almost always in sight; aboard ocean-going cruise ships you may be sailing on open stretches of water for days to reach a destination.

Aboard a rivership, the scenery is at eye level; on an ocean-going ship it isn't, and you may need to take a lift to go up and out to see it.

On a rivership, you simply step on land almost as soon as the vessel ties up. Aboard ocean-going cruise ships, you can be waiting for up to two hours or more to go ashore in some ports when the ship is at anchor, and you need to take a shore tender. There can be long queues when you return to an ocean-going cruise ship. For rivership passengers it's easy – you simply step aboard.

Aboard a rivership, you dock right in the centre of a city, town or village. Ocean-going cruise ships often have to dock in cargo terminals and other inconvenient places in insalubrious locations some distance from a city or town centre.

Riverships are more intimate than their ocean-going counterparts. They seldom carry more than 200 passengers. Ocean-going cruise ships can carry over 5,000 passengers.

Almost all cabins on a rivership have outside views; there are virtually no interior (no-view) cabins, as are typical on most ocean-going cruise ships.

Riverships often tie-up alongside at night, so you can go off into the local town to enjoy restaurants, concerts and nightlife. Most ocean-going cruise ships sail at night, so you seldom get to experience nightlife ashore.

Rivers are calm and shallow, so there is almost zero possibility of motion sickness, whereas this is likely to be more of a problem on an ocean-going cruise ship.

With ocean cruising, the ship is the destination. In river cruising, the destination is the destination!

Ocean-going cruise ships sometimes have portholes in their dining rooms that you cannot see out of when seated, but aboard rivership dining rooms, there's always a river view through large windows.

On ocean-going cruise ships, most excursions are additional cost items. Aboard most riverships excursions are usually included, although this does depend on the operator, so always check before booking.

River cruising tends to be more for the seasoned traveller and, generally, for those aged over 50. Ocean cruising caters to a broader clientele, including families and travellers with disabilities.

Cruising past Boppard on the Rhine.

Booking and budgeting

Should you book directly with the river cruise company or through a specialist booking agent? Are there any hidden extras to look for when calculating costs? And what about insurance?

Booking direct

Whether booking direct or via a cruise booking agent, check thoroughly just what is included in any offers, particularly when enticing discounts catch your eye. Make sure, for example, that all port charges, government fees and any additional fuel surcharges are included in the quote.

The internet

The internet may be a useful resource tool, but it is not the best place to book your cruise, unless you know exactly what you want. You can't ask questions, and information provided by some river cruise companies is pure marketing hype. Most sites providing cruise ship reviews have something to sell, and the information can also be misleading or outdated.

Many internet booking agencies are unlicensed and unregulated, so if you do book a cruise with one, confirm with the actual river cruise company that the booking has been made and that final payment has been received.

The internet versus travel agents

Perhaps you've found a discounted rate for your cruise online. Fine, but if a river cruise company suddenly offers special discounts for your sailing, or things go wrong with your booking, your internet booking service may prove very unfriendly. A physical cruise-booking agent, however, can probably work magic in making any discounts work for you. It's called personal service.

Most river cruise companies consider travel agents to be their distribution system (exceptions include Grand Circle Cruise Line and Saga Cruises, who only sell direct). Cruise booking agents do not charge for their services, although they earn a commission from the river cruise companies. Consider them to be your business advisor, not just a ticket agent. They will handle all matters relevant to your booking and will have the latest information on any changes of itinerary and any other relevant items.

When you have chosen an itinerary and river cruise company, look for an affiliated agency member of the Cruise Lines International Association (CLIA). This association has a full financial bonding scheme to protect passengers from failed river cruise companies.

Reservations

Riverships on Europe's waterways are small compared to ocean-going ships, carrying fewer than 200

Embarkation documents for a Viking cruise.

IDENTIFICATION AND VISAS

European citizens only need a national identity card to enter European Union countries, but those without them, such as UK and Irish citizens, must have a passport. Visitors from non-European Union countries, such as Australia, Canada, New Zealand, South Africa and the US, must have a full passport and may also need visas – some countries allow you to visit for up to 90 days without one, while others require a visa from day one. You should check this with your tour provider or the consulate/embassy of the country concerned prior to travelling, allowing at least 90 days to get the visa. Also check that your passport is not about to run out, as some countries require at least six months left (from date of entry) prior to the expiry date in order for it still to be valid.

passengers, and the most popular river cruises are often sold out a year ahead. With that in mind, book as far ahead as possible, and make any special dietary requests known, keeping any correspondence relating to the request.

After choosing a cruise, date and cabin type, you pay a deposit, typically followed by full payment within seven days (sometimes longer, depending on the river cruise company's conditions). You'll then receive a confirmation invoice. For a late reservation, you pay in full when space is confirmed (when booking via the internet, for example). River cruise companies always reserve the right to change prices in the event of tax increases, or other costs 'beyond their control'.

After the river cruise company receives full payment, your cruise ticket will be sent by post, or possibly as an e-document. Check to make sure that everything is correct (date, itinerary, etc).

Extra costs

Cruise brochures boldly state that 'almost everything's included', but in most cases it's not actually true. In fact, for some less expensive cruises (usually with older vessels) 'all-exclusive' is a more appropriate term. Your fare usually covers the rivership as transportation, your cabin, all meals and snacks, and service on board, and, possibly, shore excursions and tips. Note that even if alcoholic drinks are included, there may be an extra cost for 'premium' brands.

Port taxes/handling charges

These are (usually) included in the cost your cruise.

Air/cruise packages

If your river cruise price includes air transport, note that flights usually cannot be changed without paying a premium, because river cruise companies often book group space on aircraft to obtain the lowest rates.

If you arrange your own air/train/coach transport, the river cruise company is under no obligation to help you if you don't reach the ship on time. If you are flying overseas, allow extra time (particularly in winter) for possible flight delays or cancellations.

In Europe, air/cruise packages generally start at a major metropolitan airport; some may include first-class rail travel from outlying districts. In the US, some river cruise companies include connecting flights from suburban airports convenient to the traveller.

Cancellations and refunds

Do take out full cancellation insurance, if it is not included. Otherwise, if you cancel at the last minute – even for medical reasons – you could lose the whole fare. Insurance coverage can be obtained from

The Iron Gates Gorge on the River Danube.

Queen Isabel exterior.

your booking agent or from an independent company (it may even be included), and paying by credit card makes sense (there's a better chance of getting your money back, even if the booking agency goes bust).

River cruise companies usually accept cancellations more than 30 days before sailing, but all charge full fare if you don't turn up on sailing day. Other cancellation fees depend on the cruise and length of trip.

Travel and medical insurance

Note that river cruise companies and cruise booking agents routinely sell travel cover policies that, on close inspection, appear to wriggle out of payment due to a litany of exclusion clauses, most of which are never explained. Examples include 'pre-existing'

medical conditions – ignoring this little gem could cost you dearly – and 'valuables' left unattended on a tour bus, even though the tour guide says it is safe and that the driver will lock the door. To get the best travel insurance deal, shop around and don't accept the first travel insurance policy you are offered. Read the contract carefully and make sure you know exactly what you are covered for. Ask for a detailed explanation of all exclusions, excesses and limitations. There may be exclusions for 'hazardous sports'. These could include things typically offered as shore excursions from ships. Examples include horse riding or cycling.

Beware, too, of the 'box ticking' approach to travel cover, which is often done quickly at the travel agent's office in lieu of providing expert advice. Insurers should not, in reality, be allowed to apply exclusions that have not been clearly pointed out to the policyholder.

Before you go, make sure you know what to do if you are the victim of a crime, for example if your wallet or camera is stolen while on an excursion. If anything does unfortunately happen, obtain a police report as soon as possible. Note that many insurance policies will reimburse you only for the second-hand value of any lost or stolen item, rather than the full cost of replacement, and you may be required to produce the original receipt for any items claimed.

If you purchase travel cover over the internet, check the credentials of the company underwriting the scheme. It is best to deal with well-established names and not necessarily to take what appears to be the cheapest deal offered.

Design and layout

An overview of the different types of riverships and what to expect to find inside, depending on the type of vessel, followed by a comparison of two different brands.

River cruise companies try to attract customers by adding ever-more bells and whistles to their newest riverships and constantly challenging designers to create new ways of providing practical and attractive cabins and suites, restaurants and lounge/bars.

Overview

Riverships are long and low in the water, with fold-down masts in order to negotiate low bridges. The navigation bridge can also be raised and lowered hydraulically, and all side railings can be folded down so that the uppermost (open) deck is completely clear of all obstructions.

Public areas common to all riverships include a restaurant, an observation lounge with a bar (the social hub of any rivership), which on newer vessels incorporates a bistro-style casual eatery at the front, and an outdoor 'Sun Deck' with chairs (some under shaded canopies). Some may also have a (tiny) shop and beauty room, a fitness room and a small sauna. Most have an excellent amount of out-door deck space for viewing the scenery and hosting food-and-drink-themed events such as a once-per-cruise, mid-morning 'Frühschoppen' (Bavarian-style brunch).

There is only so much that designers can cram into the hull of a rivership, but there has been a burst of creativity in recent years (particularly by industry drivers AmaWaterways, Emerald Waterways, Scenic and Viking River Cruises), driven by the increased demand for premium (better than basic, or 'standard') facilities. The latest 135m (443ft) riverships (the maximum possible for the locks on the Rhine–Main–Danube system) for Emerald Waterways, for example, also have a dual purpose area at the aft of the vessel containing a small indoor heated pool, with a retractable glass roof that converts the area into a cinema by night. While Emerald place a pool/cinema aft and Uniworld has a small pool and bar aft, AmaWaterways has created a separate restaurant (with a full galley), and Viking River Cruises has placed its two largest suites, each with a balcony, two chairs and drinks table there.

A cabin on *Avalon Expression*.

The two-deck high atrium aboard *Viking Delling*.

Design

Depending on the river on which they operate, European riverships have either two, two-and-a-half or three accommodation decks. This is due to the restrictions placed on a vessel's dimensions by the locks and bridges on the various rivers.

There are two main types of rivership: mono-hull, and twin-cruiser. Riverships are traditionally built on a mono-hull, with or without a slightly modified split-front with bullnose (or 'Cadillac') front.

Primadonna, however, has two hulls, while *Crystal Mozart* has a double-width monohull with two sets of bows to give the impression of having twin hulls. While the increased width provides more space, the hull has to flex more to accommodate the strong currents encountered in some parts of the river. *Crystal Mozart* and *Primadonna* are limited to the River Danube because certain locks can accommodate the larger size.

As a result of their long, low-slung design, riverships have a limited amount of space for public areas. There are just two principal public rooms: a restaurant and an observation lounge (main lounge). There are, however, variations and differences between riverships, such as the location and position of the bar within the lounge, the possible addition of a small dance floor and upright or baby grand piano, and the degree of comfort and user-friendliness built into the design. Many older riverships have tub chairs (with little back support), but newer vessels have comfortable sofas and individual chairs.

Every inch of space aboard riverships is utilised to the full, and innovative design thinking, such as that used by Viking River Cruises for its Viking 'Longships', has created new levels of user-friendliness that make it difficult for older vessels (ie those built before 2000) to compete. The newest riverships are also 25m (82ft) longer than the standard older ones.

Twin-cruisers

The twin-cruiser was a design innovation when first launched in 2005 in the shape of the *Flamenco*. At time of writing there were just eight of this type in service. As is apparent from the name, a twin-cruiser consists of two sections: firstly, there is a long accommodation block, restaurant, galley and lounge, built as a separate unit that is bolted onto a smaller aft section. The latter houses the engines, engineering, propulsion and steering equipment and also includes a hydraulically operated navigation bridge that can be adjusted according to the height of any bridges encountered en route.

The rear power 'barge' pushes the front accommodation 'barge' section. The captain has a forward view over the whole of the vessel. While this is neat in theory (and should also mean that the front, lived-in section is quieter), it doesn't really work well for a rivership, because docking often requires multiple manoeuvres, and navigating around bends is challenging.

Life-sized chess board aboard *AmaCerto*.

Atrium

Some river ships (for example, the Viking 'Long-ships') have a two-deck-high atrium-style lobby with an abundance of natural light, making them feel very open and welcoming; others have a single-deck height lobby that makes them feel more closed-in and clammy.

Uniworld's atriums are grand but cluttered and perhaps overwhelming for some. Scenic's and Em-erald's are ultra-modern and open, as are those on Viking's 'Longships'. Avalon's are plain, but open.

Observation lounge/bar

At the front of most riverships there is a lounge/bar, with large panoramic windows for river viewing – especially important for sightseeing en route at the beginning and end of the cruise season in Europe, when it may be too chilly for some passengers to stay on the outside deck for long. Within the lounge, there will be a bar, which is best placed at the back of the room to leave more space for prime river viewing in the front section. If the lounge bar is towards the front of the panorama lounge, as on the *Cezanne, Der Kleine Prinz, Emerald Sky* and *Excellence Royale*, for example, only the bartender has good views, while passengers sitting on bar stools face inwards. The same is true of the Scenic riverships, where the front section has a bar and a river café, which limits the number of forward-facing (observation) seats.

Restaurants

Most riverships have one main restaurant, with large river-view windows, plus, in summer, an area outside for casual, alfresco dining. Some of the newer vessels also have an extra interior area for dining. The principal difference in the present design of rivership restaurants lies in the layout of the buffet display counter. Note that tables that are located adjacent to the doors or open entrance to the galley can be noisy, and should be avoided.

CUSTOMER CARE

In my experience, this is how the river cruise companies rate in terms of customer care:
1. AmaWaterways
2. Tauck
3. Scenic
4. APT
5. Lüftner Cruises
6. Viking River Cruises
7. Emerald Waterways
8. Uniworld Grand River Cruises
9. Travelmarvel
10. A-ROSA Cruises
11. CroisiEurope
12. Grand Circle Cruise Line
13. Vantage River Cruises
14. Avalon Waterways

Other facilities

Some riverships may also have a small plunge pool (which, in practice, is hardly ever used), a diminutive sauna, massage room and a cabin-size fitness room, although there's hardly ever time to use these facilities on a busy one-week cruise. Some of the newer riverships, notably *Emerald Sky* and *Emerald Star*, have dual-purpose indoor pools, which convert into comfortable cinemas at night.

A number of riverships have squared-off fronts, which allows designers to accommodate a dining terrace. These usually have fully opening glass doors that allow a total alfresco option – the Viking 'Longships' incorporate this feature. And, for the well-heeled, one rivership – Douro Azul's *Queen Isabel* – even has a small helicopter landing pad on the sun deck.

The top deck ('Sun deck')

The most important area for many passengers is the open top deck. This runs almost the full length of the rivership. In, or close to, the front is the navigation bridge (pilot house), cleverly constructed so that it can be lowered hydraulically into the deck below to avoid obstacles such as low bridges. Any of the canopies and side railings on the top deck are also designed to be folded down, while chairs and sun loungers simply remain on deck all the time.

Most riverships have a life-size chess game or small sunken plunge pool. Some have areas for mini golf. Viking River Cruises has herb gardens on the sun deck, with fresh herbs used by the chef, who also tends the garden.

When the top deck is in use, it provides a wonderful vantage point from which to watch the constantly changing scenery. It's also a social place, where you'll meet your fellow travellers and enjoy drinks and snacks.

In terms of the quality of the hardware on deck, there can be quite a difference between vessels. The open sun deck aboard *River Chanson* and *Royal Crown*, for example, is laid with real teak wood, but most riverships have fake turf (when it gets wet it's just soggy underfoot), or a wood-look rubberised decking material.

White plastic patio-style deck chairs are typical of budget-priced river cruise operators. The more upmarket operators, such as AmaWaterways, Scylla Tours and Viking River Cruises, provide better-quality – and more stable and comfortable – stainless steel or aluminium chairs.

Panorama (observation) lounges at the front of the vessel typically have large chairs, sofas and low coffee tables, as well, unfortunately, as a number of functional pillars that obstruct sightlines (exceptions include the *River Chanson* and *Royal Crown*), the result of old shipbuilding techniques. Although the pillars prevent the flexing that can occur in the longest riverships, the designers and builders need to re-think in terms of passenger comfort.

RIVERSHIP DIFFERENCES

There are differences between the principal river cruise companies and their riverships. River cruise operators continue trying to outdo each other – all to the benefit of savvy passengers. While most travellers look at price, there are other things that the internet and river cruise brochures *don't* highlight, which may well make quite a difference to your cruise. For example,

A trio of Viking 'Longships'.

most river cruise operators provide personal headsets for shore excursions, but Scenic goes the extra mile by providing a hand-held or lanyard-mounted GPS smartphone-style unit, which is excellent for independent sightseeing.

If you wonder why some river cruises are more – or less – expensive than others, it's all in the details, such as what is or isn't included, as well as the cost and quality of the food and staff training. For example, on embarkation day, a formal dinner may not be served – from all the hype in the brochure, you may well be expecting a gourmet meal when you first arrive, only to find instead a self-serve buffet, following the welcome aboard talk given by the Cruise Director.

General examples

The following aspects maybe where you see a difference between more and less expensive rivership cruises:

If you travel by coach (provided by the cruise or tour operator) to reach your rivership, you may be charged an extra fee if you want to sit in the first three rows.

Numerous support pillars in the lounge obstruct views (as a point of comparison, *River Chanson* and *Royal Crown* don't have any pillars of this type).

The lack of electrical outlets in cabins. There may be just one outlet, but it's taken by the telephone (if there is one) or the charger for the personal receiver used for excursions.

The quality of facial tissues. On less expensive vessels, facial tissues will probably be made of cellu-

lose – not the soft balsam tissues you may be expecting – and definitely not like the ones you use at home.

The thickness of toilet paper – 2-ply or 3-ply.

The supply (or lack of) vanity sets, including cotton buds and make-up remover pads, nail file, etc.

The washbasin in your bathroom may be big enough to wash your nose – but little else – and water may splash everywhere.

The shower head may be fixed to the wall, but at navel-height.

Drink brands on lower-priced vessels might be ones you have never heard of.

In-depth comparison

Using two brands – Scenic and Emerald Waterways – as an example, the below is a more in-depth look at how price differences manifest themselves. While both brands are owned by the same company, Scenic is more expensive, but more luxurious and more inclusive, while Emerald, the company's second brand is just that – second (but good). Here are some of the differences between them:

Scenic: Each rivership has an outdoor dip pool on the open Sun Deck. The cabins *do* have a main light switch by the bed. The bathrooms are marble-clad, tiled and more lavish, with inward-opening doors, larger washbasins and towels, magnifying shaving mirrors and retractable clothes lines. Many cabins have bathtubs and a separate shower enclosure.

Drinks are inclusive at any time (with a small extra-cost for premium drinks). There are more food

AmaCello in Cochem, Germany, on a winter cruise.

choices and a higher food budget, plus a degusta-tion 'Table La Rive'. There's also extra evening eatery Portofino (L'Amour on the French rivers).

The portable GPS receivers for (Taylor-Made) tours and self-guided excursions are excellent, and Scenic has more included shore excursions than Emerald. Aboard the newer vessels (for example *Scenic Amber*, *Scenic Jasper* and *Scenic Opal*), Royal and Panorama suites have adjustable heated bathroom floors, and three-way push-button adjustable electric beds. Electric bicycles are available, and gratuities are included.

Emerald Waterways: Each rivership has an aft heated indoor pool that converts to a cinema by night, and a retractable glass roof. There's no main light switch by the bed (they can only be turned off at the cabin entrance). The modular bathrooms are plain, have sliding doors (they are close to the bed) and a tiny washbasin. There are no bathtubs (even in the largest suites) or magnifying shaving mirrors, or retractable clothes lines.

Beer, wine and soft drinks are provided during meals; drinks consumed between meals cost extra (drinks packages are available). There are fewer food choices in the restaurant, and no extra evening alternative eateries with a different menu.

The personal 'Quiet Vox' receivers for excursions are small but heavy. Many shore excursions cost extra, and gratuities are not included, but (manual) bicycles are available.

The pool aboard *Emerald Star* at night.

OLD AND NEW

River cruise operators tend to think of their passengers as 'one-time-only' guests, but in fact the number of repeat passengers is growing. So, there's now more interest in comparing river companies and riverships. There are substantial differences between vessels built before 2000 and the latest riverships, which are typically longer and beamier (wider).

Older riverships (pre-2000) typically have

Observation lounge with low ceiling, multiple pillars and uncomfortable tub chairs
Narrow hallways
Cramped cabins with little storage space
Ceilings made of metal 'planks'
Poor soundproofing
Noisy cabins due to older type diesel engines and generators
No balconies
No Wi-fi
No refrigerator
Poor (or no) bedside reading light
Small bathrooms
Tiny shower enclosures (most with shower curtains and fixed head showers)

One restaurant, with low ceiling and cramped seating
Very limited self-serve buffets for breakfast and lunch

Newer riverships (post-2000) typically have

Larger observation lounges with built-in facilities for light eating options
Wider hallways
Larger cabins and suites (with espresso machines)
Balcony-inclusive: full or French, or both
Creative, practical cabin design
Quiet-close drawers, closet doors and toilet seats
Good storage space
Mini-fridge
Wi-fi
Dining options (main restaurant, plus a grill or another alternative)
Self-service espresso/cappuccino machines
Larger bathrooms
Larger shower enclosures (most with glass doors and flexible shower hoses)
One-piece cabin ceilings
Good soundproofing

Life aboard

From what to take with you to how to stay safe once on board, this A–Z gives the lowdown on all the practical basics that you need to be aware of during your cruise.

Air conditioning
Cabin temperature is regulated by a thermostat inside your cabin, so you can adjust it to your liking. Note that you may not be able to turn the air conditioning off completely. At the beginning and end of the season – on Christmas market cruises, for example – heating, rather than air conditioning, is provided.

Beauty salon
Just a few riverships – usually the newest – have a small beauty salon, offering haircuts and styling, manicures, pedicures, facials, waxing and, possibly, massage. It's advisable to book appointments as soon as possible after boarding, especially on short cruises. Charges are comparable to those ashore.

Bed linen
European duvets are usually provided, rather than sheets and blankets. Anti-allergenic pillows may also be available. Occupants of suites may get a choice of several different pillows.

Bicycles and walking accessories
On some cruises (for example, AmaWaterways, Emerald Waterways and Scenic), bikes are provided for passenger use. Nordic walking sticks are also sometimes available.

Captain
Most riverships have an open bridge (wheelhouse) policy, so you can visit the captain at almost any time. Exceptions to this include during poor weather or in hazardous manoeuvring conditions. Check at the reception desk if you're not sure.

Clothing
If you think you might not wear it, don't take it, as wardrobe space is really limited. In the summer, when the weather is warm to hot, pack clothes made of lightweight cottons and other natural fibres. Take a lightweight cotton jumper or windbreaker for the outdoor deck, plus sunglasses and a hat. For river cruises in winter (those for Christmas markets, for example) take well-insulated clothing, including earmuffs and

Taking in the view.

thick gloves, because it can be very cold, especially on deck when your rivership is moving.

The dress code is casual, but in the evening what you wear should be tasteful. Men might include a blazer or sports jacket. Comfortable low- or flat-heeled shoes are essential for women. Rubber soles are best for walking on deck.

Comment cards
On the last day you may be asked to fill out a comment card. Be truthful when completing it, as this feedback helps cruise providers to improve on their product. If there have been problems with any other aspect of your cruise, say so.

Communications
Most riverships (although not cruise barges) have direct-dial satellite telephone systems, so that you can call anywhere in the world while on your cruise. Wi-fi may be available in your cabin or selected areas such as the lobby or lounge or library, although the reception can be patchy when going through locks or under bridges. Connections can sometimes also be dropped when your rivership crosses borders between countries, when different telecom providers take over the transmissions and apply different rates. Some upscale lines provide iPads for guests to use, but otherwise you should bring your own tablet or computer. More standard riverships may just provide one or two communal computers with Wi-fi access, mostly with no privacy from passers-by.

Daily programme
The daily programme is a list of any activities and social events plus destination arrival and departure times. It is normally delivered to your cabin the evening before the day that it covers. For a sample breakdown of a day on a river cruise, see page 40.

Disabled travellers
River cruising is not ideal for travellers with disabilities. Some riverships do have lifts (elevators) between the main deck and the restaurant deck and/or stairlifts from the main to the upper (outside) deck, and a few riverships have wheelchair-accessible cabins, but not all.

Many landing stages are linked to steps leading up to a city or town. In some locations, riverships berth side by side, and you may have to cross several of them to get to land. Anyone in a wheelchair will have to be carried across the riverships (possibly including steps) in order to be placed on the dockside.

And it's on land where most problems arise, with many historic continental European cities having cobbled streets, steps with no ramps and few facilities aimed at those with disabilities. Budapest and Esztergom, for example, are very hilly and cobbled, making wheeling bone-shakingly difficult and uncomfortable. Bratislava is one of several cities to have numerous steps between the docking place at river level and street level, which is much higher.

Disembarkation
This is very straightforward on a rivership. The night before arrival at your final destination, place your bags outside your cabin. They will be collected and off-loaded on arrival. Remember to leave out the clothes you intend to wear on disembarkation day and to retrieve any items you have placed in the personal safe in your cabin or in the rivership's main safe.

Drinks
Some companies provide free bottled water, replenished daily. For information on drinks provided with meals and what's covered in 'all-inclusive' packages, see page 36.

Electricity
The cabin voltage is usually 220 volts, but bathrooms may have both 110- and 240-volt (60 cycles) outlets, for shavers only. Hairdryers are normally supplied in your cabin, but, if not, they will be available on request at the reception desk. Most European riverships have a deeply recessed two round pin socket, so you may need to take an adaptor.

Emergencies
A few words about safety will be given by the captain or senior officer on embarkation day. Safety instructions – ie what to do in an emergency – are provided on the back of your cabin door, in the in-cabin infotainment system, or in a documentation folder. Riverships also carry lifejackets.

Note that most door locks on riverships are operated by electronic key card or digital touch card. Aboard older riverships, an actual key may be required on the inside in order to unlock the door. It's best to leave the key in the lock, so that in the event of an emergency, you don't have to hunt for it.

Capsizing: This is rare, but riverships do bump into things occasionally due to currents or careless navigation.

Fires: Always make sure that you know the way from your cabin to the nearest emergency exit (typically aft and in the centre of the vessel), which are identifiable by their green signs. Riverships have 'low location' lighting systems, of either the electro-luminescent or the photo-luminescent types, which will lead you to the exits.

In the unlikely event that a fire does break out on your rivership, try to remain calm and think logically and clearly. If there is a fire in your cabin, report it immediately, then leave your cabin and close the door behind you to prevent any smoke or flames from entering the passageway. If you are in your cabin and the fire is in the passageway, feel the cabin door. If the door handle is hot, use a wet towel to turn it. If a fire is raging in the passageway, assess the situation and act as you deem most appropriate for your safety. If there is smoke in the passageway, crawl to the nearest exit.

Fitness facilities

Only a handful of riverships have small fitness rooms, typically including a couple of rowing machines, exercise bikes and a few weights, and possibly, although not always, a small infra-red sauna.

Identification cards/passports

When you embark, you hand in your passport (it is used for passport control, as you travel between different countries) and are given instead a personal boarding pass for identification purposes. This sometimes includes your photograph and other pertinent information and must be shown at the gangway each time you board. Your passport will be given back to you at the end of the cruise.

Laundry

Riverships do not generally have laundry facilities. You can always wash small items in your own bathroom, but be aware that there will be very little space to hang anything up to dry. Some riverships might offer a minimal laundry service, although this might be limited to passengers in suites (sometimes those in the Owner's Suite only).

Few riverships have ironing facilities.

Library

Actually, the so-called 'library' will just be a few bookshelves, usually in the lobby. You'll find a few general-interest books, some destination reference material, and periodicals, as well as board games such as Scrabble, backgammon and chess.

Luggage

While there is generally no limit to the amount of personal baggage you can take on board, storage space is very limited. Towels, soap, shampoo and shower caps are provided on all vessels, so you won't have to bring your own.

Medication

Although riverships carry first-aid kits, they do not generally have a doctor or nurse employed on board (unlike on an ocean cruise liner). However, riverships are always close to land, so any emergency medical arrangements can be made quickly, if necessary.

Take any medical supplies you need, plus spare spectacles or contact lenses and solution. In some countries it may be difficult to find certain medicines; others may be sold under different names. Ask your doctor for names of alternatives, in case the medicine you are taking is not available. Always take a supply of any medication in your carry-on luggage where flights are involved (eg if you are flying to the start point of your cruise), just in case your hold lug-

gage goes astray. If you are diabetic, ask before you book whether your chosen rivership has an in-cabin refrigerator or mini-fridge to store medication in.

Money

European riverships operate in euros (€), but for the duration of the journey, it's cashless cruising on board, so that you don't have to worry about carrying cash or cards with you. Your final payment at the end of the cruise can be made using major credit cards or cash.

Tipping: If gratuities are not included in the overall package price (they sometimes are and sometimes aren't – check the small print or ask your booking agent to be sure), the accepted standard for gratuities aboard European riverships is €8–10 (£6–12) per person, per day. Tips are given as a lump sum at the end of your cruise and divided equally between all crew members.

Pets

With the exception of 1AVista cruises, which operates a few cruises each year in Europe for owners and their dogs, pets are not allowed on board river cruises. Check with the river cruise company as to whether guide dogs would be allowed.

Reception desk

Centrally located and manned 24 hours a day, the reception desk is the nerve centre of the rivership for all information and help with any problems, plus ephemera such as postcards, stamps, river maps and items in the boutique. Your passport will normally be kept in a safe in an office behind the reception desk.

Room service

This is not generally available on riverships, as there simply aren't enough crew members to cope. Some riverships offer room service at breakfast to suite occupants. If you are poorly and confined to your cabin, you may also be offered help in the way of meals brought to your room.

Safety

Bridges: Riverships often pass under very low bridges. In some cases the space between the bridge overhead and the rivership can be so little that if you don't sit down, you run the risk of serious head injury. **Injury:** Slipping, tripping and falling can all unfortunately cause injuries on board riverships. This does not mean that vessels of this kind are unsafe, but there are some things that you can do to minimise the chances of injury.

Inside your cabin, note that on many (pre-2000) riverships, there is a raised 'lip' (typically between 15cm/6ins and 30cm/12ins) between the bathroom and the rest of the cabin. Watch out for this, as it's easy to trip over it. On deck, wear sensible shoes with

Alemannia's sun deck.

rubber soles (not crepe) when walking on the open deck and don't wear high heels.

Smokers should not throw lighted cigarette or cigar butts, or knock out pipes, over the side of the vessel. The water might seem like a safe place to throw them, but they can easily be sucked into an opening in the side or onto an aft open deck, and start a fire. It is also inconsiderate and environmentally unfriendly.

If you are injured aboard your rivership and want to take legal action against the company running the cruise, note that you need to file suit in the country of registry – so for riverships registered in Switzerland, the lawsuit must be filed in Switzerland (this is known as the Forum Clause). For more details on this, check the small print of your ticket, which will usually state at length the instances in which the cruise carrier will not be held responsible for injury. Note that passengers may not be able to sue a river cruise company in the event of injury or accident on an included or optional shore excursion, since these tours are operated by independent contractors.

Sailing time
At each destination, the vessel's sailing time will be posted at the gangway.

Security
All cabins aboard riverships can be locked. Old-style keys are made of metal and operate mechanical locks; most locks, however, will be electronically coded ones that open with plastic key cards.

River cruise lines do not accept responsibility for money or valuables left in cabins and suggest that you store them in a safe (see 'Valuables').

Shops
A small boutique on board, typically run by the reception staff, will offer a selection of maps, souvenirs, gifts and toiletries.

Smoking
Most riverships have complete no-smoking policies inside (an exception to this is the cigar lounge aboard *Premicon Queen*), but they do usually allow smoking on the open deck.

Swimming pools
A handful of the newest riverships have small swimming pools ('dip' pools), sometimes with retractable covers, so that the pool room can be used for other purposes in the evenings.

Television and film
Programming is obtained from a mix of satellite feeds and onboard videos. Some riverships receive live international news programmes, for which river cruise operators pay a subscription fee. Satellite television reception is sometimes poor because riverships constantly move out of the narrow beam of a satellite and cannot track the signal as accurately as a land-based facility.

Films are shown on the in-cabin television system and, on some of the most sophisticated riverships, in a combined pool/cinema room.

Valuables
Most riverships have a small personal safe in each cabin for storing valuables. For extra security, items of special value can also be kept in a safety deposit box at the reception desk – you will be able to access them during your cruise.

Accommodation

Your suite/cabin is your home away from home, although it will most likely be much smaller than you expect.

Design

Rivership accommodation has to be practical and functional, due to the limited space available. European riverships have either two or three accommodation decks, a result mostly of a vessel's dimensions, which are imposed by the many locks and bridges on the various rivers.

Before considering the accommodation itself, note that cabins on the lowest deck of a rivership have smaller windows (or portholes) than those on the decks above. Also, access may be via a narrow stairway or spiral staircase (an example of this is *AmaDagio*), with a handrail on one side only. Anyone with concerns about mobility limitations should look closely at the deck plan when considering these (least expensive) cabins on the lowest accommodation level.

It's not one size fits all, though. River cruise brochures list suites/ cabins in a number of different price levels, usually according to their size and location. There is a greater choice of accommodation types and sizes on the newer riverships than older ones – on Scenic riverships, there are, for example, a staggering 16 price categories, Viking has eight, while A-ROSA has just four, from standard cabins (the smallest) to owner's suites (the largest) and penthouse suites (a rather grandiose term). Basically, the more you pay, the more space you get.

Companies building riverships with less expensive materials, fitting modular bathrooms, for example, or low-quality soundproofing, large ceiling tiles (instead of a more expensive one-piece ceiling) or Ikea-style closets (instead of higher-quality units), do so to save building costs per cabin. They can then target a broader market, with more competitive pricing.

Cabins and suites

You may see different words used for what is essentially a cabin, a large cabin or a suite. These include 'stateroom', which is often used by North American companies to describe a standard cabin. Then there are 'suites', which should comprise a lounge or sitting room separated from a bedroom by a solid door, not just a curtain. Smaller 'suites' are sometimes termed 'junior' or 'deluxe', but these are simply larger cabins than standard.

Rivership cabins can vary in size from a miniscule 6 sq m (65 sq ft) to just under 40 sq m (430.5 sq ft). It's all about the micro-management of space, and, if you've ever stayed or lived in a caravan, you'll know what I mean. Suitcases can often be stored under the bed, to save valuable cabin space.

A view of a suite (with room divider open) aboard *Scenic Jasper*.

On a seven-day cruise, you probably won't spend much time in your cabin, so a suite (generally double the size of a cabin) may be a waste of money. However, a suite allows you to spread out, and it should come with a larger bathroom (with a bathtub, a separate shower enclosure and one or two washbasins). If you take a longer cruise (for example 14 days from Amsterdam all the way to the Black Sea), it may be worth the extra expense, if the budget allows.

Try to avoid cabins located directly under or adjacent to the galley (kitchen), as these can be extremely noisy, particularly early in the morning, when the chefs are preparing breakfast.

Although rivership cabins are small compared to most hotel rooms, with limited storage space, they are designed to be functional and practical. All cabins have outside river views, except for a handful of interior (no-view) ones aboard *Primadonna* and *Rossini*. Cabins on the lowest deck have only small windows, while those on the deck(s) above feature larger picture windows, some of which can be opened.

A number of the newer riverships (examples include *Avalon Illumination II, Avalon Imagery* and *Avalon Poetry II*) have cabins placed in a sideways arrangement that allows for larger bathrooms. These include a good-sized bathtub, separate shower enclosure and two washbasins (as aboard some ocean-going ships). The advantage of this arrangement is that the bed faces the river, so you wake up each morning with a great view (unless the rivership is in a lock, in which case you could feel like you are in a darkened lift). This design was first employed in 2007 on the *Premicon Queen*.

Cabin ceilings (some are nicely indented one-piece ceilings, while others are plain ceiling panels) tend to be rather low, and beds may be shorter and narrower than you have at home. Designers often place large mirrors opposite the bed to give the illusion of space (much to the horror of *feng shui* practitioners, for whom this means the reflection of negative energy).

In terms of facilities, most cabins feature a personal safe, a minibar, a television and an alarm clock/radio. Cupboards may or may not be illuminated. If you have one of the top suites, you may also have more impressive gadgets such as a personal iPad, a fancy audio system or a coffee machine. Fancier toiletries, room service and perhaps even a butler may also be part of the deal. Apart from this, and the extra space, there are few other advantages of paying more – you join the same excursions as standard passengers, for example. Some suites, such as the two Owner's Suites aboard the Viking 'Longships', have a wraparound outdoor balcony, although being located aft, these can be noisy when the vessels are moving.

Balconies, sliding windows and folding glass doors

Brochures lead us to expect floor-to-ceiling windows and doors that open (electrically, by pressing a button or by large sliding glass doors) on to some kind of balcony, but they don't tell us about the mosquitoes that can invade the Danube in the afternoon, or that riverships tie up alongside each other in busy ports (blocking the view), or that a balcony is fairly useless when a rivership moves up and down in the many locks. While a balcony of some sort may indeed be desirable, consider how much you will use it compared with the premium it costs. Since the main purpose of a river cruise is to experience the destinations, a balcony may not actually be necessary.

A real (private) balcony – that revered bit of space that lets you step outside – costs more, of course. So, is a balcony – or floor-to-ceiling (or wall-to-wall) opening glass door desirable on a rivership? In practice, it is not so useful, because sailing is often done at night; when in port, other riverships may be berthed alongside your balcony, meaning that you need to keep it closed. It's also best to keep it closed when in a lock. So, while a balcony is often useful just to 'feel' the air and temperature, and to know what clothing to choose, most people prefer to be outside on the sun deck (the top open deck) for scenery viewing. A balcony does, of course, provide a sense of exclusivity, but watch out for the mosquitoes.

Some passengers use their balconies to dry any items of clothing that they have washed – not always a pretty sight, especially if you are docked next to it.

Glossary

Step-outside balcony: A real balcony is one on which you can actually sit outside and enjoy the scenery.

'French' or 'Juliet' balcony: A 'French' or 'Juliet' balcony features a floor-to-ceiling sliding glass door that opens (or folding glass panels that open) to safety railings. This design only allows you to stick out your nose (or toes) and smell the fresh air.

Twin balcony suites: In 2010, Viking introduced an innovative new design, which became a series of over 50 Viking 'Longships'. These included several suites featuring both a real (step-outside) balcony *plus* a French balcony, with floor-to-ceiling opening glass doors – made possible due to a double-width cabin layout. AMA also has some riverships with both real and French balconies.

Panoramic opening windows: Wall-to-wall windows, such as those found aboard Emerald's *Emerald Belle, Emerald Dawn, Emerald Sky, Emerald Star, Emerald Sun* and some Scenic and Uniworld vessels (*Scenic Jasper, Scenic Opal, S.S. Antoinette, S.S. Catherine, S.S. Maria Theresa*, for example) are cleverly designed, and electrically operated by push button (it takes about 30 seconds to fully open or close the huge windows, which are around 2m/7ft across). Unfortunately, when you are seated in a chair, your view is blocked by the thick wood or steel frame of the window. Also, the weight of the huge windows can present a problem, because a rivership 'flexes' as it moves against currents, and the mechanism ceases to function.

The same is true of Avalon's vessels, whose large sliding glass doors (*Avalon Passion, Avalon Tapestry II, Avalon Tranquility II*) open on to a 'French' balcony, but these are really just large windows that open. They are, however, better than those of Emerald or Scenic because there is no viewing obstruction, other than the necessary safety railings. Placing the bed opposite the window is a bonus, because there's always a river view.

Uniworld's *S.S. Antoinette, S.S. Catherine and S.S. Maria Theresa* have push-button electric windows and a mosquito screen, while almost all CroisiEurope's riverships have small sliding windows and only a few balconies (such as aboard the nicely refurbished *Camargue*).

Cabin carpeting: This varies from vessel to vessel. Some riverships have plush carpeting with thick underlay; some have decent quality carpeting without underlay. Others have caravan-quality thin carpeting with no underlay.

Ceilings: The more expensive riverships (AmaWaterways, Scenic, Viking, for example) have one-piece cabin ceilings, while others have ceilings made of metal 'planks' (Avalon), as on so many ocean-going cruise ships, or large ceiling 'tiles' (Emerald). One-piece ceilings look more attractive.

Infotainment systems

Riverships vary considerably regarding in-cabin infotainment systems – flat-screen units that are positioned opposite the bed(s) and can be viewed from almost any angle. They typically include a shipboard information channel, television channel (including news from one of the major providers such as the BBC, CNN, Sky or Al Jazeerah), movies channel and possibly an audio channel (for CDs or pre-recorded music).

Note that when watching a movie, the picture could be interrupted when the rivership goes under a bridge or into a lock, if it's a GPS-based system. Those aboard Emerald's vessels (but not those of sister company Scenic) are like this.

Electrical sockets

The latest riverships have plenty of (220v) electrical sockets for your digital devices, but they may not always be visible. Some companies put extra sockets at floor level under the beds; others hide them in the cupboards or wardrobes; some have several on the vanity/writing desk unit or shelf, although they may be taken by the telephone and rechargeable personal receivers used for tours. Older riverships simply don't have enough sockets – you may be lucky to find just one.

Beds and bedlinen

Most of the riverships built after 2010 have twin beds that can be placed together to form a double (or queen-sized) bed. However, aboard many older (pre-2000) riverships, cabins have two beds or twin beds that are fixed and can't be pushed together. This may not be good for romantics, but the arrangement might be useful for providing 'snoring' and 'no-snoring'

beds. Examples of the latter arrangement include *Bijou, Der Kleine Prinz, River Adagio, River Allegro, River Ambassador, River Aria, River Concerto, River Harmony, River Melody, River Rhapsody* and *Swiss Ruby*.

Some riverships (such as *Amsterdam, Bellevue, Bizet, Cezanne, Prinses Juliana, Rigoletto, River Harmony, River Rhapsody, Select Explorer, Serenity, and Ukraina*) have fold-down beds, one or both of which can convert into a sofa for daytime use, giving extra space in the (really small) cabin in the daytime. Being practical and space-efficient, these are good for couples who prefer separate beds on holiday.

Some riverships have two beds in an 'L-shaped configuration (so you sleep head to head or toes to toes), which is definitely not for honeymooners! Note that beds in cabins for solo occupancy might be lower and/or slimmer than a standard single bed.

Some beds have mattresses *inside* a bed frame instead of on top of it, with square, not round, corners. The challenge here is that there is very little room to move in, and legs can easily be knocked against the sharp corners. Aboard some riverships (such as *River Voyager, Scenic Amber, Scenic Jasper* and *Scenic Opal*), mattresses have individually controlled tilt-up mechanisms. While *Serenity 2* has Tempur (memory foam) mattresses, almost all others have premium or standard mattresses.

European down duvets, high-quality bed linens and plush mattresses are what fine sleeping environments are all about. The bed linen aboard most riverships is 100 percent cotton, but on the less expensive ones it may be a 50 percent cotton/50 percent polyester mix.

Pillows

While some companies provide a choice of pillows, such Tauck's hypoallergenic pillows, other companies (including Avalon and CroisiEurope), have only a standard pillow (usually with a cotton cover and inside of polyester). Some companies (such as Ama and Scenic) provide a pillow menu with a choice of several different types, while others (such as Emerald) have a pillow menu only for the top suites. Pillow choices might include hop-filled or hypoallergenic, goose down, Hungarian goose down (considered the best), isotonic, Tempur-Pedic or copycat memory foam.

Bathrooms

Bathrooms come in various sizes, shapes and fittings, and comfort levels. Some are marble-clad; some have tiled walls and floor; some have plain modular walls (like caravan units). Some have space to sit comfortably on the toilet, while others are really cramped; some have good lighting; others have modest lighting, and a number are so dim that you can't see your hands in front of you!

Expect them to be functional rather than sumptuous – there simply isn't room to accommodate the touches of luxury you would find in a hotel suite or in the best suites aboard an ocean-going ship. A typical

Infotainment system aboard *Emerald Sky*.

bathroom includes a washbasin, toilet and shower, while bathtubs are available in some suites.

Some suites, such as the Owner's Suites aboard the Viking 'Longships', have large wet rooms, with a wooden seat in the shower enclosure. You may find little extras (Emerald's vessels have tiny blue night-lights, for example), vanity kits including cotton buds and make-up removal pads, and other toiletries. All riverships provide towels, soap and shampoo (sometimes in bottles, sometimes in wall-mounted dispensers).

Most riverships built before 2010 have shower curtains; newer vessels have more stylish – and hygienic – glass doors. Some bathrooms have fixed-head showers, but most have flexible shower hoses. One challenge, particularly for taller passengers, is that the ceiling height is limited. Newer riverships may have high-power showers with changing colours (examples include *Scenic Gem, Scenic Jade*).

Some of Uniworld's newest riverships have heated towel rails. Viking's 'Longships' have heated bathroom floors, as do all Scenic's vessels and Tauck's *Grace, Inspire, Joy* and *Savor* among others. My own frequently stated irritant is bathroom mirrors that steam up, an all-too common complaint. Well, Viking's 'Longships' and Vantage's *River Voyager* have anti-steam mirrors. Let's hope the trend continues.

Towels are normally supplied on board, so you don't have to bring them with you. Sizes vary considerably – examples include 142 x 102cm (56 x 40ins) on Viking, 132 x 71cm (52 x 28ins) on Ama, and 102 x 71cm (40 x 28ins) on Scylla/Tauck vessels.

Toilets, too, can vary in height, from a low of 41cm/16ins (Emerald) to 48cm/19ins (Avalon, and Viking, whose toilet seats are of the soft-close variety), to a high of 53cm/21ins (Ama).

Bathroom amenities

Personal amenities are provided aboard most riverships, although there are some differences. For example, Ama, Emerald, Scenic and Viking provide individual bottles of shampoo, conditioner and shower gel. Aboard the vessels of A-ROSA and Uniworld, wall-mounted dispensers for shower gel and shampoo or combined shampoo/conditioner (suites have individual items) are provided.

L'Occitane toiletries (from Provence) are often provided. Some will be in fixed dispensers on the wall of the shower (Avalon), while suite occupants may get even posher products (Hermès in suites aboard Uniworld vessels, for example).

Items including illuminated make-up/shaving mirrors, cotton make-up pads or cotton balls, nail files, sewing kits and other personal amenities may be provided aboard the better (and newer) riverships, such as those of Ama and Scenic, but not aboard the vessels of the low-priced operators. As is so often the case, the more you pay, the more you get.

Cabin numbering

Maritime tradition aboard ocean-going ships dictates that even-numbered cabins should be on the port side (the same as the lifeboats). However, aboard some riverships (Tauck's, chartered from Scylla, for example), odd-numbered cabins may be found on the port side of the vessel. Even within the same company, some riverships may have even-numbered cabins on the port side, while others may have odd-numbers. It's all a little confusing, if you're used to the traditional system. In addition, some riverships have no cabins with the number 13 (*Crystal Mozart, Danubia, Theodore Korner, Princess Christina* and *Sir Winston,* for examples), which is reassuring news for superstitious travellers.

Cuisine

Food is a major part of any successful river cruise. Here, we lift the lid on what the dining experience is really like.

Companies put maximum effort into telling you just how fabulous their food is. What is closer to the truth is that you'll be served agreeable food in comfortable surroundings. Just don't expect the variety you get on the ocean-going cruise ships.

River cruise cuisine compares favourably with the kind of 'banquet' food served in a decent hotel. River-ships cannot offer a full-on gourmet experience in the restaurant – despite what the brochures might claim – because the galley ('kitchen' for landlubbers) is small, with batch cooking used to turn out up to 200 meals at a time. At almost any time of the day or night, there is activity in the galley, whether baking fresh bread at night, preparing meals and snacks for passengers and crew around the clock, or decorating a special birthday cake.

The restaurant

All riverships have one 'main' restaurant. Many new riverships also offer a 'healthy-eating' corner as a bistro-style section (some with an indoor/outdoor option) as part of or in front of the lounge. Occasionally, small buffets or barbecues may be offered on the 'Sun Deck' (weather and temperature permitting, of course).

A section of the lunch buffet aboard *A-ROSA Stella*.

Tables for two aboard riverships are a rarity; most tables are for four, six or eight persons. When tables are unassigned – called 'open seating' – you can sit with whomever you wish. This means that you can change your dinner table partners each evening if you wish. Aboard riverships where tables are assigned, it may be difficult to change tables once the cruise has started.

Alternative eateries

The largest 135m (443ft) riverships may also have an alternative dining venue aft, which allows you to eat in a more intimate setting. All AmaWaterways river-ships, for example, have a separate 'Chef's Table', located aft, with a show galley (kitchen), where a chef prepares a high-quality multi-course dégustation menu, where everything is cooked individually, beautifully presented and paired with some excellent wines.

Meanwhile, Scenic has 'Table La Rive', a single curtained-off table in the restaurant, with a set dégustation-style menu and wine pairings.

In some riverships the forward section of the lounge may become an 'alternative' eatery in the evening, so access to the exterior forward deck may be restricted. For example, Avalon has Sky Bistro (with tablecloths and youthful wine pairing). Scenic has Portofino (aboard its riverships on French rivers its name is L'Amour), located in the forward section of the main lounge (the staff serves from a connecting stairway to the main galley area).

Several companies (Emerald and Scenic, for example) also have a 'Healthy Choice' or 'Vitality' corner for breakfast and lunch.

Note that there's no extra charge to eat in any alternative area, and spreading the diners out like this also helps to manage demand in the main restaurant from an operational point of view.

On some riverships, there are quite extensive eating options. *Alina* (2011) and *Amelia* (2012) both have two main restaurants – both of which are full-service restaurants, located at the front of the vessel, one above the other. There is also a steakhouse aft. Perhaps more new riverships will feature this approach in the future, simply because it provides a greater number of options.

The nitty gritty: It's often the case that the little details all combine to create a greater or worse end product. For example, the restaurants of *A-ROSA Stella*, *Amadeus Silver*, *Avalon Expression*, *Belle de Cadiz* and *Expression Royale* have seats without armrests, which is less comfortable than those with armrests. Aboard

River Royale buffet.

AmaCello, Mozart, S.S. *Antoinette* or *Viking Embla* (as aboard all other Viking 'Longships'), for example, most of the chairs in restaurants do have armrests.

Some riverships have a restaurant with alcove-style seating booths (examples include: AmaSonata and AmaSerena), which means that leaning over fellow passengers is necessary to serve.

Some companies (A-ROSA, for example) only have placemats and no tablecloths on restaurant tables for dinner. Emerald Waterways features placemats for breakfast and lunch, but has tablecloths for dinner. AmaWaterways and Scenic have tablecloths for breakfast, lunch and dinner. Ama, Scenic and Uniworld provide linen napkins, whereas some operators provide only paper napkins for dinner. Some companies provide paper napkins for breakfast and lunch, and linen napkins for dinner.

Also, some companies provide fish knives (Ama-Waterways, Emerald Waterways, Scenic and Viking River Cruises, for example), but most vessels cater-ing to North Americans – such as those of Grand Circle Cruise Lines and Vantage River Cruises – do not, nor does A-ROSA.

Meanwhile, AmaWaterways, Emerald Waterways, Scenic and Viking River Cruises provide proper steak knives, but most others do not. The cuisine is generally international, often with some typical dishes that represent the country or region you are visiting. Gravies and salty cream sauces are often used to mask less-expensive cuts of meat or defrosted ingredients. Portions tend to be small, however.

On budget-priced riverships you can expect portion-controlled frozen ingredients that are modified with flavour enhancers and simply reheated and plated. On more expensive vessels, you can expect to be served more freshly prepared ingredients, especially fish, better meat cuts and higher-quality fruit and vegetables. Food quality and ingredient costs vary considerably, with the general rule being the more you pay, the better-quality food you can expect.

River cruise operators work generally closely with their food suppliers to identify and remove any products that contain genetically modified food, with the exception of packages of cereal. Some owners (such as Scylla) and operators (such as the UK's Riviera Travel) even have different marine caterers and suppliers for various riverships in their fleet in order to create healthy competition and maintain standards.

On European rivers, galley standards, food supply, handling and hygiene all come under the auspices of HACCP Certification (Hazard Analysis Critical Control Point).

Breakfast: The first meal of the day, taken between around 7am and 9am, is usually a self-service buffet with a variety of cold cuts of meat and a decent range of French and other European cheeses laid out on a central display table. There may also be an omelette station (some riverships use an industrial 'egg'

SPECIAL DIETS

If you have a vegetarian, vegan or macrobiotic diet, are counting calories or want salt-free, sugar-restricted, low-fat, low-cholesterol food, or indeed have any other dietary restrictions, tell the river cruise company or your cruise booking agent before you make a booking, and ask the cruise operator to confirm that it can handle your dietary requirements. Note that food on many riverships tends to be liberally dosed with salt, and vegetables are often cooked with sauces containing dairy products, salt and sugar.

Politely hidden on the back page of menus aboard AmaWaterways' riverships is a list of possible food intolerance items (nuts, dairy items, for example) that you should make the chef aware of.

Avalon Expression bar.

mix and not real eggs). Hot food items can also be ordered from your waiter. Some riverships (including those of AmaWaterways, Scenic and Viking River Cruises) may additionally feature a 'special of the day' or other menu options.

Aboard a few riverships bread and bread rolls may be made on board (AmaWaterways, for example); but aboard most, these items may be made from frozen dough, or purchased ashore. Many rivership croissants have no taste, for example, because they are made from frozen starter dough and poor-quality butter.

Note that 'fresh' fruit juices are almost always of the pre-packed supermarket variety (and definitely not 'fresh'), due to lack of preparation space in the galley. Fruit 'smoothies' are also often featured, but note that these can contain up to 50 percent white sugar.

Lunch: This is usually a self-service buffet. The selection will include a choice of fresh green salad items with dressings (typically unimaginative) and a range of oils (olive, basil, sesame, pumpkin, walnut, etc) that can liven up your salad. The omelette station from breakfast will probably have been converted into a pasta or meat-slicing station for lunch. Requests for à la carte or 'always available' hot food items are taken by a waiter and cooked to order.

Dinner: Dinner, at about 7pm (when everyone rushes to the restaurant to find a seat if it's an open seating arrangement) is typically normally a sit-down (plated) meal served at either assigned or unassigned (open-service) tables, although the self-service buffet of A-ROSA Cruises is one exception to this. Served dinners normally consist of a choice of cold or hot starter (appetizer), a choice of two or three main courses (entrées) – one fish, one meat, one vegetarian – plus dessert and cheese (usually in that order, although cheese might be available at any time throughout the meal). You can expect river fish (other than shrimp/prawns, there may be little in the way of shellfish), and dark red meats such as venison, beef and ox, as well as lighter fare including chicken and other fowl. AmaWaterways uses fresh fish – to my knowledge, this is the only river cruise company to do so.

Drinks

River cruise companies often tout that all drinks, including alcoholic beverages, are included in the cruise price. Take a look at the selection in the bar, however, and you may notice brands you've never heard of before. Whiskies available will inevitably be of the blended variety – ask for a decent single malt whisky and you'll probably have to pay extra. ('It's not included in the included drinks, sir.') And, for that gin and tonic, you may be facing tonic, such as Royal tonic, that tastes incredibly sweet and artificial, or, alternatively, basic tonic from a hose. As for premium gins – not a chance, although I did experience a fine Black Forest gin called Monkey 47 aboard the riverships of AmaWaterways and Scenic recently.

Wine: Many river cruise companies tout their 'specially selected' wines, sometimes dubbing them 'fine wine' (Uniworld) or 'superb regional and international wines' (Scenic). If you enjoy good vintage wines, expect to be disappointed, however, unless you bring your own (most companies allow you to do this, but only for consumption in your cabin, so not during a meal).

In most cases the wines are very, very young table wines – on a par with the least expensive supermarket wines. And in terms of quantity, most river cruise operators only provide small wine glasses for both white and red wines, although a few (notably AmaWaterways and Scenic) provide large, proper glasses – by this I mean Bordeaux-sized glasses for red wines and Chardonnay-sized ones for whites – and their wines are of a better quality. Measures are up to the waiter. It's not truly unlimited, either: if you read the small print, you will find phrases such as: 'Unlimited beverages do not include premium wine and premium spirits' (Uniworld).

Of course, there are exceptions, such as the specialist wine-themed cruises of AMA Waterways, for example, which feature private tastings, exclusive vineyard visits and special brochures on the wine regions of Europe.

Coffee and tea: Riverships have self-service drinks corners, typically with a good-quality push-button espresso/cappuccino machine and a selection of teas. Most companies provide teabags rather than loose tea, although Uniworld is an exception to this. Premium riverships provide a range of teas from specialist brands such as Fauchon, Ronnefeldt, Tea Forté, Twinings or Whittard. Standard riverships in Europe may provide teas of a lesser quality by companies including Bigelow, Dilmah, Lipton or Pickwick. Coffee varies from the best Italian brands (illy, Lavazza, Sagafredo) to the unknown.

Some riverships provide only white sugar for hot beverages – a choice of white or brown at least is preferable.

Water: Water is usually provided in jugs. These are towel-wrapped aboard some of the premium riverships, but aboard most, they are not.

Excursions ashore

Excursions on a river cruise offer everything from helicopter rides and hot-air ballooning to wine tasting, horse riding and musical recitals in historic venues.

Excursions on a river cruise are a highlight for many passengers. When they are included in the cruise fare, it will be reflected in the price, but this does simplify budgeting. If you are visiting new places and want the value of a good guide, it's best to choose a company where excursions are included. Normally, this will comprise full days of activities when the rivership is in port and often a couple of evening events, too.

When river cruise operators plan and oversee optional excursions, they assume that passengers have not visited a place before and aim to show them its highlights in a comfortable manner and at a reasonable price.

Buses or minibuses are usually the principal choice of transport. This cuts costs and allows the tour operator to narrow the selection of guides to only those most competent, knowledgeable and fluent in whatever language the majority of passengers speak, while providing some degree of security and control.

Learn to read between the lines about excursions: the term 'visit' should be taken to mean actually entering the place or building concerned, whereas 'see' should be taken to mean viewing from the outside (perhaps even just from the bus, for example).

Excursions are timed to be most convenient for the greatest number of participants, taking into account the timing of meals on board (these may be altered according to excursion times). Departure times are listed in the descriptive literature and in the daily programme (delivered to your cabin and posted at the reception desk), and may or may not be announced over the vessel's public address system. There are no refunds if you miss the excursion. If you are hearing-impaired, make arrangements with the excursion staff to assist you in departing for your excursions at the correct times.

Excursions for large cities are basically superficial, although they do provide a useful introduction. On most of these tours, Audiovox or Quietvox headsets are provided. These enable the tour guide to communicate by talking into a microphone and passengers to listen wirelessly using in-ear headphones, so you don't look so much like a tourist and you can hear the commentary clearly.

To see specific sights in more detail, or to get to know a city in a more intimate fashion, go alone with a guidebook or with a small group and a private guide. (Scenic Cruises provides excellent sat-nav-style devices packed with information for self-guided visits.) Go by taxi or bus or walk directly to the places that are of most interest to you.

Going solo? If you hire a taxi for sightseeing, negotiate the price in advance and do not pay until you get back to the vessel or to your final destination. If you are with friends, hiring a taxi for a full- or half-day sightseeing trip can work out far cheaper than renting a car, and you also avoid the hazards of driving. This can be an excellent way of sightseeing, particularly if you can find a driver who speaks your language, and who has a comfortable, air-conditioned vehicle.

An excursion guide.

A day in the life of a rivership

To give you a flavour of life on board a rivership, here's a sample daily programme. There's also a summary of who's who among the crew.

After arrival at your rivership (usually mid-afternoon), you simply step aboard and check in at the reception desk, where you are given your digital touch card (or cabin key). A steward or stewardess then takes you to your cabin and explains everything about it. Your luggage will already be inside the cabin, ready to unpack. While you have dinner in the dining room, your vessel will probably depart.

Each day, when you wake up, your rivership is probably on its way to the next destination or else has already arrived and is tied up at the landing stage, ready for everyone to explore; alternatively, it may be in a lock. Note that the excursions are completely optional – you can always just stay on board and relax, if you want to, or go ashore independently.

A TYPICAL DAY ON A RIVER DANUBE CRUISE

6.30am: Fresh coffee in the lounge for early risers.
7–9am: Breakfast in the dining room.

Continental breakfast option on Viking's *Aquavit Terrace*.

9am: Arrival at the first destination.
9.15am: Leave for the morning excursion – coaches will already be outside, as close to the gangway as possible, ready to take guests on a tour of a historic castle, key town or nearby vineyard.
12 noon: Return from the morning excursion (unless you are in a major city, in which case you would spend a whole day out and about).
12 noon–1.30pm: Lunch in the dining room or a small bistro lunch on the open sun deck (weather permitting).
2pm: Arrival at the second destination.
2.15pm: Departure for the afternoon excursion eg a castle, abbey or monastery, or a historical tour with a museum visit. In a small village (such as Dürnstein, in Austria), it may instead be a simple walking tour escorted by a licensed local guide with in-depth knowledge of the locality.
4pm: Afternoon tea, cakes and sandwiches for anyone not on the afternoon excursion.
5pm: Return from the afternoon excursion.
6pm: Short briefing on the following day's programme (plus information on any changes to the schedule or docking times) in the lounge; pre-dinner cocktails and conversation.
7pm: Dinner of three or four courses is served in the dining room. Guests typically linger over an assortment of cheese and enjoy conversation around the table.
8pm: In the lounge, the resident pianist plays music for dancing or listening to. Occasionally, there might be some additional entertainment from ashore, perhaps a mini-concert (a classical trio of two violinists and a cello, for example), a small *a capella* vocal concert or perhaps some regional folk dancing. There may also be an evening excursion (such as a private concert in Vienna), if your rivership is spending longer than one day in a key destination.
10pm: Late-night snacks are available in the lounge or, if it's warm weather, perhaps outside on the sun deck, followed by bed. The lounge/bar doesn't usually close until after midnight.

BEHIND THE SCENES: HOW IT WORKS

Riverships are small, and teamwork makes it all happen. Whether you are on or off a rivership, the crew works constantly, both on the technical side (engines, air conditioning, heating and electrical items, etc) or the hospitality side – eg the reception staff dealing

Gather round for lounge entertainment.

with paperwork, acting as the main contact point for passengers, keeping track of who is on board or off the vessel, etc.

Even on the latest riverships, the maximum number of crew carried will usually be under 50. Some crews are much smaller than this – some older-style riverships have as few as 18 staff members. They work closely together, and multi-tasking skills come in handy in such a confined environment.

Captain

The captain is the ultimate authority on board. They drive the rivership and are responsible for navigation and all things technical. The captain is licensed and insured for the river(s) the vessel sails on. A deputy (second captain) is licensed and able to take over at any time – there is sometimes a lot of night sailing to do, so they take turns. The captain has several engineers to look after all electrical and mechanical items, including the air conditioning, the lighting and heating systems, and, of course, the engines themselves.

Hotel manager

The hotel manager is in charge of the overall hotel operation (and all department heads), including all things relating to passenger comfort and satisfaction, the provision of food and drinks (these may be provided by an outside maritime catering company),

placing orders for supplies and generally coordinating departments and personnel and communicating with the river cruise company's headquarters, or owner.

Cruise manager

Aboard riverships, the cruise manager makes sure that the route plan is followed, does evening recaps in the lounge, hosts social events, handles all the excursions, plans the timing for the next day's programme, and takes care of any other details such as entertainment, library books and reports.

Housekeeping

In the early morning, the cabin stewards and stewardesses will count out the number of fresh towels needed for the cabins in their sections. They will have a stock of sheets and pillowcases available in case any need changing, as well as any personal amenities that need refilling or changing.

Executive chef

The executive chef typically heads up a team of up to eight people in the galley – a small space no larger than a standard-size hotel room. At almost any hour of the day, chefs are busy preparing, cooking, grilling, sautéing or making sauces. During the night, a pastry chef prepares cakes and sweet items.

What to do if...

Here are some tips to ensure the best river cruise experience possible, and, just in case it doesn't quite go to plan, advice on what to do if you do have a problem.

...you fly internationally to take a cruise.

If your cruise is a long distance from your home, it makes sense (if time and budget allow) to fly to your cruise embarkation point and stay for at least a day or two before the cruise starts. This way you will be better rested and able to adjust to any time changes before your cruise begins. You then step aboard your rivership relaxed and ready for your holiday. As a bonus, you will get to know the departure city/town.

...your luggage does not arrive.

If your holiday package includes flights as well as your cruise, the airline is responsible for locating your luggage and delivering it to the next port. If you have arranged your own flights, you are responsible for picking your luggage up at the airport and transporting it to your cruise. Our tips include placing easy-to-read name and address tags both inside as well as outside your luggage, to increase the likelihood that it will be returned to you if it is delayed or goes missing. Also, give your airline your itinerary and a list of port agents (included with your river cruise documents), so that any lost luggage can be forwarded once it has been tracked down. (Keep this list – and contact details for insurance purposes – in your hand luggage, so that it's accessible.)

...you miss your rivership.

If you miss the rivership's departure at the port of embarkation due to late or cancelled flights or connections and you are travelling on an air/sea package, the airline will make suitable arrangements to get you to your rivership. If you are travelling 'cruise-only', however, and have arranged your own flights, then it is entirely your own responsibility to arrive on time. If you do miss the sailing, contact the rivership's agent immediately – their details will be included in your documents.

...a port of call is deleted from the itinerary.

This can easily happen on a river cruise, perhaps for security reasons, strikes or overcrowded docking spaces. Remember to read the small print in the brochure before you book. A river cruise company is under no obligation to perform the stated itinerary if they have noted otherwise in the brochure.

Dinner time in Lyon.

Waiting for passengers to embark.

...you miss the rivership in a port of call.

The onus is on you to get back to your rivership before its appointed sailing time. Miss it and you'll need to get to the next stopping point at your own cost. In Europe, the train network is fortunately so good that this is usually possible, although it's obviously more costly, inconvenient and potentially stressful.

...you leave personal belongings on a tour bus.

If you unintentionally leave something on a tour bus, and you are back on board your rivership, let the staff at the reception desk know. They will contact the excursion operator to ascertain whether any lost property has been found.

...your cabin has no air conditioning or it has heating or plumbing problems.

If there is anything wrong with your cabin, including problems with the plumbing in the bathroom, bring it to the attention of your cabin steward immediately. If things don't improve, complain to the cruise manager. If the rivership is full – and most are fully booked months in advance – it will be difficult to change to another one.

...you are unwell aboard your rivership.

Riverships do not carry their own designated medical team or unit, unlike ocean-going cruise ships. Land, however, is always accessible, so arrangements can quickly be made to access medical assistance. Almost all river cruise companies offer insurance packages that include medical cover for most eventualities. It is wise to take out this type of insurance when you book (see page 19).

Members of European Union/European Economic Area (EU/EEA) countries or those of Swiss nationality should get a free EHIC, which entitles the bearer to state health care at a reduced cost or sometimes for free. It is valid in all EEA countries, including Switzerland. You can apply online at www.ehic.org.uk. Note that EHICs do not cover private health care or repatriation.

...the food is definitely not 'gourmet' cuisine, as stated in the brochure.

If the food is not as described – for example, it promises 'whole lobster' in the brochure, but you only see cold lobster salad once during the cruise, or the 'freshly squeezed' orange juice on the breakfast menu is anything but – inform the maître d' (restaurant manager) of the problem.

...you have a problem with a crew member.

Contact the hotel manager (via the reception desk) and explain the situation. It's their job to resolve issues of this kind, although they are hopefully rare, since river cruise companies try to hire the best crew members they can.

...you're unhappy with your cruise experience.

If the cruise doesn't meet your expectations or performs less well than the brochure promises, let your booking agent and the river cruise company know as soon as possible. Be certain to read the small print, however – after you've done so, it'll probably seem as if passengers don't have many rights after all.

Cruising past Marksburg Castle on the Rhine.

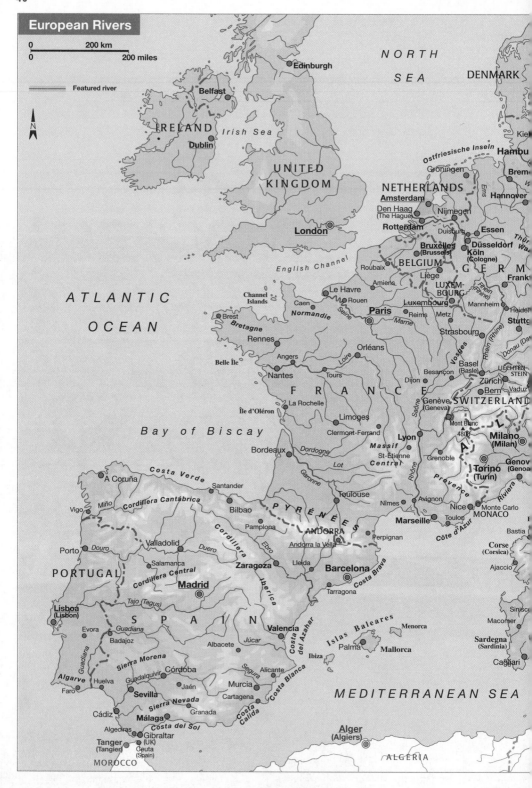

European Rivers

| 0 | 200 km |
| 0 | 200 miles |

—— Featured river

N

NORTH SEA

DENMARK

Edinburgh

Kie

Belfast

Ostfriesische Inseln   **Hambu**

IRELAND   *Irish Sea*

Groningen   **Brem**

Dublin

NETHERLANDS

Amsterdam   **Hannover**

UNITED KINGDOM

Den Haag (The Hague)   Nijmegen

Rotterdam   Duisburg   **Essen**   *Thür*

London

Bruxelles (Brussels)   **Düsseldorf**

Roubaix   **BELGIUM**   **Köln (Cologne)**   **GERM**

Liège

English Channel   Amiens   LUXEM-BOURG   **Frank**

Rhein (Rhine)

Channel Islands   Le Havre   Rouen   Luxembourg   Mannheim   **Heidel**

Caen   **Normandie**   Reims   Metz   **Stuttg**

Brest   **Paris**   Marne   Strasbourg   Donau (Da

Bretagne

Rennes   Orléans   Vosges   **Basel (Basle)**   LIECHTEN-STEIN

Belle Île   Angers   Loire   Dijon   Besançon   **Zürich**

Nantes   Tours   **Bern**   Vaduz

La Rochelle   **SWITZERLAND**

Île d'Oléron   Limoges   Genève (Geneva)

Bay of Biscay   Clermont-Ferrand   Saône   Mont Blanc 480   **Milano (Milan)**

Bordeaux   Dordogne   **Lyon**   *Massif*   St-Étienne   Grenoble   **Genov (Genoa**

Central   **Torino (Turin)**

ATLANTIC OCEAN

Lot   Rhône   *Provence*

Garonne   Toulouse   Nîmes   Avignon   Nice   *Riviera*

A Coruña   *Costa Verde*   Santander   **PYRÉNÉES**   Marseille   Toulon   Monte Carlo   **MONACO**

Vigo   Miño   *Cordillera Cantábrica*   Bilbao   **ANDORRA**   *Côte d'Azur*   Bastia

Pamplona   Perpignan   **Corse (Corsica)**

Porto   Douro   Valladolid   *Cordillera*   Andorra la Vella   Ebro   Lleida   **Barcelona**   Ajaccio

PORTUGAL   Salamanca   Duero   **Zaragoza**   *Costa Brava*

Cordillera Central   Tarragona

Madrid

Tajo (Tagus)   *Iberica*

Lisboa (Lisbon)   **S   P   A   I   N**

Evora   *Guadiana*   **Valencia**   *Costa del Azahar*   Menorca   **Sardegna (Sardinia)**

Badajoz   Júcar   *Islas Baleares*

Sierra Morena   Albacete   Ibiza   Palma   Mallorca   Cagliari

Algarve   Huelva   Córdoba   Segura   Alicante   *Costa Blanca*

Faro   Guadalquivir   Jaén   Murcia   **MEDITERRANEAN SEA**

Sevilla   Cartagena

Sierra Nevada   *Costa Calida*

Cádiz   Granada

Málaga   *Costa del Sol*

Algeciras   Gibraltar (UK)   **Alger (Algiers)**

Tanger (Tangier)   Ceuta (Spain)

MOROCCO   ALGERIA

Europe's rivers and waterways

A guide to the main river cruise routes and ports
of Europe, accompanied by diagrammatic maps.
Major ports of call come with our list of top sights.

Europe is the world's most developed and best-organised region for river cruises, and it is the heart of the European continent that is in most people's minds when they consider a river cruise. The earliest European river cruises were on the Rhine (Rhine), and later the Danube, and it isn't hard to see why. Accessible and wonderfully scenic, a trip on these great waterways instantly transports the passenger into old Europe, providing a constantly changing perspective on its history and landscapes.

A river cruise provides a unique perspective on the historic landscapes through which these waterways wend their way, past historic cities, medieval towns, fabled villages, forbidding castles, soaring cathedrals, monasteries, churches, romantic châ-

A-ROSA Stella passing the famous bridge at Avignon, France.

teaux, forests, hills, gardens, vineyards and industrial backdrops (commerce is still conducted along these rivers and waterways, so the scenery, while often magnificent, can also be industrial at times). River cruises can be combined, too, with other interests, from music – in the shape of an evening concert, attendance at a festival or through connections with a celebrated local composer – to tasting events for food and wine aficionados to film nights and more.

MAJOR EUROPEAN WATERWAYS

But on to the rivers themselves… The Rhine is justly famous for the fabulous scenery along its middle course between the German cities of Mainz and Koblenz, an utterly romantic riverscape of brooding castles perched atop steep hills covered in vineyards. Its major tributaries – the Mosel (Moselle in English), Neckar and Main – are also well-established cruise rivers. Most Danube cruises concentrate on the stretch between Passau on the German/Austrian border via Vienna and Bratislava to the Hungarian capital, Budapest – although there is also plenty of interest along the upper course in southern Germany (now linked to the Rhine via the Main–Danube Canal), as well as the lesser-known lower reaches that traverse the Balkans en route to the Black Sea. The Elbe, running from the Czech Republic through eastern Germany to the North Sea, is the other popular river of Central Europe, and itineraries along it typically explore the beautiful cities of Prague and Dresden.

OTHER WATERWAYS

Away from these major rivers, there is a variety of lesser-known waterways to explore, including the Douro in northern Portugal, the Po in Italy, and the Rhône and Seine in France. A wide range of barge cruises and other trips are also possible – barge cruising is especially popular in France.

KEY HIGHLIGHTS AND KILOMETRE DETAILS

Along most (although not all) European rivers, you'll notice white marker boards with black numbers at every navigable kilometre. These generally mark the distance from the river's source to the estuary, although on the Danube it is the other way round.

What follows in this section of the book is an overview of the key highlights you'll see on your cruise, by river, with kilometre details included, if they are likely to be marked.

SAMPLE ITINERARIES

There are many different possible itinerary combinations on European river cruises. Here are some examples of varying lengths, taken from various river cruise brochures.

7-day cruises

Amsterdam to Mainz (Rhine, Mosel)
Amsterdam, Rotterdam, Cologne (Köln), Bernkastel, Cochem, Koblenz, Rüdesheim, Mainz
Amsterdam to Amsterdam (Elbe)
Amsterdam, Volendam, Enkhuizen, Kampen, Deventer, Arnhem, Dordrecht, Rotterdam, Amsterdam
Chalon-sur-Saône to Arles (Rhône, Saône)
Chalon-sur-Saône, Mâcon, Trévoux, Lyon, Vienne, Tournon, Viviers, Avignon, Arles
Frankfurt to Frankfurt (Oder)
Frankfurt, Kostrzyn, Gorzów, Kostrzyn, Hohensaaten, Świnoujście, Szczecin, Frankfurt
Paris to Honfleur (Seine)
Paris, Melun, Conflans, Vernon, Rouen, Les Andelys, Caudebec, Honfleur
Hamburg to Dresden (Elbe)
Hamburg, Tangermünde, Magdeburg, Wittenberg, Torgau, Dresden, Bad Schandau, Dresden
Potsdam to Potsdam (Elbe)
Potsdam, Genthin, Magdeburg, Dresden, Wittenberg, Magdeburg, Brandenburg, Potsdam
Hannover to Potsdam (Elbe)
Hannover, Braunschweig, Magdeburg, Torgau, Pillnitz, Königstein, Litoměřice, Bad Schandau, Dresden, Meissen, Wittenberg, Burg, Brandenburg, Potsdam
Berlin to Prague (Elbe)
Berlin, Magdeburg, Dessau, Wittenberg, Torgau, Meissen, Dresden, Bad Schandau, Usti, Prague

10-day cruises

Amsterdam to Basel (Rhine, Mosel)
Amsterdam, Arnhem, Cologne, Koblenz, Zell, Trier, Bernkastel, Alken/Winnigen, Rüdesheim, Worms, Speyer, Strasbourg, Basel
Frankfurt to Mainz (Rhine, Main, Neckar)
Frankfurt, Nierstein, Mannheim, Heilbronn, Bad Wimpfern, Eberbach, Heidelberg, Ottmarsheim, Basel, Strasbourg, Pittersdorf, Mainz
Frankfurt to Prague (Elbe, Oder)
Frankfurt, Küstrin-Kietz, Oderberg, Potsdam, Magdeburg, Wittenberg, Meissen, Dresden, Pillnitz, Königstein, Litoměřice, Melnik, Prague
Frankfurt to Frankfurt (Mosel, Main, Rhine, Saar)
Frankfurt, Mainz, Rüdesheim, Braubach, Koblenz, Cochem, Piesport, Trier, Saarburg, Merzig, Remich,

The Douro Valley, Portugal.

Thionville, Metz, Pont-à-Mousson, Nancy

14-day cruises

Amsterdam to Vienna (Rhine, Danube)
Amsterdam, Cologne, Koblenz, Rüdesheim, Mainz, Wertheim, Würtzburg, Hassfurt, Bamberg, Nuremberg (Nürnberg), Roth, Kelheim, Regensburg, Passau, Melk, Dürnstein, Vienna
Amsterdam to Prague (Rhine, Elbe)
Amsterdam, Xantem, Münster, Braunschweig, Potsdam, Brandenburg, Magdeburg, Wittenberg, Meissen, Dresden, Pillnitz, Königstein, Litoměřice, Melnik, Prague
Amsterdam to the Black Sea (Rhine, Danube)
Amsterdam, Cologne, Koblenz, Rüdesheim, Mainz, Aschaffenburg, Miltenburg, Karlstadt, Würzburg, Schweinfurt, Bamberg, Nuremberg, Reidenburg, Kelheim, Regensburg, Melk, Dürnstein, Vienna, Ezstergom, Budapest, Kalocsa, Mohács, Vidin, Rousse (Ruse), Constanţa (Rhine)

River Danube

Winding its way from the foothills of the Alps to the distant shores of the Black Sea, this majestic waterway has long been a powerful transportation route and is a perennial favourite for river cruises.

The Danube has shaped the history of central Europe over many centuries, as an important transportation route and economic lifeline between the heart of Europe and the Balkans, although, commercially, it is less busy than the Rhine (Rhein). It has halted armies at its banks and been the inspiration for musical serenades, interludes and waltzes. Yet despite Johann Strauss's famous *Blue Danube* waltz, the river, its bed thick with sediment, is actually a murky brown, not blue – although some claim that it can have an azure sheen in the spring and autumn sunshine.

Europe's second-longest river after the Volga, the Danube flows through a range of scenery on the long journey from its source in the Black Forest to the vast delta on the Black Sea, cutting through the wooded hills of Bavaria to the steep terraces and castles of the wine-growing country of Lower Austria, then on to the edge of the Hungarian steppes and into the Balkans. The river has carved deep gorges across ancient mountain ranges, while in other places, meanders across broad, marshy plains. Sightseeing opportunities are numerous, from medieval monasteries to castles, fabulous museums and unspoilt national parks.

Towns and cities of particular interest include Regensburg and Passau in Germany; Linz and Vienna in Austria; Bratislava in Slovakia; Budapest in Hungary, and Vidin in Bulgaria. Other highlights include Dürnstein and Melk in Austria's alluring Wachau Valley and historic Esztergom in Hungary. Most cruises spend at least one night in Vienna and Budapest.

Visitors have a huge choice of itineraries, but the most rewarding is to cruise the river's entire length. There's something fascinating and addictive about the Danube, a promise of discovery and mystery as it flows eastwards through ever-more exotic lands. For many passengers, it is a first into the former Eastern Bloc. Take a shorter voyage as far as Budapest, and you'll find yourself looking longingly at the barges and cruise vessels continuing their journey through the Balkans towards the Black Sea, and vowing to come back and explore Serbia, Romania and Bulgaria.

Riverships on the Danube at Passau.

THE COURSE OF THE DANUBE

The source of the mighty Danube is marked by an ornate fountain and ornamental pool in the gardens of the Fürstenberg Palace at Donaueschingen in the hills of the Black Forest in southwestern Germany, where the two source streams, the Breg and the Brigach, unite. From here to its marshy delta on the distant Black Sea coast of Romania, the river flows through six countries and forms the border with three more, covering a distance of some 2,888km (1,795 miles). Along the way, some 300 tributaries join the river to bolster its flow. This lengthy course can be divided up into three sections.

The Upper Danube runs for approximately 1,000km (620 miles), stretching from its source to the 'Hungarian Gate', the point near the Slovakian border at which the river crosses into the wide Carpathian Basin. Along this section of the river there is considerable inclination of the river bed, and a rapid current. The first navigable point is at Regensburg.

The Middle Danube is approximately 940km (580 miles) long. From the Hungarian Gate it courses east across the plain until, at the Great Bend, it runs into the hard granite of the Börzsöny and Cserhát Hills, and swings suddenly south to Budapest. The Danube then meanders across the Great Hungarian Plain, clipping the northeastern corner of Croatia before surging across the plains of Vojvodina in northern Serbia to reach the dramatic Iron Gates Gorge on the Serbia–Romania border. Here, the river cuts through the southern spur of the crescent-shaped Carpathian mountain range.

The Lower Danube is approximately 950km (590 miles) long. The river here is broad, shallow and marshy as it forges across the Wallachian Plain (forming the border of Romania and Bulgaria) to the large delta by the Black Sea.

MAIN–DANUBE CANAL

In 793, Charlemagne had the vision of establishing a navigable waterway between the Danube and Main rivers, to be called the 'Fossa Carolina'. Thousands of Charlemagne's workers began to dig a navigable trench between the Rezat and Altmühl rivers. But the project failed due to incessant rain and the resulting 'invasion' of water. One section, now called the Karlsgraben, still exists today.

Charlemagne's vision was finally realised on 25 September 1992, when the 170km (106-mile) Main–Danube Canal was finally opened, providing the means for larger craft of up to 3,300 tons to navigate all the way from the North Sea to the Black Sea. The construction of the canal, linking the Rhine, Main and Danube rivers, is one of Europe's largest transport-engineering projects.

Costing 4.7 billion German marks at the time to build, the canal runs through rural Bavaria and rises

406m (1,332ft) via 16 locks, with up to 24.67m (80.9ft) lifting height. It was cleverly constructed to blend with the surrounding landscape, and it looks more like a river than a canal. Some 75 million German marks were invested in nature reserves and conservation projects. The canal is 55m (180ft) wide and 4m (13ft) deep, and flows into the Danube at Kelheim in Germany.

HIGHLIGHTS FROM BAMBERG (GERMANY) TO THE BLACK SEA (ROMANIA)

There are many permutations of river cruises on the Danube and many tour operators selling them, but the key stops are summarised below. These are the highlights that can be seen as you cruise downstream, from Bamberg to the Black Sea. Note that, along the Danube, distances are measured not from the source to the estuary, as is customary in Europe, but from the estuary to the source.

One thing to note is that the water level of the Danube can be too low for navigation, particularly during the warm, dry summer months, so it's worth checking with your travel provider to make sure that the water levels are sufficient for your cruise. Conversely, the water level can be too high for vessels to pass under the bridges of the upper section of the Danube beyond Passau. Normally, after the melting winter snow and spring rain, there is sufficient top-up to carry the river through the summer.

Bamberg, Germany (Km 3–6.4)

Known for its symphony orchestra and tasty smoked beer (Rauchbier), this medieval city has narrow, winding streets lined with Baroque patrician houses. The old town, the 11th-century cathedral and the Bamberg

Reiter (Bamberg Horseman) statue were declared a World Heritage Site by Unesco in 1993. The River Regnitz runs through the middle of the city, joining up with the Main 3km (2 miles) downstream.

The tombs of the Holy Roman Emperor Heinrich II and Pope Clement II are housed in the magnificent cathedral. The old Town Hall, or Rathaus, sits in the middle of a twin-arched bridge over the river and is a most impressive sight, and old fishermen's cottages can be seen close by on the river bank. In Schillerplatz, you can see E.T.A. Hoffmann's House, dedicated to the poet, musician and caricaturist, author of The Tales of Hoffmann. Bamberg is also known as the home of several well-known breweries.

The scenery as you head south towards Nuremberg is craggy and forested, giving the area the name 'Fränkische Schweiz' (Franconian Switzerland).

Nuremberg (Nürnberg), Germany (Km 67.8–72)

Half-timbered houses, cobbled streets and Gothic churches with intricate spires and grand gateways are all part of the architectural heritage of Bavaria's second-largest city, as is the almost intact 5km (3-mile) city wall with its 80 defensive watchtowers. Most of the sights are contained within the walls and are easy to find on foot, although you'll need to take a taxi, public transport or the ship's shuttle service for the 15-minute drive from the suburban dock to the old town.

One of the best views of the city and surroundings can be had from the medieval Kaiserburg (Imperial Castle), an imperial residence for 500 years. The famed post-World War II trials of Nuremberg took place at the Palace of Justice.

DID YOU KNOW...?

...that the Danube is the only major European waterway to flow from east to west?
...that the Romans called the Danube the Danuvius, from which its present name is derived?
...that the Greeks sailed up the Danube, in the 7th century? They got as far as the Iron Gates, where the rapids prevented them from further progress.
...that the Danube delta is a paradise for birdwatchers, with over 250 species including the last ibises and pelicans in Europe?
...that in 1989 an unprecedented 50,000 people assembled outside parliament in Budapest? They were part of the environmental movement protesting against plans for the construction of a hydro-electric dam on the River Danube.
...that in 1812, in Vienna, a vessel named Caroline became the first steam-driven vessel on the Danube? Its introduction was significant, and meant that, for the first time, vessels could move upstream under their own power. Prior to this date, all riverships moving upstream could only do

so by being towed – first by men, then by horses, then by locomotives; hence the term 'towpath'. Many towpaths still exist along both sides of the Danube, and today provide excellent pathways for cycling and walking.
...that the great wine route of the Wachau spans some 32km (20 miles) along the banks of the Danube, in Austria? The steep, terraced vineyards soak up the summer sun, yet the nights are cooler, making an ideal climate for a balanced wine, although the work of harvesting the grapes is a tortuous one. Many growers own small parcels of land – a hectare or two – and so making wines from the variety and quality of grapes provided is not an easy task for the region's wine makers.
...that in 2002, in Passau, the Danube reached its highest level for over 500 years?
...that only about 30 percent of the Danube is truly free flowing?
...that sailing between Bamberg and Kelheim in Bavaria takes you over the Continental Divide?

Regensburg's Cathedral Square.

Peter Henlein invented the world's first pocket watch in Nuremberg in 1510, and the world's first globe was also made here. You can see examples of early watches on display at the German National Museum of Art and Culture (Germanisches Nationalmuseum), the largest museum of its kind in the German-speaking world. Another highlight is the Albrecht Dürer House (Albrecht-Dürer-Haus), with its multimedia show depicting the life of the German painter, printmaker, draughtsman and art theorist, generally regarded as the greatest German Renaissance artist.

In 1835, Germany's first railway line was opened between Nuremberg and Fürth. Today, the Transport Museum (DB Museum) houses many locomotives, wagons and railway accessories.

It's also worth paying a visit to the Schöner Brunnen, a fountain on the Hauptmarkt. This towering, ornamented treasure was carefully covered during World War II to protect it from Allied bombing. A wrought-iron fence encloses it, and there is a bronze ring looped around one part of the fence. Turning this ring three times is supposed to grant the turner's wish. Needless to say, there is usually a line of visitors waiting to be photographed doing just that.

Nuremberg gained notoriety during the 20th century, first as the site of the Nazi party rallies, but later when the famed post-World War II trials took place (from 20 November 1945 until 1 October 1946) at the Palace of Justice. Nuremberg was chosen because the Palace of Justice was spacious (it had 22,000 sq m/236,813 sq ft of space, with about 530 offices and about 80 courtrooms; war damage to it was mini-

mal; and a large, undestroyed prison was part of the complex) following agreement between the four major powers at the time, although Russia had initially wanted the trials to be held in Berlin.

Aschaffenburg, Germany (Km 86–88)

Johannesburg Castle, set almost within touching distance right on the river bank, is simply stunning. It was the palatial residence of the archbishops of Mainz. Built of local red sandstone, it comprises four wings with corner towers and a central, square courtyard.

Miltenburg, Germany (Km 124–125)

Miltenburg is one of the best-preserved medieval towns on the River Main (its long main street, Hauptstrasse runs parallel to the Main) and is characterised by beautifully preserved or restored half-timbered houses. The town centre features a fountain dating from 1583. Miltenburg castle, built by the archbishop of Mainz around 1200, predates the first documented mention of the town, in 1237. Somewhat more recently, the town gained notoriety when Elvis Presley stayed for one night.

Regensburg, Germany (Km 2381–2377)

Founded by Marcus Aurelius over 2,000 years ago, Regensburg is one of the best-preserved of all European medieval cities, having escaped the bombing of World War II, and is the oldest city on the entire length of the Danube; the first Roman camp here has been dated by historians to AD 70, and parts of the original Roman wall can still be seen. The city's

The pretty town of Melk, Austria.

12th- to 14th-century Patricians' Houses are architecturally fascinating, and are reminiscent of the medieval tower-houses of San Gimignano in Tuscany. Riverships dock close to the centre, within walking distance of the main sights, and tours are usually a half-day, with free time afterwards.

Visit the Stone Bridge, built between 1135 and 1146 and, with 16 arches, a masterpiece of medieval engineering. The cathedral, regarded as the best example of Gothic architecture in Bavaria, has some superb stained-glass windows in its twin towers, which were added between 1859 and 1861 at the request of King Ludwig I of Bavaria, and a tranquil 15th-century cloister.

The heart of the city is Neupfarrplatz, which presents Regensburg's history in microcosm. Over the years it has been the home of Roman officers, the Jewish quarter, the marketplace, the scene of riots and protests, and of the mass burning of books by the Nazis. Between 1995 and 1998, massive excavations revealed Gothic and Romanesque synagogues, remains of the old Jewish houses and a treasure trove of gold coins.

Some 11km (7 miles) downstream from Regensburg, just outside Donaustauf, look out for a white classical temple with Doric columns on the hillside, approached by a grand staircase. This is Valhalla (Walhalla), home of the gods in German mythology – in this case, built by Ludwig I in the 1830s as a kind of Teutonic Hall of Fame, and a copy of the Parthenon in Athens.

Passau, Germany (Km 2210)

The starting point for many cruises on the Danube, Passau, located 290m (950ft) above sea level, marks the border between Germany and Austria. Ships dock right in the centre, although new berths for four riverships have been constructed at Landau, about 2km (1.25 miles) downriver from Passau, to ease the congestion that occurs at weekends, when many passengers embark and disembark.

Somewhat fancifully dubbed 'the Venice of the Danube' because of the three rivers that converge here (it is also sometimes called Dreiflüssestadt – the city of three rivers) and the Italianate style of the architecture, Passau has been a bishopric for 1,200 years. St Stephen's magnificent Baroque-style cathedral houses the world's largest cathedral organ; it has 17,774 pipes in three banks, and 233 registers, or stops. Liszt wrote his *Hungarian Coronation Mass* for this cathedral in 1857.

Passau's location as the confluence of the three rivers, the Danube, Ilz and Inn, means it often suffers from flooding. The tower of the town hall shows the high-water marks, the highest recorded being in 1501, 1595 and 1954.

Linz, Austria (Km 2139–2127)

Although the Renaissance and Baroque centre of the city, which is the provincial capital of Upper Austria, is attractive (Linz was designated a 'European Capital of Culture' in 2009), Linz is an industrial city, known for its chemical and metallurgical industries. The classic *Linzer Torte*, with a pastry base, redcurrant jam filling and crisscross pattern on the almond-encrusted top, was invented here by Bavarian baker Konrad Vogel in 1822. You can taste the real thing in one of the many street cafés in the beautifully preserved Old Town.

The cobblestoned main square is also the site of the Trinity Column – a 20m (66ft) -high white marble Baroque-style sculpture by Sebastian Stumpfegger to a design by Antonio Beduzzi; erected in 1723, it is dedicated to commemorate the dangers of war (1704), fire (1712) and the plague (1713).

Riverships dock next to the Lentos Art Museum – a magnificent glass structure housing a superb art collection.

Linz is also known for its connections with the composer Anton Bruckner, who was born at Ansfelden (now a suburb of Linz) in 1824, and died in 1896 in Vienna. Mozart also lived here for a while in 1783 as a guest of Count Thunn, during which time he composed his *Linz Symphony*. Alterdom, the magnificent baroque cathedral is where Anton Bruckner served as organist.

Melk, Austria (Km 2037.5–2037)

The mustard-yellow Benedictine Abbey of Melk, perched on a steep hill overlooking the river and vis-ible from afar, is one of the highlights of a Danube cruise. It was founded in the year 1089 by Leopold II and dominates the town, though at the same time blending in beautifully with the surrounding landscape. It was completely reconstructed in Baroque style in the early 18th century by its architect, Jakob Prandtauer, who died before its completion. The imposing abbey was completed by Prandtauer's relation and assistant, Joseph Mungengast.

The imperial rooms of the abbey once accommodated such renowned figures as Emperor Charles VI and Maria Theresa, Pope Pius VI and Napoleon – all presently immortalised in a permanent wax museum. Paul Troger frescoes can be found in the library, which houses over 2,000 manuscripts. A Gutenberg Bible, which was on display here for many years, has since been sold, and can now be viewed in the Yale Library in the US. The balconies command sweeping views of the Danube. A short organ concert is typically held for anyone on a shore excursion. The organ, built by Gregor Hradetzky (Krems), has three keyboards, 45 registers (stops) and 3,553 pipes.

Dürnstein, Austria (Km 2008)

Beyond Melk, the Danube carves its way through the beautiful, Unesco-protected Wachau Valley, a 30km (19-mile) section of steep, terraced slopes of vineyards and forested hills, which turn incredible shades of red and gold in the autumn. It is regarded by many as one of the most scenic stretches of the river. In its midst is Dürnstein, discernible from some distance away because of the jagged outline of the ruined castle on the hilltop, and the unusual Wedgwood-blue-and-white Baroque monastery tower squatting like a giant pepperpot on the river bank.

A steep one-hour walk/climb from Dürnstein itself leads to the Babenberg Duke Leopold's Kueringerburg Castle. Richard the Lionheart was incarcerated here for more than a year in the 12th century. He was released after paying an incredible 100,000 marks – truly a king's ransom in those days. There's not much of the castle to see nowadays, but the views along the Wachau Valley and over the town below are breathtaking.

Krems, Austria (Km 2003–2002)

This university town, together with its former sister town of Stein (both are located close to Dürnstein at the eastern end of the Wachau wine-growing district), grew wealthy as a result of trade in iron, grain, wine and salt. The town is an important example of successful restoration work and the centre has been a Unesco World Heritage Site since 2000. Krems was the home of the painter Martin Johann ('Kremser') Schmidt, who created numerous works in the churches of Austria.

One nearby attraction is the Stift Göttweig, an abbey set on a hillside. Its playful Benedictine architecture – its corner towers, onion domes and pastel-coloured facade – has earned it the title of 'Austria's

CHRISTMAS MARKET CRUISES

There's nothing quite like a river cruise in Europe at *Christmas*, when the twinkling fairylights and the seasonal aromas of cinnamon, gingerbread, roasting chestnuts and *Glühwein* (mulled wine) at Christmas markets in most cities and towns along the Danube, Rhine and Elbe really put you in the mood for the holiday.

Along the Danube, Vienna has a number of Christmas markets, and the window dressing of the stores along the wide Kärntnerstrasse is among the best in the world. The city's Christmas decorations are beautiful, too. Nuremberg hosts perhaps the most famous Christmas market of all. Located in the old walled section of the city, it is the oldest in Germany, dating back to the 17th century. Rows of specially constructed stalls provide the old-world setting and a magical atmosphere.

Along the Rhine, Cologne's magnificent Gothic cathedral provides an impressive backdrop to that city's Christmas market. Rüdesheim's Christkindlmarkt (Christmas market) is one of Germany's largest, with more than 100 stalls. Regensburg, often a starting or finishing point for several riverships, has its Christmas market in the town's delightful square.

AMAWaterways, CroisiEurope, Uniworld and Viking River Cruises are among the companies that operate cruises to the Christmas markets of Europe.

Monte Casino', after the Italian abbey where the Benedictine Order was first established.

Vienna (Wien), Austria (Km 1933–1928)

Vienna, located 170m (558ft) above sea level (it used to flood regularly in the winter), is built in a very strategic location, at the junction of routes from both east to west and north to south.

For centuries, the city was the seat of the mighty Habsburg dynasty, and is also the birthplace of Schubert, and of much of the music of Mozart (he composed his greatest operas and symphonies here), Beethoven and Strauss. The city exudes romance at any time of year, with its beautiful parks and Baroque palaces, elegant shops and legendary coffee houses. Most cruises spend at least one night here, giving plenty of opportunity to see the sights, attend a performance at the opera, listen to the Vienna Boys' Choir or admire the white Lipizzaner horses at the Spanish Riding School.

The Danube does not pass through the centre of Vienna – instead it runs through the northeast part of the city. Most river cruise vessels stop at the Vienna Shipping Centre (Schiffahrtszentrum), about 3km (2 miles) from the old centre. The compact, historic centre is encircled by the Ringstrasse, inside which most of the main sights are located. The following is a list of the city's top attractions:

Stephansdom: St Stephen's Cathedral, with its distinctive roof, is one of Vienna's most famous landmarks and one of the greatest Gothic structures in Europe. The interior is rich in woodcarvings, altars and paintings. Climb the steps of the south tower for a breathtaking view of the city.

Museums Quarter: The Museums Quarter is a giant cultural complex including the Museum of Modern Art (MUMOK) and the Leopold Museum, with its wonderful collection of 19th- and 20th-century art, including work by Egon Schiele, Gustav Klimt and Oskar Kokoschka. At the centre of the complex, the Kunsthalle holds temporary exhibitions.

Staatsoper: Vienna's magnificent opera house was constructed in the 1860s, and rebuilt in 1945 after suffering a direct hit in a bombing raid. It was inaugurated in 1869 with Mozart's *Don Giovanni*. The main facade is elaborately decorated with frescoes depicting *The Magic Flute*. Once a year the stage and orchestra stalls turn into a giant dance floor for the Vienna Opera Ball. If your rivership stays overnight in Vienna, you could consider an evening out at the opera, although you may need to reserve well in advance for this.

Secession Building: The Secession Building was built as a 'temple of art' to plans by Joseph Maria Olbrich in 1897. Gustav Klimt designed the *Beethoven Frieze*, on display on the lower floor, a visual interpretation of Beethoven's *Ninth Symphony*. The cubic foyer is crowned by a dome of 3,000 gilt laurel leaves. Over the entrance is the motto 'To Each Time its Art, to Art its Freedom', a riposte from the Secession artists to the conservative Academy of Fine Arts.

Schloss Schönbrunn: A short distance from the inner city lies the Schönbrunn Palace, the imperial summer residence. Leopold I wished to build a palace to rival Versailles but financial difficulties stalled his plans. It was not until 1743 that Empress Maria Theresa employed Nikolaus Pacassi to build the fabulous palace we see today. In the formal grounds are

Vienna at night.

Bratislava's 16th-century castle with earlier fortifications.

the Baroque zoo, the Palm House and the graceful Gloriette, a neoclassical colonnade perched on the crest of a hill.

Prater: The Prater, an open fairground and amusement park, is a favourite place of relaxation for the Viennese. Its main attraction is the Riesenrad, the giant Ferris wheel that was immortalised in the 1949 film *The Third Man*. This extensive stretch of parkland and woodland extends for almost 5km (3 miles).

Karlsplatz: Otto Wagner's two wonderfully elegant entrance pavilions for the Stadtbahn on Karlsplatz date from 1894 and are prime examples of Jugendstil (Austrian Art Nouveau). For the designs of the pavilions, he combined a green iron framework with marble slabs and gilded sunflower decoration, and pioneered a new form of architecture in which functionality and simplicity of ornament were the priority.

Kunsthistorisches Museum: Several famous artists helped create the interior of the Kunsthistorisches Museum. A huge number of art treasures amassed by the Habsburgs are on display, including a fine collection of ancient Egyptian and Greek Art, and works by many of the great European masters.

Belvedere: The Belvedere, a palace of sumptuous proportions, was built between 1714 and 1723 for Prince Eugene of Savoy. It is in fact two palaces, the Upper and Lower Belvedere, joined by terraced gardens. Today it houses three museums containing works of Austrian and European art and sculpture.

Hofburg: The Hofburg was the winter residence of the ruling Habsburgs. Within the confines of this vast and impressive imperial palace are the Spanish Riding School and the sleek Lipizzaner horses, and the Burgkapelle, where the Vienna Boys' Choir sing Sunday Mass. Notable collections housed here are the Collection of Court Porcelain and Silver and the Imperial Treasury, containing crown jewels and ecclesiastical treasures. The palatial National Library, also in the complex, contains more than 2 million manuscripts, printed books, maps and musical scores.

VIENNESE COFFEE HOUSES

The Viennese coffee-house tradition is deeply rooted in the country's culture and history, dating back over 300 years. Gentry and intellectuals mingled in the shady and fashionable *Kaffeehaus*. People take their coffee seriously here, and there are names for every shade, from black to white. Coffee is served in a wide variety of ways, often with the addition of alcohol or whipped cream, though always with an obligatory glass of water.

Bratislava, Slovakia (Km 1869)

Located right at the heart of central Europe close to Slovakia's borders with Austria and Hungary, Bratislava has changed its identity, and its name, more times than it cares to remember. In Habsburg times, the city was Pressburg to the Germans and Pozsony to the Magyars. Renamed Bratislava after the creation of Czechoslovakia following World War I, it emerged from the communist years to become capital of the new state of Slovakia in 1993. An am-

bitious rebuilding and restoration programme has transformed the city. The picturesque old town is clustered around a low hill on the left bank of a broad stretch of the river. The Danube is wide here – about 300m (984ft) across.

Highlights include the castle, built in the 16th century on top of earlier fortifications, the picturesque Old Town with fabulous Baroque palaces, St Martin's Cathedral, with an unusual spire topped by a tiny Hungarian crown, St Michael's Gate, the city's only surviving medieval gateway, and Pálffyho Palace, where, in 1762, the six-year old Wolfgang Amadeus Mozart gave a performance. This distinguished building now houses the Academy of Fine Arts.

Esztergom, Hungary (Km 1718.5)

Formerly the Roman settlement of Gran, Esztergom is located in the foothills of the Pilis Mountains, right on the border with Slovakia. Esztergom is famous for its vast, neoclassical cathedral, flanked by a red-brick castle, which towers over the city. The giant dome is one of the world's largest and can be seen for miles around. The castle itself was the seat of government for Hungary's kings and queens for more than 300 years when the Hungarian lands further south were held by the Ottoman Turks, while the town was the centre of the Catholic Church in Hungary, which flourished during the reign of Louis I (1342–82), a role it retains today. The Gothic-style cathedral was built in the 19th century to replace its predecessor, ransacked by the Turks in 1543 after they pushed northwards, although the red-marble Bakócz Chapel inside survived. Both Beethoven and Liszt performed here.

Budapest, Hungary (Km 1647)

Budapest is the perfect destination for river cruises, because the Danube flows right through the heart of the city for some 10km (6 miles), with Buda (and Obuda) on the west bank and Pest on the east bank connected by eight bridges.

Often referred to by the local inhabitants as the 'Pearl of the Danube', Budapest goes beyond the attractions of its fabulous, romantic setting. It is the cultural heart of the nation and a city of international standing that still possesses some of its late 19th-century flair and romance. Nostalgia can be found in the sumptuous spas offering the simple pleasure of bathing in thermal waters, and in the grand old coffee houses.

Riverships dock in a superbly convenient (and also picturesque) location. If your one leaves at night, you'll see the city's historic buildings in all their illuminated splendour – a real treat, especially if you stand outside on deck with a glass of Champagne in hand.

Budapest also marks the starting point for the second half of river cruises (typically of 14 days or more) that travel all the way to the Danube Delta at the Black Sea.

City highlights include the following:

Parliament Building: Strongly reminiscent of the Palace of Westminster in London, the Parliament Building (Országház) is one of Budapest's most famous sights. The neo-Gothic pile, which was completed in 1902, extends along the Danube for some 268m (292 yds).

Chain Bridge: When it was completed in 1849, the Chain Bridge (Széchenyi Lánchíd) linked the two halves of the city, Buda and Pest, for the first time (there are now eight Danube bridges in the Hungarian capital, as well as more on the outskirts). Count István Széchenyi, the 19th-century reformer and innovator, brought in engineers from Great Britain to construct the graceful span, which is beautifully floodlit at night.

Gellért Hill: Rising steeply from the Buda riverfront, the craggy, wooded heights of Gellért Hill (Gellért-hegy) can be seen from almost anywhere in the city (not least from where the riverships dock). Naturally, the views are tremendous, extending as far as the distant Matra mountains on the Slovak border on a clear day.

Heroes' Square: At the end of Andrássy út, one of Pest's major thoroughfares, is the wide open space of Heroes' Square (Hősök tere), with its 36m (118ft) Millennium Monument, erected in 1896 to mark 1,000 years of the Magyar state. The square is flanked by the Palace of Art and Museum of Fine Arts and behind the former is the world's largest hourglass, the Timewheel, unveiled in May 2004 to mark Hungary's admission into the European Union. Some 8m (26ft) in diameter, the structure 'turns' once a year to send the sand running anew.

Váci utca: Long, narrow and pedestrianised for much of its length, Váci utca (pronounced vah-tsee oohtsa) is a busy and fashionable shopping street, which also has a range of bars, cafés and restaurants. At its northern end is the square of Vörösmarty tér. At No. 7 is one of the city's main meeting places and home to Gerbeaud, doyen of the city's prosperous café society since 1884 and a major tourist attraction in itself.

Museum of Fine Arts: Hungary's pre-eminent art gallery, the Museum of Fine Arts (Szépművészeti Múzeum) has a huge collection, focusing on European art from 1300–1800. Highlights include works by the Spanish school including El Greco, Goya and Velázquez.

Matthias Church: The focal point of the old town of Buda, high above the river, the Matthias Church (Mátyás-templom) is named after Hungary's most popular medieval king, Mátyás Corvinus Hunyadi (1458–90). The Habsburg emperor Franz Josef I was crowned king of Hungary here in 1867. The unusual geometric patterns on the roof, the stained-glass windows and other details date from the 19th century, but parts of the building are far older. Outside the church in Trinity Square (Szentháromság tér) is the mighty equestrian statue of St Stephen.

Fisherman's Bastion: Overlooking the Danube and just in front of the Matthias Church, the fairytale spires and turrets of the Fisherman's Bastion (Halászbástya) afford the classic view of Budapest. Built onto the castle walls in the early 20th century purely for ornamental reasons, the monument's name is a reference to the fishermen who heroically defended the ramparts here against invaders in the 18th century.

Hungarian National Museum: The large Hungarian National Museum (Magyar Nemzeti Múzeum) is the most important museum in the city. St Stephen's Crown, the symbol of Hungarian sovereignty, was returned here in 1978, having been stolen by the Wehrmacht in World War II. Inside, amid monumental architectural and ornamental details, the whole story of Hungary unfolds – from prehistory right up to the 21st century. On display are prehistoric remains, ancient jewellery and tools, Roman mosaics, a 17th-century Turkish tent fitted out with grand carpets, and a Baroque library. There are some notable royal regalia, although the crown, orb, sceptre and sword have been moved to the Parliament Building.

Central Market Hall: A good place for souvenirs is the upstairs section of the cavernous Central Market Hall (Nagy Vásárcsarnok) at the Pest end of Freedom Bridge.

Budapest's Chain Bridge and Parliament Building.

Lower Danube

Gellért Baths: At the southern edge of Gellért-hegy, the Gellért Baths (Gellért gyógyfürdő) comprise medicinal baths as well as regular swimming pools, all decorated in opulent Art Nouveau style. The unisex indoor pool has a vaulted glass ceiling and Roman-style carved columns, while the thermal baths feature marble statues, fine mosaics and glazed tiles.

Kalocsa, Hungary (Km 1515.4)

Kalocsa is a pretty town in the middle of the Puszta region, located on a terrace overlooking the Danube, 10km (6 miles) from the river itself (passengers are taken by coach) and famous for growing the paprika that gives Hungarian goulash its distinctive flavour. It's an important agricultural and tourism centre, surrounded by pepper fields, and the shops are packed with paprika souvenirs, from painted eggs to colourful pottery and embroidered linen.

Some 1,000 years ago, Kalocsa was the seat of the archdiocese, and the Archbishop's Palace, whose permanent exhibition of ecclesiastical relics and treasure is open to the public. The House of Folk Art Museum and the Károly Visky Museum feature the colourful local painting for which the region is famous, while for something different, the world's only Paprika Museum documents the history of paprika production in Hungary, from growing to different pepper types and the processing technique.

Belgrade (Beograd), Serbia (Km 1170)

Belgrade, capital of Serbia (and of the former Yugoslavia), is strategically located on the southern edge of the great Carpathian Basin, at the confluence of the River Danube and River Sava, and has a turbulent history. It is one of the oldest cities in Europe and nowadays forms the largest urban area in southeastern Europe after Athens. The ravages of communism and damage from the war in 1999 are still visible, and the city is noticeably less colourful (and wealthy) than Budapest, but vibrant nonetheless, with a busy, pedestrianised centre.

Iron Gates Gorge (Km 949.7)

The Iron Gates (Porţile de Fier) are a highlight of any Danube itinerary. The river cuts through the southern spur of the Carpathian Mountains where they meet the northern foothills of the Balkan ranges, forming an emphatic natural boundary between Serbia and Romania. The 'true' Iron Gates is in fact a single narrow gorge, which boats enter at Km 949, but the name is generally given to the entire stretch of river between Km 1,059 and Km 942 – a series of gorges linked by wider stretches of river. There are towering cliffs on either side, although these are less impressive than they were before the river level was raised in the 1970s. Parts of the river bed here are among the world's deepest, with depths up to 60m (196ft).

At the eastern end of the Iron Gates, at Km 942, is the enormous Djerdap Hydro-electric power station complex. There are actually two power stations (one belonging to Serbia and the other belonging to Romania), two double-level locks, and a barrage supporting a railway and road bridge. The whole project involved much re-siting of infrastructure, the reconstruction of 13 river harbours and the relocation of many inhabitants (8,400 within Serbia and 14,500 within Romania) at the time of its construction, which, when completed in 1972, had cost an estimated $500 million. The dam raised the Danube's water level by some 33m (100ft), and removed the treacherous currents and whirlpools at a stroke. On the negative side, the higher water has hugely diminished the grandeur of the landscape, obliterated a number of historic towns and villages (notably the Turkish island enclave of Ada Kaleh, a short distance downstream from Orşova), and the river's diminished flow is no longer sufficient to flush pollution – chemical toxins and other waste – downriver and out to sea.

The first gorge is the Golubac, 14km (9 miles) in length. The town of Golubac was flooded by the power-station project, but nine massive towers – the ruins of a castle that was, for more than two and a half centuries, a base for the Turks for their raids to the north and west until they left in 1688 – can still be seen on the Serbian side. After a broader section, the second gorge – the Gospodin Vir – extends for a further 15km (9 miles). Beyond is the famous Kazan gorge, 19km (12 miles) long, where the river flows between towering cliffs soaring 700m (2,300ft) through a chasm only 150m (492ft) across.

Vidin, Bulgaria (Km 790)

Vidin, on the Bulgarian side of the river, occupies the site of an old Celtic settlement and is one of the country's oldest towns, dating back to Roman times. The dramatic fortress of Baba Vida, built in the 14th century, is the best-preserved example of medieval architecture in the country and looms impressively on the bank of the Danube as you approach. In fact, the whole town used to be famous for its fairytale minarets, towers and domes, although its skyline suffered from the building of ugly concrete apartment blocks during the communist era. Most tours combine Baba Vida with a visit to the amazing village of Belogradchik, cut directly into sandstone rock.

Bucharest (Bucureşti), Romania

There is no kilometre marking for Bucharest, the capital of Romania, but that's because the city is ac-

---

MUSIC

Music is inextricably linked to the River Danube. Johann Strauss and Franz Schubert were born in Vienna. Brahms, Beethoven, Haydn, Mahler and Mozart were all inspired by this culturally rich city. Vienna's huge *Zentralofriedhof* (cemetery) has a Musician's Corner, where Beethoven, Brahms, Gluck, Schubert, Strauss (The Younger), Strauss (The Elder), Franz von Suppé, Arnold Schoenberg and Salieri are buried. The following composers all have connections with this area:

Béla Bartók was born on 25 March 1881 in Nagyszentmiklós, Hungary. He died on 26 September 1945 in New York, US.

Ludwig van Beethoven was baptised on 17 December 1770 in Bonn, Germany. He died in Vienna on 17 July 1787.

Alban Berg was born on 9 February 1885 in Vienna, Austria. He died on 24 December 1935 in Vienna.

Johannes Brahms was born on 7 May 1833 in Hamburg, Germany. He died on April 3, 1879 in Vienna

Josef Anton Bruckner was born on 4 September 1824 in Ansfelden, Austria. He died on 11 October 1896 in Vienna.

Franz Josef Haydn was born on 31 March 31 1732 in Rohrau, Lower Austria. He died on 31 May 1809 in Vienna. The Haydn Museum, located at Haydengasse 19 is open to the public and highlights the places that were important in the composer's life. This is the house where he composed *The Creation* (1796–8) and *The Seasons* (1799–1801).

Zoltán Kodály was born on 16 December 1882 in Kecskemét, Hungary. He died on 6 March 1967 in Budapest, Hungary

Franz Liszt was born on 22 October 1811 in Raiding, Hungary. He died on 31 July 1886 in Bayreuth (Germany). Budapest is where you'll find many of his pianos, in the Liszt Museum (Vörösmarty u. 35).

Wolfgang Amadeus Mozart was born on 27 January 1756 in Salzburg, Austria. He died on 5 December 1791 in Vienna.

Antonio Salieri was born on 18 August 1850 in Legnago, Italy. He died on 7 May 1825 in.Vienna.

Arnold Franz Walter Schoenberg was born on 13 September 1874 in Vienna. He died on July 13, 1951 in Los Angeles, US.

Franz Peter Schubert was born on 31 January 1797 in Vienna. He died on 19 November 1828 in Vienna. The house where he was born and where he spent the first four years of his life has been restored and now has a museum on the first floor.

Johann Strauss ('The Younger'), composer of *The Blue Danube* waltz, was born on 25 October 1825 in Vienna. He died on 3 June 1899 in Vienna.

Johann Strauss ('The Elder') was born on 14 March 1804 in Vienna. He died on 24 September 1849 in Vienna.

Richard Georg Strauss was born on 11 June 1864 in Munich, Germany. He died on 8 September 1949 in Garmisch-Partenkirchen, Austria.

The Iron Gates Gorge.

tually located somewhat inland from the river (about a one-hour coach journey from Rousse). A visit to Nicolae Ceaușescu's truly monumental Parliament Palace, the world's second largest administrative building (after the Pentagon), may be included on your excursion itinerary. Just a handful of the 3,000 rooms can be visited. You will probably also see Revolution (formerly Royal Palace) Square, where the famous riots started that led to the collapse of the communist dictatorship in December 1989.

Rousse (Ruse), Bulgaria (Km 495)

Rousse is the largest and most important river port in Bulgaria, set in gorgeous, rolling countryside brilliant with sunflowers in summer and golden wheatfields in autumn. The city itself was once the garrison of the Roman Danube fleets and was known as Sexaginta Prista – 'Sixty Ships'. Today, it's an industrial centre, and across the river you can see the grimlooking factories of Giurgiu in Romania.

Most of the attractions are outside the centre. A short drive away is the Rusenski Lom National Park, where a tributary of the Danube has carved a sheer-sided gorge through the uplifted limestone. Tours include a visit to the imposing Basarbovo Monastery, sprawling across a steep hilltop.

Giurgiu, Romania (Km 493)

Capital of Giurgiu County, southern Romania, the city is located about 65km (40 miles) south of Bucharest. Romanian crude oil is loaded here for shipping, via a pipeline that connects it with the oil fields of Ploesti. A bi-level, combined highway and railway bridge, the 2,224m (7,296ft) -long Friendship Bridge (Km 489), one of the longest bridges in Europe, which connects Romania with Bulgaria, was opened in 1954.

Cernavoda, Romania (Km 483)

Almost on the Black Sea, this is the starting point of the Danube-Black Sea Canal, which was completed in 1984. It is about 65km (40 miles) long and 640m (195ft) wide, and passes through the vineyards of Murfatlar, the best-known wine-growing area of Romania. The town's railway bridge, built in the 1890s, has 68 arches and rises up to 40m (131ft) above the surface of the water. When built it was one of the most modern and largest bridge installations in the world.

Oltenița, Romania (Km 430)

This little town is home to a building yard for river-ships. In former times, however, it was a quarantine station.

The Chilia Arm

The most northerly of the three branches of the Danube, the Chilia also transports more water than the other two. Approximately 120km (75 miles) long and as much as 990m (3,250ft) wide for most of its course it marks the border between Romania (right bank) and Ukraine (left bank). For the last 17.5km (11 miles) before reaching its Black Sea confluence, it flows exclusively through Ukraine.

Izmail, Ukraine (Km 80)

This port city was designed and built from scratch during the Soviet era. Its highlight is the sumptuously decorated cathedral.

Kilija, Ukraine (Km 40)

Ukraine is on the left bank, and Chilia-Veche (formerly Chilia, in the province of Odessa Oblast), Romania, is on the right bank. Chilia is thought to be one of the oldest settlements on the Danube, and, at earlier times, was only about 5km (3 miles) from the Black Sea. Today, the river must run about 40km (25 miles) to reach the sea.

Vilkovo, Ukraine (Km 15.5)

Located on the left bank, many of the houses belonging to this fishing village are built on stilts. With its many canals and small islands, it is often referred to as the 'Venice of the East'. The residents are fiercely religious, and its two churches (the Nikolaevskaya Church of the Orthodox, and the Nikolaevsakaya Church of the Old Believers) are lavished with care and attention. Along the shoreline, the houses have beautifully attended, colourful gardens.

The Sulina Arm

The shortest of the three branches of the Danube, the Sulina (often called the Sulina Canal) is the most important for commercial shipping. The depth of the arm is maintained to enable commercial ships to reach Tulcea (and its shipyards) on the Black Sea.

Sulina, Romania

Formerly named Porto Franco, Sulina was the headquarters of the Danube Commission during the 19th century. No longer an important seaport, today it is a minor town, seemingly abandoned by the modern world.

The Sfantu-Gheorghe Arm

This 104.5km (65-mile) -long arm forks off to the south just a few kilometres east of Tulcea, but it is not traversed by Danube passenger riverships.

Constanța, Romania (Km 0)

The official end of the River Danube, this port city is the capital of southeastern Romania, and located about 200km (125 miles) east of Bucharest. Reached via the Danube–Black Sea Canal, it is the country's principal seaport and its most important commercial centre, which is slowly being modernised. At journey's end in Constanța, riverships tie up at the Gare Maritime in the heart of the city.

THE DANUBE-KOSOVO CONNECTION

Since 1992, the 10 countries connected to the Danube had built up trade in shipping goods from the Black Sea to the North Sea. However, the Kosovo war in 1999 had devastating effects. Several bridges, including the three principal ones in Novi Sad, the capital of Vojvodina in northern Serbia, were blown up by NATO. The network of pipes to carry purified water from the west bank to homes on the other side of the river was also destroyed. Mines were also laid in the riverbed.

River cargo vessels, tugs ('pusher' vessels) and barges were trapped on either side of Serbia. Under the rules governing the Danube Shipping Convention, companies with riverships, tugs and barges can trade only with another country belonging to the convention. About 10 percent of the 700 or so regular trade vessels on the Danube were put out of work by the war, and many maritime employees were laid off.

Economically, ports along the river lost about $1 million per day in revenue and shipping. Bulgaria and Hungary probably suffered most from the effects of the war, which had nothing to do with them. Much of the agricultural and mineral exports had to go by road and rail, adding to shipment costs and time, and this made some products uncompetitive.

The Kosovo War also affected several river cruise companies forced to cancel all voyages scheduled to start downriver (the Danube flows east to west) in Passau or other German cities, to cross the region of conflict and end up at the Black Sea ports.

After the war, a temporary pontoon (built in September 1999) was placed across the river, using disused barges. It prevented the use of the river as a through traffic point, reportedly done deliberately in order to obtain UN funding to rebuild the three bridges, although sanctions against the Milosevic regime also provided reasons for the delay.

In August 2001 the Danube Convention officially declared the river open again for through traffic – once each week, following the removal of bridge debris, mines and other ordnance, and the rebuilding of the three principal bridges. The three principal bridges are: Sloboda Bridge, opened in 1981 for road traffic; Zezeli Bridge (formerly called Marshall Tito Bridge), completed in 1961 for pedestrians and light traffic; and the Petrovaradin Bridge, built in 1946 for railway traffic). Three replacement bridges have now been constructed and opened (one is a permanent structure).

The Rhine and its tributaries

The Rhine (Rhein) is a magnificent river for cruising, with its vineyard-clad slopes and generous peppering of romantic castles. The Mosel, Neckar, Main and Saar tributaries are of interest too.

'Old Father Rhine', as the Germans lovingly call it, is Europe's most important commercial waterway, flowing for some 1,320km (820 miles) from source to estuary. The Rhine has long been Europe's busiest river, with some of the densest shipping traffic in the world, yet its waters and turbulent past have inspired poets and romantics for centuries. The mystery of the river comes alive in the folklore tales of Lorelei and the Nibelung, the music of Wagner and Beethoven, and in the countless legends surrounding the fairytale castles and fortresses that line its banks.

Although it is essentially seen as a German river, the Rhine crosses several international boundaries, passing through no fewer than six countries – Austria, France, Germany, Liechtenstein, the Netherlands and Switzerland – on its journey from the Alps to the North Sea. Although the stretch known as the Middle Rhine, or the Romantic Rhine, with its towering cliffs, castles, vineyards and dense forests, is the best-known section, the river has many other faces as it flows along the German–French border, or cuts a course across the flat, agricultural landscapes of

On the Rhine at Cologne.

the Netherlands in the final stages of its journey north. The most scenic section is the 65km (40-mile)-long gorge between Bingen and Koblenz, which is almost always part of a Rhine river cruise.

Together with the Bodensee (Lake Constance), the Rhine forms a reservoir of drinking water for approximately 30 million Germans. It irrigates mile upon mile of vineyards. It has been an essential transport route through Europe since prehistoric times and has given rise to a string of prosperous towns and cities along its banks. A cruise on the Rhine is rarely without something to draw the eye. Heavily laden barges chug their way north or south, pleasure cruisers ply the waters from one beauty spot to the next, and hikers, swimmers and cyclists enjoy the river's banks and beaches. In parts, there is abundant birdlife to spot, spectacular castles to identify and bridges, statues and monuments all charting the river's history.

THE COURSE OF THE RHINE

The source of the Rhine is a mountain brook that trickles out from the craggy Gotthard Massif in southeastern Switzerland. This is where two small streams, the Hinterrhein and Vorderrhein, unite to form the Alpine Rhine (Alpernrhein). The waters then flow along the borders of Liechtenstein and Austria and into the beautiful sweep of Lake Constance, emerging from the other side of the lake to tumble over the Rhine Falls, Europe's biggest waterfall, near Schaffhausen in Switzerland, where the river plunges 21m (69ft). The river is joined here by the Aar, doubling its volume.

The next stretch, known as the High Rhine (Hochrhein), forms the Swiss–German frontier. At Basel, the river executes a sharp right turn, the 'Rhine Knee', to head northwards, cutting a course through a broad valley along the French–German border. Close to the city of Karlsruhe, the French border is left behind and the river enters its German heartland. After holding a northerly course for some distance, it twists to the west between Mainz and Bingen, an area known as the Rheingau, before forcing its way through the Binger Loch (Hole of Bingen), a steep gorge that marks the beginning of the Middle Rhine (Mittelrhein), or Romantic Rhine. The river then flows northwest through the Uplands (Rheinisches Schiefergebirge) along its most scenic stretch with steep vine-clad slopes, deep gorges and dramatic castles towering over the water.

Below Bonn the river becomes the Lower Rhine (Niederrhein). It then travels through the flat territory of Germany's heavily industrialised Westphalia and the neighbouring Netherlands, where it divides into a number of delta arms, the principal ones being the Lek and the Waal, before finally disgorging into the North Sea.

The Rhine is fed by a number of tributaries, the most important being major rivers in their own right, such as the Main and the Mosel. River cruises operate on both of these, usually in conjunction with the Middle Rhine, and also on the pretty Neckar, which flows through one of Germany's biggest tourist attractions, the city of Heidelberg.

CASTLES ON THE RHINE

The Rhine is home to the highest density of castles in Europe. Most date from the Middle Ages or earlier, and legends, deeds of chivalry, internment and torture of every kind are connected with almost every one of them. Many were built by the feudal lords to protect their land; others were built to take advantage of the views of the traffic on the Rhine and later became toll-collection points. Between Mainz and Bonn, especially in the narrow slate gorge between Bingen and Koblenz, a distance of only 56km (35 miles), there are more castles than in any other river valley in the world.

The following castles can all be clearly seen from a rivership as it motors quietly along the Rhine. Many are in excellent condition and have been converted into hotels, although some have fallen into ruin.

Bonn to Koblenz

Km 647.6 (right): Godesburg Castle
Km 645.3 (left): Königswinter Castle
Km 643.7 (left): Drachenburg Castle and Drachenfels Castle (ruin)
Km 640 (right): Rolandseck Castle (ruin)
Km 623.9 (left): Arenfels Castle (now a hotel)
Km 621.9 (right): Rheineck Castle (now a hotel)
Km 618 (left): Hammerstein Castle (ruin)
Km 592.3 (left): Ehrenbreitstein Castle (now a youth hostel)

Koblenz to Bingen

Km 585.2 (left): Lahneck Castle
Km 585.2 (right): Stolzenfels Castle (now a hotel)
Km 580 (left): Marksburg Castle
Km 556.9 (right): Rheinfels Castle
Km 556.5 (right): Sterrenberg Castle and Liebenstein Castle
Km 555.9 (left): Katz Castle (now a hotel)
Km 549.1 (right): Schönburg Castle
Km 546.5 (left): Gutenfels Castle
Km 543.1 (right): Stahleck Castle (with a water-filled moat and inner wall)
Km 541 (right): Fürstenberg Castle (ruin)
Km 539.8 (left): Nollig Castle (ruin)
Km 539.4 (right): Heimburg Castle
Km 537.4 (right): Sooneck Castle

Rheinstein Castle.

DID YOU KNOW...?

...that the name 'Rhine' comes from the Celtic word *renos*, meaning 'raging flow'?
...that there are more castles in the Rhine Valley than in any other valley in the world?
...that the Middle Rhine Valley (an 80km/50 mile stretch) became a Unesco World Heritage site in 1992?
...that since 1855 there has been a signal-box for river shipping at the top of the Mice Tower (Mäuseturm) near Schloss Ehrenfels (Ehrenfels Castle) on the Rhine, just downstream from Rüdesheim?
...that the composer Schumann (1810–56) attempted to drown himself in the Rhine in 1854? He lived in Düsseldorf for four years and was appointed conductor of the municipal orchestra in 1850.
...that the Roman Emperor Caracalla used to go to the spa at Baden-Baden to cure his rheumatism?
...that salmon once thrived in the Rhine? Sadly, dams and industrial pollution have all but killed the salmon population here. In 2001, despite €20 million having been spent on breeding wild salmon, only 60 fish were detected in the river; some €50 billion was spent in cleaning up the polluted river. Compare this with the more than 250,000 wild salmon recorded caught on the Rhine in 1885, and you can see why wild salmon (so much better tasting than the farmed variety) is now a rarity.
...that the first stone bridge across the Mosel was built in 1363 for pilgrims on their way to Rome?
...that in Switzerland, 25 percent of all freight arrives by water?
...that the German for 'lock', as in watergate, is *die Schleuse*?

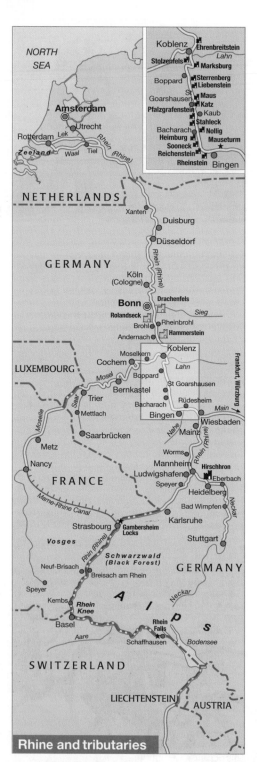

Rhine and tributaries

Km 534.5 (right): Reichenstein Castle (in use today as a hotel)
Km 533 (right): Rheinstein Castle
Km 530.4 (left): Ehrenfels Castle (ruin)

Principal tributaries

The Main: Some 524km (325 miles) long, the Main starts at Kulmbach from the confluence of the brooks known as the White and Red Main, which have their sources in the Fichtel Mountains and in the Franconian Alb. The riverships typically cruise on the section between Frankfurt and Würzburg, passing forested hills, lush meadows and historic towns.

The Mosel (Moselle, in English): At 535km (332 miles) long, the Mosel is the longest of the Rhine's tributaries. It is narrower and, some say, prettier or more intimate than the Rhine. It rises in the Vosges Mountains at some 735m (2,410ft) above sea level. Mosel means 'little Maas' in French, a reference to the fact that, in prehistoric times, its bed joined that of the Maas. The river was only developed into a navigable waterway as recently as 1964, an event made possible by the signing of a contract between France, Germany and Luxembourg, following which a system of 14 locks was constructed.

The Mosel twists and turns in a series of sharp bends as it cuts its way through a deep valley, the sides lined with steeply terraced vineyards, before merging with the Rhine at Koblenz, at an altitude some 676m (2,218ft) lower than its source. On its journey it forms the border between Luxembourg and Germany for a distance of 36km (22 miles). The Mosel is navigable from Thionville in France to Koblenz, a distance of 270km (165 miles).

The Neckar: This is one of the longest tributaries to flow into the Rhine. Its source is in the Baar in a region between the Black Forest and the Swabian Alb (the region in which the Danube also has its source), to the east of the Rhine in Baden-Württemberg, north of Lake Constance. The river is 367km (228 miles) long and navigable for 203km (126 miles), although some stretches have canals that enable cargo vessels to make their way through the 26 sets of locks as far upstream as Plochingen.

The Neckar flows through some of Germany's most beautiful countryside, castles guarding every curve of the river, and vines and forests sloping right down to the banks. The whole valley is one of Germany's great summer playgrounds, with pleasure boats, canoes, punts and dinghies out on the water, and cyclists and hikers enjoying the scene from the banks.

After a journey of 367km (228 miles) past great towns and cities including Stuttgart and Heidelberg, the river cuts briefly across the flatter, more industrialised Rhine plain and disgorges its contents into the major river at the city of Mannheim.

The Saar: Another of the Rhine's longest tributaries, the Saar flows through France and Saarland on its way from the Vosges mountain range to the Mosel. Some 246km (153 miles) long, it is navigable from

Dillingen to the confluence in Konz. It was integrated in 1989 into the European waterways network with additional locks and canals. One of these canals cuts off a magnificent horseshoe-shaped loop of the river near Mettlach. The hill (called Cloef) adjacent to the river provides an excellent vantage point for photographs of this spectacular bend.

HIGHLIGHTS BETWEEN AMSTERDAM (THE NETHERLANDS) AND BASEL (SWITZERLAND)

Amsterdam, The Netherlands (Km 0)

At the start of the Rhine Canal is cosmopolitan, easy-going Amsterdam. The city lies near the sea on the narrow land strips between Lake IJssel and the North Sea. The River Amstel runs through the centre of the city, which consists of a horseshoe-shaped network of over 100km (62 miles) of man-made canals that connect about 90 islands and 400 stone bridges. Whether you arrive by air, or by train, the riverships berth close to the central railway station, along the Oosterdokskade or Ruijterkade Oost (ocean-going cruise ships sail from a different terminal in Oosterlijke Handelskade).

The city is one of Europe's most enjoyable destinations, unique in many ways – not least for its balance of past and present. Perhaps no community has ever had such a glorious explosion of wealth and culture as Amsterdam during the 17th century, the city's Golden Age, yet this is a place that has always looked forward rather than back. The modern city is exuberant, with a tremendous range of cultural life from world-class art galleries to wacky street theatre.

Here are its highlights:

Canal ring: Amsterdam's horseshoe-shaped network of canals is the city's most distinctive feature and a must-see for visitors – lined with tall, elegant mansions from the 17th and 18th centuries. The canal ring (Grachtengordel) encompassing the three parallel waterways of Herengracht, Keizersgracht and Prinsengracht is the most scenic stretch.

Maritime Museum: This excellent museum (Scheepvaartmuseum) documents and celebrates Amsterdam's illustrious maritime history.

Rijksmuseum: Home to arguably the greatest collection of Dutch art in the world, the Rijksmuseum is housed within a magnificent Victorian Gothic building that has recently undergone a vast programme of renovations.

The collection is varied, but most visitors come to see the works of the Dutch masters from the 15th to the 17th centuries. Among the collection are 20 works by Rembrandt, including *The Night Watch*. Johannes Vermeer is well represented, as is Frans Hals, the founding artist of the Dutch School, along with a collection of Dutch artists who were influenced or schooled by the masters. The museum also has a collection of work by non-Dutch artists, including Rubens, Tintoretto and El Greco, along with porcelain, furniture, sculpture and decorative arts, and Asiatic art.

Van Gogh Museum: The world's largest permanent collection features a selection of paintings by Van Gogh hung in chronological and, to a degree, thematic order – though the location of individual works may change from time to time.

An Amsterdam canal.

Royal Palace: Dominating Dam Square in the heart of Amsterdam is the 17th-century Koninklijk Paleis (Royal Palace). The rather heavy exterior belies an elegant series of rooms inside with some notable works of art. The square itself is a hub of activity and meeting point.
Anne Frank House: A staircase leads into the backrooms where Otto Frank, his family and friends hid for two fraught years, from 1942 until August 1944. The house is a monument to all the victims of Fascism and anti-Semitism and something of a place of pilgrimage.
De Looier antiques market: A vast indoor antiques market selling anything from memorabilia to handmade pottery, and old dolls and toys.

Utrecht, The Netherlands (Km 31)
The fourth-largest city of the Netherlands is also the capital of Utrecht Province in the country's central section. Magnificent churches abound here (Domkerk, or St Martin's Cathedral, St Jacobuskerk, St Janskerk and St Pieterskerk), and there's also a large, historic university, founded in 1636.

Amsterdam–Rhine Canal (Km 913.4)
The canal, which opened in 1952 and is 72km (48 miles) long, connects the city and port of Amsterdam with the Lek River, making Amsterdam an important port for the trans-shipment of cargo. Considered to be the most heavily used canal in Europe, it has four locks.
(Start of the Rhine kilometre markings).

Düsseldorf, Germany (Km 744.2)
The capital of North Rhine-Westphalia and its administration centre, Düsseldorf is best known for its iron and steel production and as a centre for banking. It is also famous for its beer, with a number of microbreweries and some hundreds of pubs in the atmospheric Altstadt (Old Town), and for its shopping, particularly along the Königsallee.

The Fine Arts Museum is worth a visit, as is the Ceramic Museum, and the Lambertus Basilica, begun in 1288 (its spire is twisted), and the Castle Tower, which houses a museum of navigation. The city has long been famous for its Christmas market. The Bolkerstrasse, one of the city's liveliest streets, was the birthplace of the poet Heinrich Heine, author of *Die Lorelei* (see page 72).

Cologne (Köln), Germany (Km 688)
Cologne is one of the most important traffic junctions and commercial centres in Germany and the most important economic centre on the Rhine. Riverships berth at landing stages in the heart of the old town centre, with its fine riverfront promenade and views along the Rhine.

It's a busy modern city with a strong sense of historical heritage. Already established as an important centre in Roman times and resurgent in the Middle Ages, today's city centre is still dominated by its glorious twin-towered cathedral. Repeatedly bombed in World War II, Cologne preserved its historic street pattern when it was rebuilt and, although most buildings are modern, much of its traditional atmosphere survives. It's a lively place, best experienced for those with stamina during the merrymaking of Karneval (Lenten Carnival) time. The historic core of Cologne is large, bounded by the semicircular boulevard of the Ring running along the line of the old city walls, although the epicentre of city life is to be found in the

Katz Castle and Lorelei rock.

busy squares around the cathedral. Shoppers will enjoy walking the Hohe-Strasse, close to the docking area.

Cologne is also noted for its very own 'Original' Eau de Cologne toilet water (its brand name is 4711, which was the maker's former address).

Dom: With its awesome dimensions, the cathedral (Dom) is the unmistakable landmark of the city, its two mighty towers the defining symbol of Cologne's skyline. Construction began in 1248 and resumed in 1880, the final result remaining true to the original plans. A winding staircase of 509 steps leads to a viewing platform 95m (312ft) up in the south tower, where the view amply rewards your efforts.

Fischmarkt: There are few reminders today that the people of Cologne once bought and sold fish, but adjacent to the river is the city's old harbour area and the former fish market. The late-Gothic buildings surrounding the square, now lined with bars and restaurants, have been preserved in their distinct, original style.

Römisch-Germanisches Museum: Containing treasures from over 2,000 years ago after the Romans had established their camp of Colonia here, the city's Roman-Germanic Museum was built over the famous Dionysus Mosaic.

Wallraf-Richartz Museum: Cologne's oldest museum showcases art from the 14th to the 20th centuries. The collection represents every period and school, from Dutch and Flemish masters to French Impressionists, with works by Dürer, Rembrandt, Rubens, Degas and Cézanne, among many others.

St Gereon Basilica: This medieval church is known for its intricate floor mosaic of David and Goliath and its unique decagon-shaped dome. It contains the tomb of St Gereon and other martyrs.

Bonn, Germany (Km 654.8)

The Rhine flows through the suburbs of Bonn, the former German capital. The Romans named it Castra Bonnensia 2,000 years ago, when it formed part of their Rhine Valley defences, although its real development did not begin until the Middle Ages. The city became the residence of the electors and archbishops of Cologne in the 17th century, and was the capital of West Germany before reunification and the eventual reinstatement of Berlin as the home of government in 1999. Today, Bonn is a university town, and has several museums on the riverbank in the 'Museum Mile', including the Kunst- und Ausstellungshalle (Art and Exhibition Hall), with exhibitions of art, technology, history and architecture, and the Kunstmuseum (Museum of Art).

Beethoven was born in Bonn in a house that, since 1890, has been a museum (Beethovenhaus). You can see original handwritten manuscripts, his instruments (including a piano complete with amplified sound to allow for his deafness), listening horns and life and death masks.

Cologne at night.

Drachenfels Castle, Germany (Km 643.7)

According to legend, it was at the foot of the sheer Drachenfels (Dragon's Rock) cliff that Siegfried, the hero of the *Nibelungen Saga*, slew the dragon and then bathed in its blood in order to render himself invulnerable. The castle is now a ruin, and is reached by funicular from Bad Godesburg. The view is magnificent.

Rolandseck Castle (Km 640)

Rolandseck was originally a fortress that also served as a customs station. It is now in ruins, but old archways can still be found on the grounds, the principal one being Rolandsbogen (Roland's Arch). The Rolandsbogen got its name from the legend of the young knight Roland, who is said to have looked yearningly down from this window at the Nonnenwerth convent, on an island in the middle of the Rhine, where his beloved was incarcerated. She had taken her vows because she had believed that he would not return from the Crusades. He did come home, but she was not allowed to leave the nunnery, and the couple died apart, their love unfulfilled. It is said that a tunnel led from the castle to the Nonnenwerth convent, but the castle was destroyed in the 17th century, and the last remaining archway of the ruin collapsed in 1839. The poet Ferdinand Freiligrath had the idea that the Rolandsbogen should be restored – and it was, in 1840. It now rests some 150m (492ft) above the Rhine, covered in a thick growth of ivy.

Andernach, Germany (Km 613.3)

This place was known as 'Backerjungenstadt' ('city of baker's apprentices'), because legend has it that it was once under siege, and baker's apprentices threw bees' nests on the attackers from the city walls. Its historical town hall, with its Jewish baths, can be visited.

Ehrenbreitstein Castle, Germany (Km 592.3)

Located opposite the mouth of the Mosel, where it flows into the Rhine at Koblenz, this squat, solid-looking fortress was built around 1100 on a site that is 116m (380ft) above the water, with incredible views over both

The curious Pfalzgrafenstein (or Mäuseturm) Castle.

rivers, the Eifel Hills and the city of Koblenz. It was acquired in 1152 by the Electorate of Trier and expanded, becoming a fortress around 1500 with the addition of more fortifications. By 1750, after several breaches by the French, the fortress was made impregnable by the brilliant architect Balthasar Neumann. Today, the castle houses the National Collection of Monuments to Technology, and also serves as a youth hostel. Ehrenbreitstein Castle is also one of the sites for the annual Rhine in Flames celebration (see page 71).

Koblenz, Germany (Km 591.5, Rhine/Km 0.30, Mosel)

A former Roman trading settlement, Koblenz grew up at the confluence of the Rhine and the Mosel and lies on the massif of the Middle Rhine Highlands. It is bordered by North Rhine-Westphalia to the north, Hesse to the east and Saarland to the south. The Rhine cuts it diagonally from southeast to northwest.

Stolzenfels Castle, Germany (Km 585.2)

Located just south of Koblenz and surrounded by thick forest, this handsome, imperial yellow castle was originally built in the 13th century to defend the nearby silver mines. The castle was destroyed by the French but rebuilt in 1852 by the Prussian Crown Prince Friedrich-Wilhelm IV, in neo-Gothic style. In the castle's chapel, important works from the period of High Romanticism can be found in the murals. It is one of the best-known castles along the Rhine.

Marksburg Castle, Germany (Km 580)

This beautiful, mystical castle is the only one in the entire Rhine Valley never to have been destroyed, and is easily the most visited, as it gives the best insight into medieval life. It dates back to 1150, towering majestically 170m (557ft) above the town of Braubach. The original founder, one of the nobles of Braubach, named it after St Mark. A successor, Eberhard von Eppstein, had the castle extended and further fortified in 1219, and it was occupied after 1220 by vassals of the Counts Palatine. In 1283, the castle was acquired by the counts of Katzenelnbogen.

At the end of the 19th century it passed to the German Castles Association, which has its headquarters and archives here. The library houses over 12,000 volumes. A tour of the castle will take you through not only the citadel itself, but also the impressive kitchens in the Gothic Hall building. There is a gruesome torture chamber in the cellar of the older hall building, where a great assortment of grisly instruments of torture can be viewed.

A complete replica of the castle can be seen today in an amusement park in Japan. It appears that the Japanese offered to buy the original ruin, have it dismantled and shipped to Japan, for the price of 250 million marks, but were refused by the German Castles Association – hence the replica.

Boppard, Germany (Km 570.5)

A charming riverfront city, Boppard (of Celtic origin) is located at one of the bends in the Rhine. It has a medieval town hall, Roman castle (eight of the original 28 towers still exist, as do the medieval town gates), several convents, stylish villas and half-timbered houses. Grapes (mostly Riesling) are grown on slopes that are among the steepest in Germany – these are used by 14 full-time cooperatives that obtain more than 500,000 litres (approximately 110,000 imperial gallons) from the cultivation.

Liebenstein Castle and Sterrenberg Castle (Km 566.5)

Not far from Boppard are the ruins of two 12th-century castles, Sterrenberg and Liebenstein, built close together. These were inhabited by two brothers, who hated each other so much that they erected a wall between the castles. The story goes that they made up their differences, and for fun, decided to wake each other with an arrow shot every morning. Inevitably, one killed the other by mistake with a badly aimed arrow.

Lorelei, St Goarshausen, Germany (Km 554.6)

Nobody can pass through the medieval wine-growing village of St Goarshausen without learning the legend of the Lorelei (see box). Here, the river carves its way through a steep, narrow gorge, with its bed descending to 25m (82ft) in places, winding around jagged rocks and creating powerful whirlpools, which have sucked many a ship below the surface. The gorge, with its 132m (433ft) cliffs, is so narrow that the railway line that runs alongside the river has been cut into rock tunnels. A bronze statue of the maiden Lorelei looks down on the river from where, as related by the poem by Heinrich Heine in 1824, the mysterious nymph would once appear, captivating sailors with her beauty and her hypnotic singing before luring them onto the rocks to their death. The poem *Die Lorelei*, set to music in 1837, is seen as the epitome of Rhine Romanticism. A visitor centre

RHINE IN FLAMES

Time it right and you could be part of the fabulous 'Rhein in Flammen' (Rhine in Flames) celebration, which typically takes place in August each year. There are, in fact, three such celebrations, but by far the best is on the section of river between Boppard and Koblenz. Almost 100 riverships take part each year, strung one behind the other in convoy, like a string of sausages (the river police organise this), and measuring over 3km (1.8 miles) in length.

As the convoy moves from Boppard to Koblenz, past numerous towns and villages along the way, fireworks light up the night sky, with all the local towns and villages vying to create the best display. On reaching Koblenz, the convoy stops and turns round to face Ehrenbreitstein Castle (see page 69), the magnificent fortress across from the mouth of the Mosel River. The castle is gloriously lit in red spotlights, with smoke rising all around it, so that it seems to be on fire. It is an unforgettable sight. For more information, see www.rhein-in-flammen.com.

stands on the top of the rock today, although the entrance fee is hardly worth it, as there is little inside (it's much better to cruise past the rock).

Pfalzgrafenstein Castle (Km 545)

This is undoubtedly one of the most curious castle creations in the world, a six-storey tower clinging to a tiny island in the middle of the swirling waters and resembling a ship. The castle was erected in 1326 by King Ludwig I of Bavaria purely for collecting customs duties from passing vessels on the Rhine. Anyone who couldn't pay would be sent down a rope to the 'dungeon' – a platform floating at the bottom of a deep well. Since 1946 it has been the property of the state of the Rhineland-Palatinate. Although it has been repaired and restored, purely for tourism purposes, the castle was in use as a signal point for Rhine shipping until the 1960s.

Reichenstein Castle, Germany (Km 534.4)

In the 19th century, Reichenstein was called Falkenburg Castle. It was erected to protect the property of Cornelimunster Abbey near Aachen in the 11th century. It has been destroyed and rebuilt several times, the last time in 1899. Nowadays, it is in use as a hotel.

Rheinstein Castle (Km 533)

Originally constructed as an imperial castle for customs and toll collection, it also protected the surrounding estates. One of the oldest castle buildings on the Rhine – it dates back to the 9th century – it has an astounding position: the steely-grey castle appears to be part of a huge, jagged slab of rock high on the hillside.

Rheinstein belonged to the archbishops of Mainz, who named it after their patron saint, Bonifatius, although its original name was Vogtberg. It fell into ruin in the 16th century, and in 1823 Prince Friedrich of Prussia paid 100 Reichsmarks for what was left of it, renaming it Rheinstein. His great-granddaughter sold it in 1975, in an advanced state of dilapidation, to an Austrian singer from the Tyrol. It is now preserved thanks to donations from tourists, a society founded by the singer and income from its rental.

Mäuseturm, Germany (Km 529)

Below the mouth of the Nahe, close to Rüdesheim and Bingen, a slender red-and-yellow tower looking like something out of a Disney cartoon perches on a small island. The legend relates how the original tower was built by the evil, hard-hearted Archbishop Hatto of Mainz in 1208 as reinforcement for the customs castle, Ehrenfels, which stands in ruinous state on the opposite hillside. The tower's strategic position allowed the archbishop to fleece passing traffic on the Rhine. To bolster his income, peasants were levied a corn tithe, which he collected in a large barn in Mainz. After a bad harvest, the hungry populace went to Mainz and asked for grain. Archbishop Hatto, having promised to help, then proceeded to lock them up in his tithe barn and set fire to it.

Everyone inside perished, but the story goes that some mice escaped. The archbishop departed to his castle on the island by boat from Bingen, opposite Rüdesheim, but the mice followed him... and then ate him alive, even though he had had his bed suspended by chains from the ceiling, so that it was well above the floor.

The edifice thus became known as the Mice Tower (Mäuseturm), although its actual title was once Mautturm (Customs Tower). Under France's King Louis XIV, the castle was burnt down, although fortunately it was restored by the King of Prussia in 1855 and used as a signal tower for shipping, to warn ships of the treacherous whirlpools and rocks of the Hole of Bingen. It remained in this manner until 1974, when the channel was deepened, and since then it has been inhabited only by bats, and, so the legend goes, the ghost of the evil archbishop.

Rüdesheim, Germany (Km 526.7)

This was the terminal point of the old 'Merchant Road' that originated in Lohr and circumvented the waterfalls that once made this stretch of river treacherous. It is famous for its wine growing districts on the Rüdesheim Hills, located at the foothills of the Niederwald Forest and Taunus Mountains. A cable car will take you to the top of the Rheingau hills, where the famous Niederwald Denkmal monument – a statue of Germania built to commemorate the founding of the German Empire in 1871 – is located.

Four castles were constructed to protect this important merchant centre and traffic route, one of which, Bromserburg, belonged for a while to the Knights of Rüdesheim; today it is a wine museum. A number of taverns and drinking houses line its narrow streets, particularly Drosselgasse.

One fascinating attraction in Rüdesheim is Siegfried's Mechanisches Musikkabinett (Siegfried's Mechanical Instrument Museum). This unusual museum, located in the Bromserhof (parts of which date back to the 15th century), is famous for its outstanding collection of priceless mechanical musical instruments. All 250 instruments have been collected from the period spanning 150 years prior to 1930 and have all been restored. Siegfried Wendel, the museum's owner, is always on hand and frequently plays some of the instruments for visitors. It is open from March to December.

Mainz, Germany (Km 498.5)

Mainz, located on the west bank of the Rhine opposite the mouth of the river Main, is over 2,000 years old (it was founded as the Roman camp Moguntiacum). It is the capital city of Rhineland-Palatinate (Rheinland-Pfalz), and has a history as seat of electors and bishops. Much of the city was devastated by bombing in World War II and has been rebuilt. In the Old Town, visit the six-towered

THE LORELEI

Near St Goarshausen, at one of the most notorious bends in the Middle Rhine Valley, the Lorelei is a large, almost perpendicular slate rock 130m (427ft) high that produces an echo. In days of old, so it is told, noblemen occupied the area in order to squeeze taxes from passing traffic – from every vessel and merchant needing to travel beyond its grasp.

Back then, Lorelei herself, a siren, could be seen occasionally on the hilltop. Echoing through the landscape, a mysterious voice belonging to the maiden chanted the now-famous poem, as fishermen passed within her grasp. She lured them on to the craggy rocks, and to a fate unknown.

The charming maiden's beauty and reputation spread throughout the land, until one day it reached the ears of the son of the Duke Palatine. Yearning for passion, the young man left his father's palace in secret and journeyed by boat to win the maiden's heart. It is said that at sunset he and his followers reached the gorge and were spellbound by the singing of the Lorelei. He caught a glimpse of her hair and enchanting figure at the top of the steepest cliff.

Magically, the strength to row vanished from their arms as they stared at the figure. It seemed as if the boatswain had lost memory of his duties. The young prince, somewhat impatient, jumped into the waters to reach the lovely maiden and take her hand. With a cry of 'Lorelei', he sank into the busy, swirling waters, never to be seen again.

The Duke ordered his son's betrayer to be captured. The rock, soon surrounded by the Duke's revengeful soldiers, became a silent witness. One captain took the bravest of his soldiers with him to the top of the hill. 'Unholy woman, now you can pay for your sins,' he commanded, blocking the monster's path to her grotto. 'That does not lie with you,' she replied and cast her pearl necklaces into the floods below. They rose out of the water – as high as the cliff top – and carried the fairy away into the grey evening night. Lorelei was never seen again, but if you go today to the rock and stare at it, a manifold echo may taunt you.

The Lorelei has been the subject of a number of literary works, including, most famously, Heinrich Heine's 1824 poem, which has been set to music by more than 20 composers. Although Heine made the poem so renowned, he was not its creator. That honour goes to the German romantic poet Clemens Brentano, who, in 1801, included the ballad of Lore Lay in his novel, Godwi.

Christmas market in Düsseldorf's Altstadt.

cathedral, originally constructed in AD 975 and a highlight of ecclesiastical architecture in the Upper Rhine region.

Mainz is also home to the Gutenberg Museum, which tells the history of printing. The city is also one of the main centres of the Rhine wine trade. There are several museums and palaces to explore, but one sight not to miss is St Stephen's Church, with its stunning stained-glass windows by the French painter Marc Chagall.

Worms, Germany (Km 443.2)

One of the oldest cities in Germany, Worms was originally inhabited as an imperial residence on the banks of the Rhine and the centre of the Burgundian Empire that was destroyed by the Huns. Today, the city is known as a wine-trading centre. The vineyards surrounding the city produce the grapes used for making 'Liebfraumilch', a trade name for the much-maligned semi-sweet white wine that is from the Palatinate, Rhine-Hesse (Rheinhessen), Nahe and Rheingau wine-growing regions. Passengers typically disembark at Worms to take a tour (by bus) to Heidelberg (see page 76).

Mannheim, Germany (Km 415–425)

The city was founded in 1606 in a circular layout that covered only the peninsula at the strategic confluence of the Neckar and the Rhine. The city, which developed from the fortress that is aligned with the Rhine, was created by the Palatine Elector Frederick

IV and has grown into a modern finance and insurance centre. It also has a university.

Speyer, Germany (Km 400)

This is typically used as a short stop so that passengers can leave the vessel to take a tour to Heidelberg (see page 76), although Speyer has a few noteworthy sights, including an immense Unesco-protected cathedral, one of the most important Romanesque buildings from the time of the Holy Roman Empire, and the Jewish baths. The city was burned down on the order of Louis XIV in 1689. After it was returned to Germany in 1816, it became the government seat of Bavaria Palatinate until 1845.

Gambersheim Locks, France (Km 309)

The Gambersheim locks are a relatively recent construction, put into operation in 1974. They are operated from Strasbourg and are the largest inland waterway locks in France. There are two chambers, each with a length of 270m (885ft), and the locks are in operation 24 hours a day, all year round (it takes about 15 minutes to pass through them). About 20 million tons of goods pass through the locks each year, as well as numerous riverships.

Strasbourg, France (Km 294.3)

The medieval city of Strasbourg is the seat of the Council of Europe, the European Commission on Human Rights and the European Science Foundation, and is also capital and cultural centre of the Alsace

The Rhine in Flames celebration.

region of France. The port is the largest on the Upper Rhine, and a large network of docks provides freight and other services.

Strasbourg's centre is surrounded by the River Ill, and is mainly pedestrianised, particularly the area known as Petite France, where the river splits into a number of canals. At the end of Petite France, look out for the Ponts Couverts, a series of wooden footbridges dating back to the 13th century (but no longer covered).

The focal point of it all is place Gutenberg, named after Johannes Gutenberg, the inventor of the printing press, who lived here during the 15th century and whose statue stands at the centre of the square. A highlight of any visit is the massive hulk of the Cathédrale de Notre Dame, the tallest medieval building in Europe, its viewing platform reached by a wearying 332 steps up inside the tower. It's worth the climb for the vista of the Black Forest (and, in the other direction, the Vosges Mountains) beyond the colourful roofs of the old town. At noon, crowds are drawn to the astronomical clock inside the cathedral, adorned with a Parade of the Apostles, which dates from 1838.

Many river cruises start and end in Strasbourg, and the Gare Fluviale is located adjacent to rue du Havre, a short walk from the heart of the city on an arm of the Ill.

Basel, Switzerland (Km 165–169)

Basel, the navigable limit of the Rhine, is the starting point for many cruises. The city has grown up either side of the river, with the industrial Kleinbasel section to the north and the lovely old part, Grossbasel, on the south bank. Basel has a real international flavour; it is, after all, where three countries – France, Germany and Switzerland – meet. Situated at the 'knee' of the Rhine, it is the location of the oldest university in Switzerland, together with some 30 museums and an inviting old town – a jumble of medieval buildings along the hilly river bank (a short walk from the cruise boat landing stage). Basel is also steeped in Roman history.

The focal point of the city is the Rathaus (Town Hall) and marketplace, around which are several late Gothic, Renaissance and Baroque guildhalls. The 13th-century Romanesque Münster (Cathedral) is an unusual shade of red, its slender towers built from sandstone quarried from the nearby Vosges Mountains.

There are several museums worth visiting, including the Kunstmuseum, where you can view two Picasso paintings (The Seated Harlequin and Two Brothers), purchased by the people of the city in 1967, together with four others the artist donated.

Basel is famous for its music festivals and industrial trade fairs, the most famous being the Autumn Fair, which has been held each and every year since 1471.

HIGHLIGHTS ON THE MOSEL

Moselkern, Germany (Km 34)

This small, sleepy hamlet provides a stopping point for riverships, so that passengers can take a tour to Burg Eltz, a castle set not on a hillside but deep in the forest. The castle is unusual in that it is really a collection of three houses. A drawbridge-like entrance from a steep winding forest road helps to add to the atmosphere.

Cochem, Germany (Km 51.3)

One of the loveliest and most picturesque of all the towns along the Mosel, Cochem is located at the beginning of a 20km (13-mile) bend in the river. The walled Old Town is laced with narrow alleys. The skyline is dominated by the Imperial Castle, which has a rectangular keep *(donjon)* and numerous small towers. Worth a look is the Capuchin monastery, built in 1623, and restored for use today as a cultural centre. The Baroque Town Hall is also of note, as are the old gabled houses overlooking the Market Fountain. The Mosel Wine Week takes place here in mid-June each year, and the wine taverns along the river front have 'green wine' (very young wine) available all year round. Behind the waterfront are more taverns, which are recommended for their friendly atmosphere.

Bernkastel-Kues, Germany (Km 129.4)

Bernkastel-Kues is comprised of two villages (Bernkastel and Kues), one on each side of the Mosel (and joined by a bridge) at the confluence of the Tiefenbach

(meaning 'deep stream'). The riverships dock on the Kues side. This is big wine-growing country, and the Middle Mosel Wine Festival is staged here in the first week in September. There is also a Wine Museum in the town. The ruins of a fortress called Lanshut dominate the town, which is filled with gorgeous half-timbered houses; the lowest floor of many houses is typically smaller than the upper floor because taxes used to be charged based on the amount of ground the house covered. During winter Christmas market cruises, the picture-postcard setting is magical.

Trier, Germany (Km 181.5–191.4)

Trier is the principal city of the Mosel Valley and the oldest in Germany; growing up around a ford used by the Germanic-Celtic Treveri tribe before being officially founded in 16 BC by the Roman Emperor Caesar Augustus, who named it Augusta Treverorum. Trier, which lies in the Middle Rhine Highlands, is bordered by Luxembourg and Belgium to the west, North Rhine-Westphalia to the north and Saarland to the south.

One of the best-preserved and most important Roman edifices in Germany is the 2nd-century, four-storey Porta Nigra (Town Gate), built of sandstone (originally without mortar) and today protected as a Unesco World Heritage Site. You can visit the Constantine Baths, and other remaining Roman relics such as a 20,000-seat amphitheatre and Roman bridge. A cross dating from AD 958 can be found in the Stadtmuseum (town museum); there is a replica in the market square, while close by is the Petrus Fountain, constructed in 1595. It is also famous as

Sunset in Petite France, Strasbourg.

the birthplace of Karl Marx (1818–83), whose house still stands in Bruckenstrasse.

Trier is at the heart of the Mosel wine-producing region and close to one of the area's largest breweries: Bitburger. It is also known for its Christmas markets.

Nancy, France (Km 149.2)

Five palaces, two fountains, a triumphal arch, a cathedral and a grand square are among the attractions backdrop of this delightful town, which is located in an important manufacturing region of France. At its heart is place Stanislas, a vast, impressive square with splendid iron gateways, gilded lanterns and a huge fountain with wrought-iron screen (features that were introduced by the former, exiled King Stanislas of Poland). On one side of the square is the Musée des Beaux-Arts, home to a collection of paintings from Old Masters to the 20th century. Other highlights include the rose-filled Parc de la Pépinière.

HIGHLIGHTS ON THE NECKAR

Heidelberg, Germany (Km 22.7)

Heidelberg, located just over 20km (13 miles) upstream on the Neckar from Mannheim, is the epitome of German Romanticism, nestling on the south side of the river and set against the forested hills of Oldenwald, and dominated by a sprawling red-sand-

MUSIC

Several composers were born or died in the region of the River Rhine.

Johann Sebastian Bach was born on 21 May 1685 in Eisenbach, Germany. He died on 28 July 1750 in Leipzig, Germany.

Ludwig van Beethoven was baptized on 17 December 1770 in Bonn, Germany. He died on 26 March 1827 in Vienna, Austria. The house in which he was born is close to his statue, which is located in front of the post office.

Cristolph Willibald Gluck was born on 2 July 1714 in Erasbach, near Berching, Germany. He died on 15 November 1787 in Vienna.

Paul Hindemith was born on 16 November 1895 in Hanau, near Frankfurt-am-Main, Germany. He died in the same city on 28 December 1963.

Engelbert Humperdinck was born on 1 September 1854 in Sieberg, Hannover, Germany. He died on 27 September 1921 in Neustrelitz, Germany.

Georg Phillipp Telemann was born on 14 March 1681 in Magdeburg, Germany. He died on 27 June 1767 in Hamburg.

Wilhelm Richard Wagner was born on 22 May 1813 in Leipzig, Germany. He died on 13 February 1883 in Venice, Italy.

stone castle complex. This venerable city is the old capital of the Electorate of the Palatinate, although its history goes back a good deal further than that – some 600,000 years, in fact: the jawbone of *Homo heidelbergensis*, the oldest human remains discovered in Europe, was found near here. Thousands of years later, Celts and Romans settled the area. Count Palatine Ruprecht I founded Germany's oldest university here in 1386, and for 500 years the Electoral College, which was responsible for electing the German kings, was based in the city. Heidelberg Castle, constructed with a moat and several keeps, is considered to be the most magnificent castle ruin in all of Germany, and attracts several million visitors a year.

The castle took 400 years to build and encompasses many different architectural styles. It was destroyed by the French during the Wars of Succession between 1689 and 1693, then subsequently rebuilt only to be destroyed again in 1764 when freak lightning struck and burnt it to the ground. Today, some parts lie in ruins, while other sections have been restored to be used for concerts and banquets or to house museums. The whole complex can be reached on foot by steps and walkways that lead up to it from the city, spread along the river below, or via a funicular railway. Highlights include the Friedrich Wing, with impressive statues of the German kings, and the Heidelberg Tun, one of the world's largest wine vats. The castle houses a fine restaurant with views over the castle courtyard. Try the local duck speciality – you'll receive a handwritten card from the chef showing the number assigned to the portion of duck you have just eaten.

Within the castle complex, the Otto Henry Palace is a richly decorated Renaissance building constructed in 1556. Although only the facade remains, it is a splendid reminder that this was the first such Renaissance building to be built in northern Europe. Inside is the Deutsches Apotheken-Museum, containing old medical instruments and medicine bottles.

The city below is full of wonderful Baroque and Renaissance buildings, and remains an important university town, with its population swelled by 28,000 students, so there's always a lively buzz during termtime. Other things to see include the Heiliggeistkirche (Church of the Holy Ghost), the wonderful Renaissance facade of the Hotel Ritter and the Old Bridge (the Karl Theodore Brücke) over the Neckar, which the writer J.W. von Goethe believed to be one of the wonders of the world, thanks to its breathtaking view.

Eberbach, Germany (Km 57.4)

This market town is home to one of the best-kept medieval monasterial establishments in all of Germany, the Eberbach Abbey (Kloster Eberbach). The abbey was built in two stages, from 1145 to 1160, then from 1170 to 1186. Architectural scholars will enjoy the remarkable monks' dormitory, which was

Romantic Heidelberg.

built as a double-naved, ribbed vaulted room with a slightly rising floor; columns were shortened accordingly, and the finished article provides the illusion that it is much longer than it really is (approximately 85m/279ft).

Bad Wimpfen, Germany (Km 100)

Located at the mouth of the River Jagst, Bad Wimpfen is a saline health spa that is extremely popular with German health seekers. From the river, there is a superb view of the old Staufer Palace, with its spires, Romanesque arcades and red roof. The town itself is extremely pretty, with richly decorated half-timbered houses and narrow streets.

Stuttgart, Germany (Km 179–189)

Wealthy in financial and cultural terms, Stuttgart is the capital city of Baden-Württemberg. It is known as the spiritual home of Mercedes-Benz, building of which was started here by two remarkable pioneers, Gottlieb Daimler (1834–1900) and Karl Benz (1844–1929). At night, the famous trademark of Mercedes – a three-pointed star within a circle – can be seen illuminated high above the city.

Definitely worth a visit for automobile-lovers is the Mercedes-Benz Museum, with over 100 vintage and veteran cars on display. Also worth seeing is the Linden Museum, with its many sections displaying ethnological collections from around the world, and the Staatsgalerie, one of Germany's finest art collections. The city itself has a handsome centre with many 16th-century buildings.

HIGHLIGHTS ON THE SAAR

Mettlach, Germany (Km 37)

Mettlach is best known as the home of the ceramics manufacturer Villeroy & Boch, whose offices are housed in the former Benedictine Abbey of St Peter. The abbey was completely rebuilt from 1728 onwards, but earlier excavations at the site revealed buildings that date from AD 700. Some of the scenery along the river around the town is spectacular, notably adjacent to Cloef (see page 67).

Saarbrücken, Germany (Km 90.6)

Saarbrücken, the capital of the Saarland, lies on the River Saar at the mouth of the River Sulz. Dating back to Celtic and Roman times, it was first mentioned in the record books in AD 999. The city is the centre of the Saar coal-mining region, and iron- and steel-making are important industries, as are food processing and brewing and other industries. Architectural highlights include the Protestant Baroque-style Ludwigskirche, built in yellow and red sandstone from the region, and the grand, harmonious Ludwigsplatz on which it stands.

River Elbe

From the Czech Republic to Germany's sandy North Sea coast, an Elbe cruise offers a range of landscapes and some fascinating cities, most notably Prague, Dresden and Berlin.

The Elbe runs for 1,165km (724 miles) from its source in the Czech Republic to the North Sea coast of Germany, passing through a wide range of scenery en route. From the highlands of Bohemia it curves west then north to the dramatic sandstone massif south of Dresden, continuing through the hills and vineyards of Saxony to reach the marshy woodlands of the Lüneburg Heath and the flatlands of the North European Plain. The history of the river is inextricably linked with division. In earlier days, it divided the Slavs and the Germans; later, a stretch of the river separated the former East and West Germany. From the Czech border to beyond Wittenberg the Elbe flows through the heart of the erstwhile German Democratic Republic (East Germany), its towns and villages still perceptibly less prosperous than those ones further west.

Great cities have grown up along its banks, including beautiful Baroque Dresden, and Hamburg, Germany's most important sea and river port. An Elbe cruise also travels a short distance along the Vltava River to the fairytale Czech capital, Prague, and much further north, along the Havel tributary to Berlin, until 1990 the city divided between East and West and now the united country's cosmopolitan capital. Fascinating historic towns along the river's course include Wittenberg, where Dr Martin Luther began the Protestant Reformation, Dessau, heart of the Bauhaus movement, and Meissen, world-famous for its fine porcelain.

Elbe cruises are available in a variety of permutations, usually between Berlin and Prague. Some continue north all the way to Hamburg; some even take in the coast and islands of the North Sea. All offer an opportunity to spend a couple of days in both Berlin and Prague, which is highly recommended.

KIEL CANAL

At Brunsbüttel, near the estuary, the Elbe passes the mouth of the Kiel Canal (also known as the Kaiser Wilhelm Canal), a 98km (60-mile) man-made waterway connecting the North and Baltic seas. It was constructed by the German government in the late 19th century across the northwest of the state of Schleswig-Holstein, from Brunsbüttelkoog to Holenau, on the Kieler Bucht of the Baltic Sea, and became an international waterway following the signing of the Treaty of Versailles in 1919.

A Viking rivership on the Elbe.

DID YOU KNOW...?

...that the longest inland beach is on the River Elbe? Well, sort of. On 14 July 2002, between 80,000 and 100,000 people took part in the first International Elbe Swimming Day. The celebration was organised in 52 towns from the source of the Elbe in the Czech Giant Mountains to the mouth of the river in the North Sea. It was run by 'Project Living Elbe', together with the German organisation Deutsche Umwelthilfe, among other partners. The event, a swimming success, was designed to bring people's attention to the river, which, only a few years previously, had been extremely polluted. What was a sewer has been turned into a river in which one can swim, with the addition of more than 200 water treatment plants along its length.
...that in 2002 the Elbe reached its highest level since 1845?
...that the Rhine Falls at Schaffhausen are the widest in Europe?
...that both the Czech and German names for Elbe derive from Indo-Germanic *albi* or the Latin *albus*, meaning 'shining' or 'white'?

Major tributaries

The 440km (273-mile) -long Vltava (known to the Germans as the Moldau) is a Czech tributary of the Elbe, although its source lies in the Bohemian Forest in Germany. It joins the Elbe at Melnik, a short distance north of Prague, the Czech Republic's capital and the most important city along its shores.

Another tributary is the 343km (213-mile) -long Havel, which originates in the Mecklenburg lakes in northern Germany. It flows through Berlin to Potsdam and Brandenburg and enters the Elbe near Havelberg.

The Oder–Havel Canal is reached via the Berlin Lakes. Because the lakes and the Oder have a height difference of 36m (118ft), in 1934 a special vessel lift (Niederfinow) was completed in order to raise a rivership the required height in under five minutes.

HIGHLIGHTS ON THE ELBE FROM HAMBURG (GERMANY) TO PRAGUE (CZECH REPUBLIC)

On a river cruise between Hamburg (on the River Elbe) and Prague (on the River Vltava, a tributary of the Elbe), you are likely to visit some of the following towns and cities:

Hamburg, Germany (Km 623)

Best-known, somewhat unfairly, for its raunchy nightlife, Hamburg is actually a very dignified and elegant city, the notorious Reeperbahn red-light district aside. It is Germany's main seaport, despite the fact that it is some 110km (70 miles) inland, on the right bank of the Elbe where it meets the River Alster.

The city is crisscrossed by canals and has numer-

ous green squares and corners, with lively street cafés. Exploring the canals and waterfront on a boat tour is one of the most restful ways to get around. Otherwise, things to see include the Rathaus (Town Hall), built in neo-Renaissance style in 1887 and set in one corner of the Binnenalster, an inland lake.

On Sunday mornings, head for the Fischmarkt, a noisy, atmospheric marketplace where everything from fish to household clutter is sold. The city has numerous museums, including the Kunsthalle, which houses one of Germany's finest collections of art, with exhibits from the 13th to the 20th centuries. Hamburg is also good for shopping; there are a lot of high-quality boutiques, while the major department stores are located in Jungfernstieg, Mönckebergstrasse and Spitalerstrasse.

Berlin, Germany (River Havel, no km marker)

Germany's capital actually lies on the River Havel, which passes through a complex system of lakes and locks, so river cruisers usually berth at Potsdam and passengers are brought by coach to the city centre. Berlin has metamorphosed since the fall of the Wall in 1990 into a buzzing, thriving metropolis, drawing artists and entrepreneurs, movers and shakers into its midst. Innovative architecture, ultra-chic shopping along the Kurfürstendamm, grand boulevards and lavish monuments collectively create one of Europe's most exciting capitals – and the nightlife is legendary, too.

Most itineraries allow a couple of days in Berlin, to take in the grand neoclassical buildings along Unter den Linden, the Brandenburg Gate and the Reichstag, and the Museuminsel (Museum Island), now a Unesco World Heritage Site. Slightly more off the beaten track are some of the multicultural suburbs such as Kreuzberg, arty and newly gentrified Prenzlauer Berg or the patrician Charlottenburg, or the nearby lakes and forests.

Brandenburger Tor: The Brandenburg Gate has played varying roles in the history of Berlin. Napoleon marched through here on his triumphant way to Russia, and when the Berlin Wall fell in 1990, the gates came to symbolise freedom and unity. The sandstone structure is based on the gateway to the Acropolis in Athens.

The Reichstag: The Reichstag, restored to prominence with the return of the goverment to Berlin in 1999 and crowned by a spectacular glass dome designed by Lord Norman Foster, was originally built in the late 19th century in Italian Renaissance style. A broad spiral ramp enables visitors to watch parliamentary proceedings from above.

Museuminsel: Between the River Spree and Kupfergraben lies Museum Island, which ranks as one of the world's finest museum complexes. The stunning diversity of displays includes everything from ancient archaeological artefacts to early 20th-century German and European art.

Kurfürstendamm: Inspired by the Champs-Elysées in Paris, Ku'damm (as it's usually known) is the most popular boulevard in Berlin, and is flanked by a series of exclusive hotels, department stores and cafés. In the 1920s it became the meeting-place for Berlin's intellectuals.

Checkpoint Charlie: From 1961 until 1989, Checkpoint Charlie was the only crossing point between East and West Berlin. Today, the former border crossing has become a shrine to the Berlin Wall's memory. Nothing remains of the actual military installation today, although a small guardhouse was rebuilt in the middle of the street. For more information on the general history of the Wall, visit the nearby Museum Haus am Checkpoint Charlie 5 at Friedrichstrasse 44.

Tangermünde, Germany (Km 388)

Tangermünde is a former Hanseatic League town with many fine examples remaining of Gothic brick architecture and half-timbered houses.

Magdeburg, Germany (Km 326–333)

Magdeburg is located about mid-way on the Elbe, southwest of Berlin, positioned at a natural crossroads on the Elbe at the junction of six railway lines and seven arterial roads. The city is linked with Berlin and the lower River Oder by a system of canals, and to the River Rhine by the Mittelland Canal. It was almost destroyed in 1945, but is now a superb example of a traditional German town, albeit reconstructed. The town's museum houses the *Magdeburg Rider*, Germany's oldest equestrian statue, created in 1240. There is a replica of it in front of the town hall. Other notable city sights include the world's third-tallest wooden structure, a 60m (197ft) -high 'Millennium Tower' (Jahrtausendturm), constructed as an exhibition centre in time for the turn of the century. Famous former residents of Magdeburg include the composer Georg Philip Telemann.

THE ODER

Renowned as a sanctuary for birdlife, the Oder is a little-cruised river that forms the border between Poland and Germany for a distance of 186km (116 miles). Its isolated river valley is green and lush, lined with meadows and ancient forests, as well as expanses of grass and moorland. Apart from the occasional sleepy hamlet, the only signs of human life are cyclists and hikers. But this was also the region in which the Russians broke through the German lines in World War II to commence their final assault on Berlin, and it is rich in history.

Cruises operating on the Oder usually start in Berlin, travel east along the Havel to join the Oder, and then sail either south to Wroclaw (Breslau) or north to Szczecin, close to the river's mouth on the Baltic Sea.

Wittenberg, Germany (Km 215)

Not to be confused with another town with almost the same name (Wittenberge – located further along the Elbe), Wittenberg is a sleepy town, brought to life by hordes of visitors who come here to see where the Protestant Reformation began. The mooring is some distance from the town, so it's best to take a coach tour.

Dr Martin Luther, an Augustine monk and university lecturer, famously nailed 95 theses to the door of the Palace Church on 31 October 1517, an act that is defined by historians as beginning the Reformation. Three years later, Luther was excommunicated by the Pope. Luther's house can also be visited, as can St Marien's Church, where he preached. An oak tree marks the spot where he burnt the papal bull condemning his doctrines. Nearby is Luther Hall, a museum dedicated to the Reformation.

Meissen, Germany (Km 80–83)

Meissen is a lovely old town, dominated by the slender Gothic spires of its cathedral and the hulking Albrechtsburg Castle, built in 1525. There has been a settlement since AD 968, but the town really rose to fame in 1710 with the advent of porcelain manufacture.

Augustus the Strong, Elector of Saxony (where he was known as Frederick Augustus I) from 1694 to 1733, had earlier employed the renegade alchemist Friedrich Böttger to make gold, partly in order to raise much-needed funds for the state, and partly (of course) out of personal greed. Not surprisingly, this scheme had failed, but in 1709 Böttger realised that valuable white porcelain could be made from nacrite, of which there were large deposits nearby, and the castle was quickly turned into a factory. The famous blue-glaze technique was discovered in 1740, and the porcelain soon became known all over the world. The castle houses an art collection today, with a number of early Meissen pieces.

Pillnitz, Germany (Km 50)

One of Saxony's architectural treasures, Pillnitz Palace – built to rival Buckingham Palace and Versailles – houses an impressive collection of fine jewellery and porcelain.

Dresden, Germany (Km 50–61)

The Elbe runs for 25km (16 miles) right through the middle of this venerable German city, the capital of Saxony once again since 1990 and world-renowned for its fabulous art treasures, which have given it the epithet 'Florence on the Elbe'. There are water meadows and green parks close to the centre giving a marvellous feeling of open space. The river cruise landing stage is right in the centre of the city, and most boats spend the night here, a good opportunity to see the beautiful sandstone buildings illuminated by dramatic floodlights.

Dresden will always be remembered for the devastating bombing in 1945, which flattened the city centre and cost some 35,000 people their lives. For years, the Frauenkirche (Church of Our Lady) was left ruined, as a reminder of the destruction, but it has now been rebuilt as an exact replica of its former self. The city centre is now a Unesco-protected site and has almost been fully restored, thanks to a 50-year rebuilding project.

Dresden is a very attractive city and, for many, is a highlight of an Elbe cruise. The Town Hall Tower, standing at 100m (330ft), will always by law be the tallest building. The 13th-century Kreuzkirche, meanwhile, rebuilt in 1764 after the Seven Years War, is said to contain a fragment of the Holy Cross, and is a superb example of Baroque architecture.

Another beautiful Baroque building is the meticulously restored 18th-century Zwinger Palace, a superb collection of graceful pavilions on the south bank of the Elbe, known for its superb art collection of Old Masters, including pieces by Raphael and Rembrandt.

Music-lovers should see the incredible Semper Opera House, in which performances are given from September to May. On the opposite side of the river (the left bank) is the quadrilateral Japanese Palace, built to display Augustus the Strong's superb collection of Meissen porcelain and tableware.

The River Moldau starts at Km 0.

Meissen at night.

Königstein, Germany (Km 17)

Once you've passed the spa town of Rathen, set against a natural amphitheatre of cliffs, the dramatic medieval Königstein Fortress comes into view, 360m (1,180ft) above the river. Riverships usually stop here for a brief visit, taking passengers by coach to the fortress. Königstein has been rebuilt and strengthened several times, and in its day was considered impregnable; a well was dug 150m (490ft) into the rock in case of siege. Inside, you can see the living quarters and workshop of Friedrich Böttger, the alchemist who discovered the secret of making true porcelain in 1709. Prior to this, Böttger was incarcerated here from 1706 to 1707 when the castle served as a jail – the Elector of Saxony, Augustus the Strong, had held him in 'protective custody' in order to be the beneficiary of the alchemist's quest to manufacture gold. Other prominent prisoners included the social democrat August Bebel and the poet Frank Wedekind.

Prague, Czech Republic (Km 45–55)

The starting or finishing point for most Elbe/Vltava cruises (although the vessel actually docks at Ústí, 70km/43 miles to the north), the romantic city of Prague is located on a curve of the winding River Vltava, a tributary of the Elbe, and known to Germans as the Moldau. Graceful bridges span the river, including the famous Charles Bridge, the Lesser Quarter clinging to one side and the Old Town to the other, surveyed from above by the 10th-century Hradčany (Prague Castle). The city has inspired composers including Mozart, Smetana and Dvořák, as well as poets, writers, revolutionaries and intellectuals. It's still a great university city and seat of learning, with nightlife to match in the legendary bars and pubs.

If your river cruise ends in Prague, try to stay for at least a couple of days, so that you have plenty of time to visit the highlights, which include the following:

Charles Bridge (Karlův most): Slightly curved and spanning the Vltava between the Old Town and the hill leading up to the castle, Charles Bridge is a Gothic masterpiece, with the added impact of some fine Baroque sculpture. The first stone bridge was constructed here during the second half of the 12th century, in place of the wooden structure that was situated further to the north. The 30 statues adorning the bridge were added over a period of 250 years. The oldest and most significant statue is that of St John of Nepomuk, which was installed in 1683. Many are now replicas, and the valuable originals can be seen in the Lapidarium of the National Museum. The bridge is usually very crowded with sightseers; for a more atmospheric experience visit early in the morning or late at night.

Prague Castle (Hrad): With its commanding position high above the river, the castle has been key to every epoch in the city's history. It is the most extensive complex of buildings in the city, containing St Vitus Cathedral, the Royal Palace and many other monuments. It also serves as the seat of the president of the republic.

St Vitus Cathedral (Katedrála sv. Víta): Prague's magnificent Gothic cathedral contains not only chapels and tombs, but also some fine stained glass,

Prague and its bridges.

including the window designed by Art Nouveau artist Alphonse Mucha. The main attraction inside the cathedral is St Wenceslas's Chapel, built by Peter Parler in which the national saint, Wenceslas, was interred. The saint's sacred place is exceptionally ornate; walls are decorated with polished jasper, amethysts, agate and emeralds, as well as fine gilding and frescoes.

Jewish Quarter (Josefov): The Jews of Prague suffered persecution from the Middle Ages, but found some freedom in their ghetto, now preserved as the Jewish Quarter and a memorial to their tenacity. The earliest mention of Prague's Jewish community comes from a document by the Jewish merchant Abraham ben Jakob, dated 965. The ghetto, built in about 1100 and surrounded by a wall, soon became one of the largest Jewish communities in Europe. Major sites include the Old-New Synagogue, the oldest remaining synagogue in Europe in which services are held. Nearby, the Old Jewish Cemetery is both a moving and fascinating place and was the last resting place for Jews between the 15th and 18th centuries. The number of graves is much greater than the 12,000 gravestones would suggest – this was the only place where Jews could be buried, so graves were layered one above the other. The Jewish community was destroyed in World War II, when thousands were sent to their deaths. Today there are around 1,500 people of Jewish descent in Prague.

Loreto Church: The Loreto Church is dedicated to the Virgin Mary and is the most famous pilgrimage church in Prague. The ornate facade and frescoes in the cloister date from the 18th century. In the tower is a glockenspiel with 27 bells, which play a Czech hymn to the Virgin Mary every hour. The highlight is the Treasure Chamber, which contains the remarkable Diamond Monstrance, a gift from a Bohemian nobleman. It was made in 1699 by Baptist Kanischbauer and Matthias Stegner of Vienna and is studded with over 6,000 diamonds.

Old Town Square (Staroměstské náměstí): Prague's picturesque Old Town Square is the natural mid-point of the Old Town, and the heart of Prague. Memorial tablets on the Town Hall Tower are reminders of various important events that have taken place here over the centuries. In the 12th century the Old Town Square was a central market place and a major crossroads on central European merchant routes. Over the next few centuries many buildings of Romanesque, Baroque and Gothic styles were erected. The Jan Hus monument in the centre of the square is in honour of the 15th-century reformer who stood up against the corrupt practices of the Catholic Church.

Astronomical Clock: The astronomical clock on the Town Hall Tower dates from 1410. It consists of three parts. In the middle is the actual clock, which also shows the movement of the sun and moon through the zodiac. Underneath is the calendar, with scenes from country life symbolising the 12 months of the year, painted by Josef Manés (these have now been replaced with replicas). The performance of the upper part of the clock is what draws the hordes of tourists. On the hour the figures play the same scene: Death rings the death knell and turns an hourglass upside down. The 12 Apostles proceed along the little windows that open before the chimes, and a cockerel flaps its wings and crows.

Týn Church: The landmark pointed towers of the Týn are one of the icons of Prague, looming 80m (260ft) above the Old Town. The building was erected between 1365 and 1511, and features many noteworthy Bohemian Baroque works of art and the oldest baptismal font (1414) in Prague. To the right of the high altar is the tombstone of the famous Danish astronomer Tycho Brahe, who worked at the court of Rudolf ll. The church is a source of great national pride, and the facade, particularly when floodlit at night, is one of the finest sights in the Old Town.

National Gallery (Národní galerie): In Sternberg Palace, within the castle complex, is the National Gallery, which houses a fine collection of European art. There are three levels; the ground floor houses German and Austrian art from the 15th to the 18th centuries; the first floor comprises the art of antiquity, icons and the art of the Netherlands and Italy of the 14th to the 16th centuries; the second floor has Italian, Spanish, French, Dutch and Flemish art of the 16th to the 18th centuries. Albrecht Dürer's large-scale *Feast of the Rosary* is perhaps the most famous exhibit.

Wenceslas Square (Václavské náměstí): Nearly a kilometre (two-thirds of a mile) long, Wenceslas Square is not really a square at all, but a wide boulevard. Nowadays, the former horse market is dominated by hotels, bars, restaurants, cafés, banks and department stores. It is a busy area, along which half of Prague seems to stroll. The historic square is crowned by the giant equestrian statue of St Wenceslas, erected by Josef Myslbek in 1912 after taking 30 years to plan and design.

National Theatre (Národní divadlo): This is the city's main cultural venue and a potent symbol of the Czech spirit. In 1845 the ruling Habsburgs turned down the request for a Czech theatre. In response, money was collected on a voluntary basis, and the building of the theatre was declared a national duty. Built in an Italian Renaissance style in 1881, the theatre was destroyed in a fire just before it was due to open. Under Josef Schulz's direction, using many notable artists including Vojtěch Hynais, it was quickly rebuilt with the aid of endowments and donations and opened in 1883. The auditorium is only open to the public during performances.

North German port cities

Some river cruises also visit sea ports that lie within protected areas of the coastline. In the 19th century, wealthy Berliners came to the region to recuperate in fashionable coastal bathing resorts.

Cuxhaven (Km 730): The citizens of Cuxhaven in Lower Saxony once controlled all shipping in and out of the River Elbe. Today, however, it is one of the largest fishing ports in Germany and the centre of its fish processing industry. It is also home to Germany's oldest lighthouse, built in the 14th century on the island of Neuwerk.

Lauterbach, Isle of Rügen, Germany: Although few people think of islands when Germany is mentioned, Rügen is, at 926 sq km (357.5 sq miles), Germany's largest island, separated from the mainland by a narrow channel, although joined to the mainland by a 2.5km (1.5-mile) -long bridge. It is the port for Lutbus, an elegant, all-white city that formerly had a royal residence, although its castle was demolished in 1960. Today, you can stroll around the castle gardens. The popular bathing resorts of Baabe, Binz, Göhren and Sellin are located on the southwest of the island.

Wolgast, Isle of Usedom, Germany: Another 'island', Germany's second largest and its easternmost, lies near the mouth of the River Oder, and the border with Poland. It is a mix of old established verdant forests (part of the national park) and white sandy beaches. Wolgast itself lies on the mainland at the point where a road bridge connects it with the island.

Stralsund, Germany: Located on the Baltic Sea coast and surrounded by three lakes, this port city, founded in 1209, features some fine architecture of Gothic red brick buildings, similar to those of nearby Lübeck. Although it has been the subject of many battles in the past, this important centre of maritime navigation has today been restored to its former glory.

Zingst, Germany: Sitting on a small peninsula, much of which is a national park (Vorpommersche Boddenlandschaft), the town has the character and charm of a typical German village untouched by time. Nearby, there are long sandy beaches and forests.

MUSIC

Several famous classical composers lived and worked between Hamburg and Prague, and Lutheran chants were always heard throughout the region.

Antonín Leopold Dvořák was born on 8 September 1841 in Nelahozeves (then Bohemia, now part of the Czech Republic), between Usti and Prague. He died on 1 May 1904 in Prague.

Leoš Janáček was born on 3 July 1854 in Hukvaldy, Moravia (then part of the Austrian empire, now in the Czech Republic). He died on 12 August 1928 in Ostrava (now part of the Czech Republic).

Bohuslav Martinů was born on 8 December 1890 in Policka, Bohemia, Austria-Hungary (now in the Czech Republic). He died on 28 August 1959 in Liestal, Switzerland.

Felix Mendelssohn was born on 3 February 1809 in Hamburg, Germany. He died on 4 November 1847 in Leipzig, Germany.

Bedřich Smetana was born on 2 March 1824 in Litomyšl, then Bohemia (now in the Czech Republic). He died on 12 May 1884 in Prague.

Robert Alexander Schumann was born on 8 June 1810 in Zwickaw, Saxony (now Germany). He died on 29 July 1856 in Endenich, near Bonn, Prussia, Germany.

River Rhône

A trip along the Rhône incorporates the gastronomy of Burgundy and Lyon, Roman ruins in Vienne and Arles, the magnificent historic papal city of Avignon and cowboys in the Camargue.

The evocative names of Burgundy, Avignon, Lyon and Mâcon conjure up all kinds of enticing images, from fields of yellow sunflowers and purple lavender to ruby-red wines, truffles, rich cheeses and plates of charcuterie, not to mention magnificent Roman antiquities and colourful market towns. The Rhône flows through the gastronomic heart of France, carving its way across some of the most beautiful wine-growing country, as well as handsome, historic cities such as Avignon and Arles.

The Rhône has always been an important trade route, linking northern Europe to the Mediterranean and forming a means for armies from the south to move north through the continent. It is 813km (505 miles) long, and starts its journey in the Swiss Alps, just upstream from Lake Geneva. It descends westward through a long valley between the Alps and the Jura Mountains to Lake Geneva, and then enters France. The final section is from Lyon to the Golfe du Lion and the Mediterranean, which it enters through a two-armed delta that begins at Arles and extends for approximately 40km (25 miles) to the sea. The arms

River Royale on the Rhône.

are known as the Great Rhône and the Little Rhône, with the unnavigable salt marshes and lagoon of the Camargue between them.

A Rhône river cruise starts either from Lyon, the country's gastronomic capital, located in the heart of the country between the Saône and Rhône rivers, or from Chalon-sur-Saône. In the reverse direction your journey will start from Arles or Avignon in Provence. If you are a devotee of French cuisine, it is worthwhile considering a stay of at least an extra day or two in Lyon. A visit on the third Thursday of November is always lively, since that's the date that Beaujolais Nouveau, cultivated near Lyon, is released for sale each year.

HIGHLIGHTS FROM CHALON-SUR-SAÔNE TO THE CAMARGUE

Chalon-sur-Saône (Km 141)

This important inland port in the heart of Burgundy is located at the confluence of the River Saône and the Canal du Centre in a region famous for its wine. Chalon is often the start for excursions to Dijon, considered by many to be the underrated capital of Burgundy (Dijon has a wide range of restaurants, an excellent city museum and a stunning array of Flemish-influenced architecture in its beautiful city centre). Chalon's town's heart is place St Vincent, with its colourful half-timbered houses and cathedral, the oldest parts of which date from the 11th century. It was also the birthplace of photography in 1822; Kodak still has a presence here. Nicéphore Niépce is credited for having invented photography in 1816, and the Musée Nicéphore Niépce, located on quai de Messageries, slightly downstream from the Pont St-Laurent, covers every conceivable aspect of photography, including cameras employed on the Apollo space missions.

Mâcon (Km 80)

Nestled neatly into the west bank of the River Saône at the end of a 14th-century bridge (Pont St-Laurent),

DID YOU KNOW...?

...that the Rhône is the only major river that flows directly into the Mediterranean?
...that the river has famously fierce currents? Climatic conditions (eg the mistral) and seasonal changes (eg bringing meltwater from the Alps) create extra navigational difficulties.
...that the French for 'lock' is *écluse*?

Mâcon is located at the southern end of the Burgundy wine region and plays an important part in its wine trade. May is the month when Mâcon hosts the Burgundy wine sales. The Unesco-protected Benedictine Abbey of Cluny, 25km (15 miles) northwest of Mâcon, is the highlight of a visit to this area, although wine lovers could travel to the region to taste the local wines.

Lyon (Km 0–12)

The gastronomic capital of France, Lyon actually lies on a little peninsula between the Rhône and Saône rivers. It was founded more than 2,000 years ago and is today the second-largest city in the country, and its most important educational centre outside Paris. The city's reputation for wonderful food is completely deserved, and there are countless local specialities to try, among them *quenelles de brochet* (mousse of pike) and a huge array of magnificent charcuterie. Notable Michelin-starred chefs connected with the city include Paul Bocuse, Guy Lassausaie and Philippe Gavreau.

There's also an eclectic collection of museums in the city, including the Musée Historique des Tissus et des Arts Décoratifs – a wonderful textile museum with some rare exhibits – and the Musée des Beaux Arts, its collection ranked second in France only to that of the Louvre.

A visit to Lyon also usually includes a trip up Fourvière Hill, either a clamber up steep steps or a funicular ride. At the top, you can visit the Basilique de Notre-Dame and gaze out over the city's rooftops, past the two rivers to the vineyards beyond. River-ships tie up close to some magnificent architecture, including one of the city's historic universities.

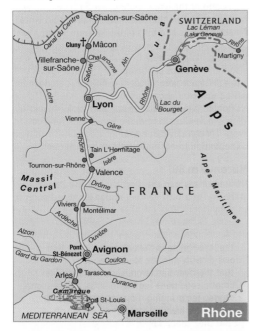

Vienne (Km 28)

This town's position, between the Beaujolais and Burgundy wine regions, makes it the gateway to the countryside around Lyon. Most notable, however, is the town's amazing Roman heritage: Vienne has one of the best-preserved Roman amphitheatres in France, on the slopes of nearby Mt Pipet, seating 13,000 and still used for theatrical performances. The Temple d'Auguste et de Livie in the town itself is also an arresting example of 1st-century Roman architecture. Vienne is well known for its jazz festival, which normally takes place in July.

Tournon-sur-Rhône (Km 91)

The scenery as the river carves its way south is rugged and mountainous, dotted with castles and jagged rock outcrops, although vineyards are still the main feature along the banks. Tournon is one of the region's most attractive cities, nestling on the left bank of the river (Tain-l'Hermitage is on the opposite bank) and overlooked by its 10th-century castle, built into a rock.

An excursion from here – not to be missed – is a 32km (20 mile) ride on a nostalgic steam-hauled train to the Ardèche region (between Tournon and Lamastre), a wild, limestone upland of craggy cliffs, gorges and caves in the Doux Valley, with red wine and lavender among its main products.

There are also excursions by coach to the Gorge de l'Ardèche: a road runs along the top of the red-rock gorge, the river a silvery ribbon hundreds of feet below, and there are various lookout points and peculiar rock formations. Between Tournon and the city of Valence, the Rhône is reinforced by the turbulent waters of the Isère, flowing in from the Alps to the northeast.

Tain-l'Hermitage (Km 91)

Tournon and Tain-l'Hermitage are connected by a bridge, created by the celebrated engineer Marc Seguin, in 1825. He used cables made from iron wires for the first time; the original bridge was taken down in 1965, but today you can still walk across a replica bridge, dating from 1849. A food market is located in the town centre on place du Tourobole (named after the sacrifice of the bulls in ancient times), while close by is the delightfully decadent Cité du Chocolat Valrhona, a haven for chocolate lovers. If your rivership docks overnight, take a stroll along the embankment – a favourite pastime for locals and visitors alike.

Viviers (Km 166)

This hilltop town – a Unesco World Heritage site and one of the best-preserved Medieval towns in southern France – occupies a strategically important position. It has a long history, dating to when the Celts occupied the location. It is divided into two parts, established when it became a bishopric in the 5th century. The Upper Town, which can only be accessed through the 40m (130-ft) -high Tower of St Michael, remained an ecclesiastical domain for over 1,000

View of Lyon from Fourvière Hill.

years. It has outstanding views over the Rhône. The Lower Town includes the magnificent Maison des Chevaliers, built by an important government official in the mid-16th century. The Lower Part was the home of artisans and tradesmen, and is remarkably well preserved.

This quiet town retains its old-world charm today, with medieval houses and its impressive cathedral of St Vincent. Some riverships stay overnight, when the illuminated town is beautiful, and mysterious.

An excursion may be offered to Montélimar, known as the centre for nougat-making in France (it was created here in the 16th century). Almond trees were imported here from Asia, and nougat is made from ground almonds, mixed with local honey, sugar and egg whites, before being boiled and then allowed to set.

Some riverships may make a stop at Châteauneuf-du-Pape. The town is about 5km (3 miles) from the landing stage, from where an excursion to the town and its environs may be offered.

Avignon (Km 241)

The river broadens out as it enters Provence and nears the Mediterranean, although the scenery is still undulating and becomes rich with colour – yellow sunflowers all summer long, and ranks of purple lavender spread across the hilltops, scenting the air.

The beautiful university city of Avignon is totally encircled by medieval walls and known as the 'City of Popes'; in the 14th century, this was the residence of the papacy for 70 years. The ravishingly handsome medieval Palais des Papes at the centre is one of the great wonders of France, and was once considered the heart of the Christian world. Nearby are the remains of the famous bridge, Pont

MUSIC

Several French composers were born or died in the region of the River Rhône.

Claude-Achille Debussy was born on 22 August 1862 in St-Germaine-en-Laye, France. He died on 25 March 1918 in Paris.

Clément-Philibert-Léo Delibes was born on 21 February 1836 in St-Germain-du-Val, France 1836. He died on 16 January 1891 in Paris.

Olivier Messiaen was born on 10 December 1908 in Avignon, France. He died 27 April 1992 in Clichy, near Paris.

Darius Milhaud was born on 4 September 1892 in Aix-en-Provence, France. He died on 22 June 1974 in Geneva, Switzerland.

Jean-Phillippe Rameau was baptised on 25 September 1683 in Dijon, France. He died on 12 September 1764 in Paris.

Edgard Victor Achille Charles Varèse was born on 22 December 1883 in Paris. He died on 6 November 1965 in New York, US.

St-Bénezet – originally built in 1189 – which juts out across a branch of the river (only four out of the original 23 arches remain). It was reduced to its present condition by terrible flooding in 1667. It is the subject of one of the most famous French nursery rhymes, *Sur le Pont d'Avignon ('On the bridge of Avignon')*. The city has a terrific buzz on warm summer nights, with outdoor cafés and bars lining the streets and free entertainment provided by buskers and street artists, especially during the Theatre Festival in July.

Not far from Avignon (about 16 km/10 miles) is Châteuneuf du Pape. It was Pope John XXII of Avignon who planted the vines in the grounds of what was his summer home. Today, the cuvée red wines (a blend of the temperamental granache and other grape varities) are among the most respected in France. Some riverships may dock at the town itself.

Tarascon (Km 267)

Your rivership might stop at the fortified medieval town of Tarascon, from where you can visit Arles on an excursion. The river runs right through the centre of the commune, which is located between Arles and Avignon. Among the main attractions are the 15th-century Château de Tarascon, built on the edge of the Rhône, and a 12th-century collegiate church of St Martha. Provençal fabrics can be seen in a museum located in a 14th-century building in the town centre (the Charles Demery fabric factory is in the town). If your rivership happens to be in Tarascon on a Tuesday, it's worth visiting the market.

Pont St-Bénézet and Palais des Papes, Avignon.

Arles (Km 282) and the Camargue

The Romans built their first bridge across the Rhône here, and this helped to create a vital link between Italy and Spain. The small town – one of the most attractive in Provence – is located on the banks of the river. It boasts many Gallo-Roman ruins, including Les Arènes, an amphitheatre that has a capacity of 20,000 and is still used for bullfights and plays. A visit to the animated place du Forum, in the heart of town, is a must. Vincent van Gogh, who lived here for 444 days between 1880 and 1890, immortalised in vibrant colours many of this city's highlights.

The river splits into two arms just before Arles; the Petit Rhône flows to the southwest, while the Grand Rhône continues south for about 48km (30 miles) and empties (after coursing through the Camargue's marshes and silt) into the Mediterranean Sea. From Arles, you can take an excursion (it may be included in the cost of your holiday) to the Camargue, the delta of the River Rhône and one of Europe's finest nature reserves, with its unspoiled landscape and wildlife (renowned for its wild, pink flamingos, black bulls and white horses). You may be able to see the *gardians*, modern-day Camargue cowboys who tend the bulls.

Just 32km (20 miles) from Arles is Nîmes, where denim (serge de Nîmes) was created. It was the 16th-century name given to the tough fabric produced in the city and used as material for making sacks. Transported to America via Genoa, it was chosen by a German immigrant in San Francisco – Levi Strauss – as sturdy material for clothing for gold prospectors in the 'Gold Rush' in about 1850.

River Seine

A voyage along the Seine offers beautiful scenery, from romantic Paris to bucolic Normandy and historic Rouen to the pretty port of Honfleur. Gastronomic delights and wine tours add to the appeal.

From the iconic French capital to Honfleur, one of the most picturesque of all French ports, the Seine has been witness to some of the most remarkable characters throughout history: Joan of Arc, Van Gogh, Seurat and Claude Monet. A cruise along this slow-flowing river is a gentle voyage through some of France's most mellow countryside, of farmland and meadows, historic towns and sleepy villages. It is also a gastronomic adventure, in the land of brie and camembert cheeses, Calvados liqueur and Normandy cider.

The Seine is is 780km (485 miles) long, and its source is 471m (1,545.2ft) above sea level on Mont Tasselot in the Côte d'Or region of Burgundy. It is the longest navigable waterway in France, and carries more commercial traffic and freight than any other river or canal in the country. It flows northwest of Dijon, Burgundy, through the dry chalk plateau of Champagne then through Paris, Giverny, Rouen and across Normandy before emptying into the English Channel not far from Le Havre. The estuary is wide and extends for 26km (16 miles) between Tancarville and Le Havre. The relatively flat Seine is slow-flowing and hence eminently navigable. On its journey, it is joined by the Aube, near Romilly, the Yonne, near Montereau, and the Marne, its greatest tributary, near Paris.

Riverships can go all the way to Paris all year round – the reason why the port of Paris trans-ships more than 20 million tons of cargo each year.

HIGHLIGHTS FROM PARIS TO HONFLEUR

Paris (Km 0)

The major highlight is, of course, Paris, perhaps the most romantic city in Europe.

It is cut through the middle by the slowly meandering River Seine and edged with gentle hills. The Seine is the capital's widest avenue; it is spanned by a total of 37 bridges, which provide some of the loveliest views of Paris. The fascination of the French capital is eternal and has long been a magnet to artists, writers, philosophers and composers. Its grand architecture, fine cuisine and haute couture combine to make Paris one of the most glamorous European capitals. Ile St-Louis, in the middle of the River Seine and at the heart of the city, is the official start of kilometre markings along the River Seine.

There are too many city highlights to cover here in full, so what follows is a classic top-10 big sights. If you know the city already, less obvious delights include the Marais area, with its show-stopping place des Vosges, or the adjacent, more edgy, Bastille. Otherwise, head to the literary St-Germain, explore the city's other key waterway, the Canal St-Martin, or, if shopping appeals, the so-called grands magasins (department stores), including Galeries Lafayette and

River Baroness cruising along the Seine.

DID YOU KNOW...?

...that the name Seine comes from the Latin name 'Sequana', the goddess of the river?
...that the Seine is the third-longest river in France, after the Loire and the Rhône?
...that Joan of Arc's ashes were supposedly scattered in the Seine at Rouen?
...that the first steamboat on the River Seine was in 1816? However, it actually frightened the people along the river banks because the vessel's steam engine sprayed out smoke and sparks.
...that the composer Puccini set his 1918 opera *Il Tabarro* (The Cloak) aboard a barge on the Seine?
...that in 1991 the banks of the Seine in Paris were declared World Heritage sites? Unesco calls the French capital 'a river town', with banks 'studded with a succession of masterpieces'.

Printemps. Alternatively, if the weather allows, simply relax in the elegant Parisian parks, such as the Jardin du Luxembourg or the Tuileries or else just along the arty banks of the Seine itself.

Key sights include

Musée du Louvre: One of the largest palaces in Europe has assembled an incomparable collection of Old Masters, sculptures and antiquities. There are 380,000 objects in the collection, of which around 35,000 are displayed. It has three wings, and the superb collections are divided up into seven different sections, each assigned its own colour to help you find your way around. Highlights include Leonardo da Vinci's Mona Lisa.

Tour Eiffel: No visit to Paris would be complete without a trip to the Eiffel Tower, symbol of the city and of France herself. The metal giant looms over the area southwest of the centre. This icon of iron girders was chosen as the centrepiece to the World Fair of 1889. The first two floors are negotiated on foot or by lift, and then another lift goes up to the top. From here you will see a spectacular city panorama, best viewed one hour before sunset.

Notre-Dame: The cathedral's position on the banks of the Seine is an unforgettable setting. Just as Gothic cathedrals were considered symbols of paradise, so the entrance facade, with its series of sculptures, was considered to be the gateway to heaven. The stories of the Bible are depicted in the portals, paintings and stained glass of the cathedral. The scale exceeded all earlier churches – Paris became the capital only a few years before the foundation stone was laid, and the building was designed to reflect the power of the state and its church. Construction work on the cathedral began in 1163 and was finished around 1240. The exquisite 13th-century north and south rose windows are star attractions.

Arc de Triomphe: Built between 1806 and 1836, this triumphal arch is the epitome of French grandeur. The many statues on the main facade glorify the insurrection of 1792 and Napoleon's major victories.

Centre Georges Pompidou: Made entirely of glass and surrounded by a white steel grid, the Pompidou Centre is the main showcase for modern and contemporary art in Paris. Now a much-loved city icon, Richard Rogers and Renzo Piano's 'inside-out' design was controversial when it was unveiled in 1977.

Sacré-Cœur: Perched on the Montmartre hilltop is the virginal-white Basilique du Sacré-Cœur, its Byzantine cupolas as much a part of the city skyline as the Eiffel Tower. It can be reached by walking up 250 steps or by taking a funicular cable car. When the lights are turned on at night, the Sacré-Cœur resembles a lit wedding cake.

Musée d'Orsay: France's national museum of 19th-century art is housed in the former Gare d'Orsay, an ornate Beaux-Arts train station, opened in 1900 to serve passengers to the World Fair. It's an immensely dramatic setting, worth visiting for its own sake. But the museum's contents are unmissable too: there is a major collection of paintings by the Impressionists, plus works by Delacroix and Ingres.

Musée Rodin: Housed in the Hotel Biron is the Rodin Museum. Auguste Rodin came to live here in 1908 and stayed until his death in 1917. Here you can admire Rodin's famous works, The Kiss and The Thinker, reputedly based on Dante contemplating the Inferno.

Sainte-Chapelle: This is a masterpiece of Parisian Rayonnant Gothic architecture on the Ile de la Cité. The beautiful 13th-century stained glass, magnificently displayed in 85 major panels, is without equal anywhere in Paris.

Versailles: Located southwest of Paris lies the grand Palace of Versailles. Take the RER line C5, which will drop you a short distance away. Allow a full day to visit the château and its magnificent formal gardens.

Conflans–Ste-Honorine (Km 68)

Situated on the confluence of the Oise and the Seine, Conflans was an important shipping centre from 1855 onwards, when a chain was laid along the bed of the Seine allowing barges to be hauled upstream to the capital. Highlights of the town include the Montjoie Tower and St-Maciou church. A religious festival is held here for three days each June, and riverships flock to attend. Many riverships also moor here overnight.

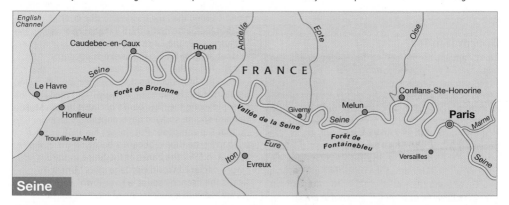

Monet's house and garden at Giverny.

Melun (Km 110)

About 45km (28 miles) from Paris, Melun (the Romans called it Melodunum) is, like Paris, located on both banks of the Seine, on the northern edge of the forest of Fontainebleau. Its ancient church of Notre-Dame stands on an island between two branches of the river. The town is a centre of commerce for the agricultural district of southern Brie. The famous brie de Melun is made here – quite different in texture and taste to the bries of Coulommiers, Meaux and Montereau.

Located about 6km (4 miles) from Melun is the 17th-century royal Château de Fontainebleau, home of French kings and emperors from François I to Napoleon and well worth a visit, if time allows.

Giverny (Km 147)

World-famous as the setting for the water-lily pond and graceful arched bridge immortalised by the painter Claude Monet, who lived here for 43 years, Giverny is one of France's most-visited sights, receiving 500,000 tourists a year, some of them clutching easels and paint, hoping to recreate the master's work. You can visit the house and, of course, the garden, which is especially glorious, even if the throng of tourists does take a little of the shine off it. The Musée d'Art Americain Giverny, located just along the main road in the village and showcasing the works of US-born Impressionists who were inspired by Monet, is also worth a visit.

Rouen (Km 238–245)

Rouen is known as the 'City of 100 Spires', and you can see its graceful skyline as you approach along the river. Until the 17th century, it was the second-largest city in France, and is still important today as France's fourth-largest port. Although badly damaged during World War II, the city has been extensively restored – in particular the 700 or so half-timber-framed buildings on the right bank of the river in the old quarter. The spot everybody wants to see, though, is the marker on the pavement in the place du Vieux Marché, where Joan of Arc was burnt at the stake as a witch in 1431.

Other sights include the magnificent Cathédrale Notre Dame, the western facade of which was painted by Monet (the work is housed in the city's Musée des Beaux Arts), and the medieval Eglise St-Maclou, which contains some superb wood carvings. Also look out for the Gros Horloge, a splendid, gold-faced clock mounted on a building, which creates a bridge across one of the narrow streets.

Caudebec-en-Caux (Km 309.5)

The medieval town of Caudebec-en-Caux is only a short cruise downstream from Rouen, through pretty Normandy scenery of woods, orchards and fields. The main attraction is the Eglise Notre Dame, the construction of which was started by the English when they had conquered the town in the 14th century, but completed by the French in 1439 after they had won the town back. The church is in Flamboyant Gothic style, with intricate stone carvings, flying buttresses and graceful spires. Tours of the town also include a visit to Jumièges Abbey, which was consecrated in 1067 in the presence of William the Conqueror.

Honfleur (Km 355)

The Seine broadens out into a wide estuary as it approaches the coast, and is busy with commercial traffic. Honfleur is a charming old port city on the southern shore of the Seine Estuary, opposite the port of Le Havre; most cruises turn around here and head back to Paris. It was from Honfleur that French settlers set out for the new lands of Canada in the 16th century. The town really is the stuff of picture postcards, particularly around the inner harbour, the Vieux Bassin, where narrow medieval houses overlook a colourful yacht and fishing harbour.

It's no surprise that the light, the space, the old coloured buildings and the boats have attracted artists for years, including Boudin and many of the Impressionists. You can see their work in the Musée Eugène Boudin, which has an ethnographic section detailing the history of the town as well as several rooms containing paintings, mainly from the 19th century, of the town, including some work by Monet. Buying French bread and cheese or duck pâté and having a picnic on a bench beside the river is highly recommended here.

Bordeaux Region

Think of wine, cognac, oysters, truffles, châteaux and grand architecture and you'll be in the heart of alluring Bordeaux.

RIVERS DORDOGNE, GARONNE, GIRONDE

Just below the city of Bordeaux, the Dordogne and the Garonne rivers (the latter starts in southwest France and mostly flows northwest from the Spanish Pyrenees) meet to form the Gironde. This is actually an estuary rather than a river and is under the constant influence of the Atlantic tides in the Bassin d'Arcachon – Europe's largest estuary.

The area is renowned for its fish farming and oyster cultivation (up to 10,000 tons of oysters are harvested in the Bassin d'Arcachon each year). Special flat-bottomed boats – called *pinasses* – are used due to the shallow, marshy water and the remarkable profusion of bird life.

It is the Gironde (about 72km/45 miles long and 3 to 11km/2 to 7 miles wide, it includes Gironde Island) that provides the gateway to Bordeaux. The river divides the famed wine-growing region into two distinct sections: the Left Bank and the Right Bank. Strong tidal currents can be challenging for navigation, and there are numerous sandbanks, shallows and other obstructions to negotiate.

Bordeaux region cruises on the Garonne are relatively new, but itineraries include excursions to the stunning ancient commune of St-Emilion, and the chateaux and estates of one or more of the famous wine makers such as Pauillac. Both the Garonne (including the Dordogne) and Gironde wend their way through charming picture-postcard landscapes.

Graves and Médoc wines are made in the low-lying gravelly land to the south of the Gironde. The gently sloping right bank, which consists of limestone and clay, to the north, is home to some of the most famous wine districts such as Pomerol and St-Emilion.

About Bordeaux cruises

Cruising the tidal rivers Garonne, Gironde and Dordogne can prove challenging for river cruise operators because they are influenced by the sea, particularly by the huge estuary of the River Gironde, which has tides of up to 7m (23 ft).

Among the companies that feature Bordeaux region cruises include: AMA Waterways, Avalon Waterways, CroisiEurope, Grand Circle Cruise Line, Scenic, Uniworld and Viking River Cruises.

Bordeaux

The vineyards covering the rolling hills along the banks of the rivers of the Aquitaine region are renowned for

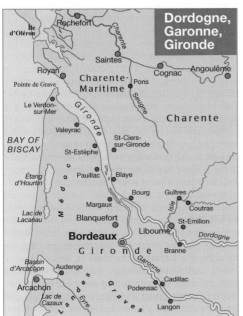

Dordogne, Garonne, Gironde

Bordeaux by night.

Vineyard in St-Emilion.

their remarkable wines. The city of Bordeaux is at the heart of 'wineland'.

With over 8,500 châteaux in the region, it's no wonder that Bordeaux has become world renowned as the capital of the wine world. Bordeaux itself is the ninth largest city in France. It is situated on a bend in the River Garonne, and is the capital of Aquitaine and the Gironde *département*; it is also a major university city. Bordeaux was founded over 2,000 years ago, when it was known as Burdigala. Formerly known as *la belle au bois dormant* (Sleeping Beauty), Bordeaux is, today, the centre of the wine trade and home to the world's main wine fair, Vinexpro. The city is also famous for its *macarons* (macaroons), filled with buttercream, caramel or preserves.

Bordeaux has a population of about 250,000 and is an absolute delight since its park-like waterfront regeneration was completed in 2013. Riverships moor directly alongside the city centre, on a broad stretch of the river, close to the St-Michael basilica and magnificent Cathédrale St-André, charming pedestrian-only boulevards, and place des Quincones, one of the largest squares in Europe.

Blaye

The 17th-century citadel (small fortress) town of Blaye is situated on the right bank of the Gironde. It was built to protect the Bordeaux region from invasion via the Bay of Biscay. Blaye lies opposite a small island named the Ile Paté, home to Fort Paté. These two fortress locations form part of a trio of fortifications known as the 'Fortifications of Vauban' group (Vauban was Louis XIVs outstanding military engineer), the other being Fort Médoc on the opposite side, the left bank – all were listed in 2008 as Unesco World Heritage sites.

The citadel is a short walk from your rivership's landing place. Today the thick-walled moated fortress contains tunnels, a museum, and a well-established market town. Over time, the town outgrew its walls, and then started to spread along the riverfront. Warehouses for wine storage, wine cellars, coopers' shops

and wine-transportation agents sprung up to service the growth of the wine business. Blaye is not far from the vineyards of Pomerol and St-Emilion.

Libourne

This charming little fortified town was created in 1270 and originally named Leyburnia, after Roger de Leybourne (1215–71), of Kent, England. It is strategically located where the Isle and Dordogne rivers meet. Today, Libourne is a pretty and dynamic little town and the wine-making capital of the northern Gironde. Located close to Pomerol and St-Emilion, it is a sister (and often a rival) to Bordeaux as a distributor and exporter of the region's fine wines. Other attractions include the fish market, one of the largest in the region, held every weekend in the main square, place Abel Surchamp.

Bourg (Bourg-en-Gironde)

This lovely ancient town is located high on a hilly outcrop at the confluence of the Dordogne and Garonne rivers. It is enclosed by ramparts with streets that tumble down to the harbour front and marina.

Cadillac

Located on the Garonne, directly opposite Sauterne, the charming Aquitaine medieval bastide town of Cadillac was founded in 1280. Its attractions include the imposing Château des Ducs d'Epernon, a horseshoe-shaped palace that dominates the town.

St-Emilion

This stunning Dordogne town, whose heyday was considered to be in the Middle Ages, was named after the monk Emilion. It is now a Unesco World Heritage Site, with highlights including numerous wine merchants and a remarkable subterranean church, hewn out of soft limestone bedrock. The largest of its kind in Europe, it measures 35m (115ft) long, 20m (66ft) wide and up to 11m (36ft) high. If you like wine, and have some spare time (perhaps if you are not on an organised tour), do visit 14th-century Cloître des Cordeliers – a former Franciscan friary, where sparkling wine is made and aged in the labyrinth of underground passages.

River cruise companies provide an excursion that will take you to the cobblestoned town square, and include a visit to the Eglise Monolithe, whose tower is 52m (172ft) tall. Climb the 196 steps to the top to get some magnificent views over the town and its fortifications.

Arcachon

Long considered the jewel of France's western coastline in Aquitaine, Arcachon is located on the northern tip of Europe's longest coastal beach, some 55km (34 miles) southwest of Bordeaux. Its bay is known for hosting Europe's largest sand dune, the Dune du Pilat, which is almost 3km (2 miles) long and home to an array of nature habitats, as well as being an important oyster-growing area.

River Loire

Enchanting, but shallow and challenging, only specialised vessels are able to navigate its extremes.

With a length of 1,012km (629 miles), the River Loire drains an area of 117,054 sq km (45,195 sq miles) – that's over one-fifth of France. The Loire flows from the Cévennes Mountains to St Nazaire, on the Bay of Biscay in the west. It forms the southwest border of Burgundy, and along its axis stand the main towns of the Nièvre *département*: La Charité-sur-Loire, Pouilly-sur-Loire and Cosne-Cours-sur-Loire. Like most rivers it has attracted settlements and trade since prehistory – when boats were fashioned from tree trunks to navigate the river.

A rich array of wildlife inhabits the River Loire and its sandbanks – so much so that a strip of 20km (12 miles) is now a protected nature reserve. The temperate climate along the river's valley is due to the influence of the Atlantic and this provides a remarkably diverse range of wildlife and fauna. The stretch between Chalonnes and Sully-sure Loire is also a Unesco World Heritage Site because of its 'outstanding cultural landscape'. But it is the glorious châteaux and their gardens that visitors come to admire.

The river's path through Burgundy begins in the Brionnais in eastern France, not far from the medieval village of Semur-en-Brionnaise, one of the most beautiful villages in France. The river carries on to Digoin, known as the 'town of water' with the rivers Arroux, Bourbince, Vouzance and Aronce converging on the Loire, making it a boater's haven. With a marina for 100 craft, the Canal du Centre, Canal Latéral à la Loire and Canal de Roanne à Digoin converge here.

One of the most interesting and scenic aspects is that of the Pont-Canal, which resembles a viaduct, except that it is a 'viacanal', which crosses the Loire and joins the Canal du Centre with the Canal Latéral at a great height. You can watch the activity from the 'Observaloire' centre on the river bank.

The inspiration for *Sleeping Beauty* came from the turreted castle of Ussé. Today, the big attractions are the storybook villages, historic towns and fortified châteaux, not to mention the wonderful array of wines that are produced in this beautiful environment (France's third largest AOC region).

At present, among the river cruise companies, only CroisiEurope cruises the Loire, with the custom-designed, mid-ship side paddlewheel vessel *Loire Princesse*, built in 2015.

Taking in the view from the *Loire Princesse*.

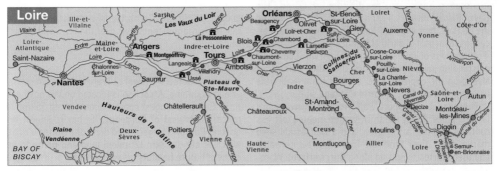

River Po

A cruise on the Po is a great way to see some of Italy's most breathtaking cities and sample the regional cuisine. Few towns are on the river itself, so most excursions involve a bus trip.

With a length of 670km (416 miles), the Po is,the longest river in Italy. It starts in the northwest near the border with France, rising on Monte Viso near the southern end of the Cottian Alps. It then flows eastward through Italy's heartland and empties into the Adriatic Sea to the south of Venice. It is fed from numerous small rivers from the Alps, including the Adda, Mincio, Oglio and the Ticino. Today, it runs through the north Italian provinces of Lombardy, Emilia-Romagna and the Veneto.

After the fall of the Roman rulers in the 8th century, many people moved inland, away from the River Po delta. The dykes fell into disrepair, and the river formed its own course. It was approximately 400 years ago that the Po Delta shaped itself into a sort of triangle. The longest arm of the triangle was formed by the coastal dunes. As the lagoons silted up, the coastline moved at the rate of 500 yards every 100 years towards the sea, which created the river's ever-increasing delta.

Although the plain was mostly marshland, the canalisation of the area was started as long ago as the 12th century, although it was only between 1604 and 1660 that a canal was dug to divert the river, so that it flows directly into the sea; the mouth of the main arm was blocked off and all river traffic was halted. So much silt is brought by the river and deposited in the fertile deltas at its mouth that it is reported to be advancing into the Adriatic Sea at a rate of 60m (196ft) per year.

Today, the shallow, slowly meandering River Po is navigable from Nizza Monferrato, a city in northern Italy's Piedmont region, to the Adriatic Sea, through some of Italy's loveliest unspoiled land.

Po floods

However, all is not always serene and calm. In 2000, some 43,000 persons were evacuated in Italy following flooding from heavy rains in the western and central plains of the River Po. The floodwaters moved eastwards along the river, closing factories and schools and disrupting telecommunications, and a state of emergency was declared by the Italian government. The floods affected Cremona and Mantua, both of which were highlights of River Po cruises.

River Countess in Venice.

CRUISING THE PO

Given the historical riches of the region, it may seem surprising that there aren't more river cruises on the Po. There are reasons for this, however: the Po is not an easy river for larger boats to navigate, as its depth changes constantly; capacity is therefore limited to smaller vessels. Indeed, riverships that draw very little water have been specially constructed to navigate this scenic route.

Cruising along the Po River is centred around Venice and its lagoon, which was created by the estuaries of three rivers, the Adige, Brenta and Po, and is separated from the Adriatic Sea by a row of

DID YOU KNOW?

...that the Latin name for this river was Padus?
...at its widest point, the river measures 503m (1,650ft)?
...that in 2005 the Po hit global headlines when it was found to be carrying the equivalent of almost 4kg (8.8lbs) of cocaine daily, way above official estimates for cocaine consumed? (This figure indicates around 40,000 doses of cocaine daily for the region, whereas the official statistics are about 15,000 doses per month for young adults in the region.)

Mantua's Piazza dell' Erbe.

sand bars. It is about 51km (32 miles) long. Most Po cruises operate a long summer season, from late March to early November. Spring is a wonderful time to visit, before the cities get too crowded and Venice becomes clogged with tourists and, more to the point, its canals begin to smell less than fragrant. October is also a good month, as the trees begin to turn, a gentle mist hangs over the fields at sunrise, the searing heat of the days lessens and the long lines of tour buses thin out.

In February, it's Carnival in Venice, a glamorous and frenetic annual festivity that typically lasts for about two weeks. River cruise companies usually operate special Venice and lagoon cruises during this period.

Note

At the time this book was produced and published, cruises along the River Po had been put on hold. In the aftermath of the capsizing of *Costa Concordia* in 2012 the Italian authorities implemented new safety regulations in April 2012. Both *Bellissima* of Nicko Tours and *Michelangelo* of CroisiEurope are presently restricted to cruising the Venice Lagoon and the Po delta, as the authorities require additional certification for the open water stretch between Chioggia and the mouth of the Po, which leads to the Adriatic Sea.

HIGHLIGHTS FROM MANTUA TO VENICE

There are no kilometre markers along the Po. Cruising distances are short, and most of the time is spent sightseeing away from the boat.

Mantua (Mantova)

Mantua, hometown of the poet Virgil, is fortunate to be located close to three lakes. The old centre

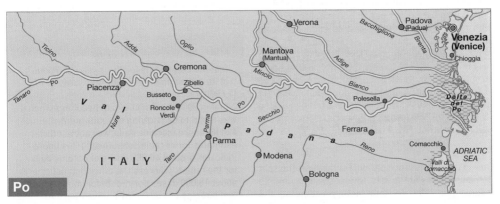

Juliet's House, Verona.

perches serenely on a peninsula that juts out into the lakes. Sadly, the nearby petrochemical plants have brought pollution, but the setting is nonetheless picturesque. The city itself has ancient stone churches, small shops, lovely squares and pavement cafés. The most impressive squares are the Piazza dell'Erbe with its marketplace, the medieval Piazza del Broletto, and the attractive, cobbled Piazza Sordello.

Mantua was the seat of the powerful Gonzaga dynasty in the 14th century, when this was a flourishing centre for the arts. The 500-room Palazzo Ducale compound is testament to the family's great wealth, with a huge collection of Renaissance art and frescoes. The Palazzo's most important fresco cycle is in the Camera degli Sposi, in which Andrea Mantegna's frescoes depict the court life of Ludovico Gonzaga in intricate detail, right down to his favourite dog and the court dwarf.

The Palazzo Te, built by Federigo Gonzaga for his mistress, stands outside the walled part of the city and, with its sweeping gardens, is located opposite the cathedral; this elegant country palace served as an inspiration for Versailles (Paris), the Nymphenburg (Munich) and Schönbrunn (Vienna).

Cremona

Cremona is indisputably the world's violin capital, its fame dating back to the period between the 16th and 18th centuries, when great names such as Nicolò and Hieronymus Amati, Giuseppe Guarneri and, most famous of all, Antonio Stradivari, who was born here in 1644, set out to create the perfect stringed instrument. An excursion will probably take you to one of the workshops of a present-day violin maker as well as to the Museo Stradivariano. Cremona is also famous for its 12th-century cathedral and square, as well as for having Italy's tallest bell tower.

Ferrara

During the Renaissance period, Ferrara was the seat of many patrons of the arts. Impressive monuments include the 13th- to 15th-century cathedral, the

Palazza Schifonoia (which contains frescoes from the 15th century) and the Castello Estense. The centre of the city has been designated a World Heritage site. Typically, there may be an excursion from Ferrara to visit Bologna, depending on itinerary and operator.

Piacenza

The streets of the city of Piacenza were originally laid out in a rectangular grid by the Romans, but, sadly, no Roman monuments have survived. The cathedral, built in the Lombardy-Romanesque style between 1122 and 1253, is a splendid example of the period. Cereal growing and viniculture form most of the economy of this city, which is also a major transportation centre on the road between Milan and Bologna.

Bologna

Although some distance from the river (around 45km/28 miles south), the city of Bologna is well worth a visit, if offered as an excursion. The city is of great historical interest and has excellent shopping, particularly for food.

Located to the north of Florence, Bologna is the principal city of the Emilia-Romagna region and lies at the foot of the northern Apennine mountain range, some 55m (180ft) above sea level. In 1088, the first university in Europe was established here; by the 12th century, many wealthy families were resident in the city. In the competitive spirit of the age, each family attempted to outdo their neighbours by building a large tower on their properties – needless to say, the bigger the tower, the more important the family. At one point there were 180 of these medieval skyscrapers looming over the city, 15 of which still stand.

Highlights include the Piazza Maggiore and the neighbouring Piazza Nettuno, both in the heart of the city, surrounded by graceful Renaissance and medieval buildings. Both piazzas are great gathering-places, full of outdoor cafés and street artists, and buzzing with life. Between the two squares is a huge bronze of *Neptune* by the French sculptor Giambologna.

Bologna's beautiful Basilica di San Petronio is one of the largest churches in the world. Look out for the

PARMESAN

True parmesan cheese *(parmigiano-reggiano)* is manufactured from 15 April to 11 November in Parma (also in the provinces of Bologna and Mantua). It is made from skimmed cow's milk (32 percent butterfat), which is mixed with rennet and cooked for 30 minutes. After going through several rounds of draining and drying, it is coated and formed into cylindrical shapes weighing about 30kg (67.5lbs), with slightly convex sides. It takes about one year to mature and has a yellow, crumbly consistency.

carvings depicting scenes from the New Testament by Jacopo della Quercia, and frescoes by Giovanni da Modena. Within walking distance from here is the Pinacoteca Nazionale, in the old university quarter, with works by Giotto, Raphael's *Ecstasy of St Cecilia* and some minor El Grecos and Titians.

Verona

Another highlight along the Po is the Romanesque city that inspired Shakespeare's *Romeo and Juliet* (and *The Two Gentlemen of Verona*), offered as a half- or full-day tour and, during the Opera Festival season of July and August, as an evening event.

Verona lies on the winding Adige River, which descends from the Italian Alps to run parallel with the Po before emptying into the Adriatic just to the north of the Po Delta, on a plain at the foot of the Lessini Mountains, approximately 105km (65 miles) west of Venice. The compact medieval centre lends itself to slow wandering, its shopping streets lavishly paved with smooth marble, and some of the 600-year-old facades decorated with intricate frescoes.

The city was the seat of the Scaligeri family, one of northern Italy's most important dynasties, throughout the medieval period. Towards the end of their rule, the family built Castelvecchio, a solid-looking fortress, damaged in World War II but subsequently restored.

The Roman Arena, a stunning creation in rose-coloured marble on the Piazza Bra, dates to the 1st century AD and is the third-largest Roman amphitheatre in existence. If you get a chance to go to the opera, take it; the atmosphere inside is amazing, and the evening really is a special occasion, with well-known Italian operas performed under the stars and fans flocking from all over the world.

An even bigger lure for most, though, is Casa di Giulietta (Juliet's House) on Via Cappello, just off Via Mazzini, the main shopping street. The star-crossed lovers are fictional, although they are based on real families, the Cappello and the Montecchi. Whether these families were actually feuding, however, is questionable. You can see the famous balcony and recite the immortal lines, but the chances of photographing the old house without a coach party in front of it are slim.

Verona is also known for its regional wines, Bardolino, Recioto, Soave and Valpolicella, and has a good supply of outdoor cafés where you can sit with a chilled Soave and a plate of antipasti, read the paper and watch the world go by.

Padua (Padova)

An historic university town (Galileo was professor of mathematics here in 1592), Padua lies on the River Bacchiglione, west of Venice. Highlights include its great basilica, St Andrew's, built to house the body of the saint after which it is named (the town's patron saint) and completed in the 14th century. The high altar is decorated with magnificent bronzes by Donatello. Padua is home to the oldest botanical garden in the world, founded in 1545. It's also worth paying a visit to the food market, the Mercato Sotto il Salone, for its wonderful variety of produce.

Parma

Set in wooded, gently hilly countryside south of the Po on the Torrente Parma tributary, Parma is famed for

Old wooden boats in a Chioggia canal.

its hams and cheeses. Parma itself deserves recognition for more than gastronomy; Verdi composed many great works here, while the conductor Toscanini was born here. The cathedral is famous for Correggio's *Assumption of the Virgin* in the cupola, which took six years to paint. The other important sight is the Galleria Nazionale in the Palazzo della Pilotta, the 17th-century home of the wealthy Farnese family. The gallery contains work by Correggio, Francesco Parmigianino, Fra Angelico, Leonardo, Canaletto and Van Dyck.

The cobbled lanes around the old centre are lined with delicatessens selling Parma ham and parmesan cheese. There's also a colourful produce market in Piazza Ghiaia, south of Palazzo della Pilotta. Genuine parmesan cheese comes from two towns, Parma and Reggio Emilia, which between them have an official logo that should be embossed on the side of the cheese. The unique qualities of both the cheese and Parma ham are attributed to the humid microclimate of the immediate area around Parma. The salty chunks of meat are actually taken to cure in Zibello, on the banks of the River Po.

Chioggia

Chioggia is located on an island at the southern end of the Venice Lagoon, about 24km (15 miles) south of Venice. It is Italy's largest fishing port and hugely reminiscent of Venice itself, with its winding, narrow streets and canals, and old-world charm. The most notable buildings are the 11th-century cathedral and the churches of San Martino (1392) and San Domenico (14th century), both of which house valuable paintings.

Venice (Venezia)

Beautiful, dreamy, romantic Venice, straddling 118 islands on the edge of the Venice Lagoon, has inspired poets, artists, musicians and lovers, and brings endless superlatives to the lips of visitors today. No matter that is it sinking at an alarming rate, floods frequently, smells of drains in the hot summer months and the canals are as clogged with traffic, albeit waterborne, as the streets of Rome. Venice is on every river cruise passenger's must-see list

River cruise vessels moor along the Giudecca Canal, between the ocean cruise terminal and the entrance of the Grand Canal. You can walk from the mooring points to St Mark's Square in 20 minutes. Our key highlights are listed below:

Rialto Bridge (Ponte de Rialto): This famous bridge crosses the Grand Canal at what used to be the busiest trading centre in the city – the Rialto market district. Two rows of shops lie within the solid, closed arches – the feature which gives it its unique appearance. This is a great place to pause and watch the river traffic, and admire the majestic sweep of palaces and warehouses swinging away to La Volta del Canal, the great elbow-like bend in the canal.

St Mark's Basilica and Museum (Basilica & Museo di San Marco): The basilica is the centrepiece of St Mark's Square and is the most famous of the churches in Venice – a place the aesthete John Ruskin called 'a treasure heap, a confusion of delight'. Best visited in the morning, the basilica, which was modelled on Byzantine churches in Constantinople, remains a glorious confusion. Despite the sloping irregular floors, an eclectic mix of styles both inside and out, the five low domes of unequal proportions and some 500 non-matching columns, St Mark's still manages to convey a sense of grandeur as well as jewel-like delicacy.

Attached to the basilica is a museum housing some of St Mark's finest treasures. The star attraction is the world's only surviving ancient *quadriga* (four horses abreast), known as the *Cavalli di San Marco* (The Horses of St Mark). These are the gilded bronze originals believed to have crowned Trajan's Arch in Rome, but later moved to Constantinople, where Doge Dandolo claimed them as spoils of war, bringing them back to Venice. Replicas adorn the facade in order to protect the originals from corrosion.

Doge's Palace (Palazzo Ducale): For nine centuries, the magnificent Doge's Palace was the seat of the

---

PROSCIUTTO

Langhirano is a town about 20km (12.5 miles) to the east of Parma, known as the place where Pio Tosini (who died in 2002 aged 95) argued that the silky air-cured ham produced in the town, and refined for the last century, should be known as *prosciutto di Langhirano*. He lost, and the speciality became known by its present tag, *prosciutto di Parma* (Parma ham).

Langhirano is located between a small mountain range and plains with a small stream to the north – ideal conditions for nature to provide the cure.

After being salted twice, hams then rest for 24 days at 1–4ºC (34–39ºF), before being passed through a pummelling tunnel to take away any excess salt and relax the tissue to allow the remaining salt to penetrate evenly. The last drop of blood is removed by a 'squeezer' – a person who literally squeezes the hams, before they are sent to rest for 70 days.

The hams are then hung and pre-cured for three months. Each prosciutto is then serially stamped, starting with the number of the farmer who bred the pigs, then the number of the abattoir, and the curer. When the ham has cured for one year, the Consorzio di Prosciutto inspects it using a pointed piece of porous horse bone from the femur (leg bone) to decide whether it is good enough. When the inspector has given his approval, the ham receives its Ducal stamp before being dispatched.

Beautiful Venice.

Republic, serving as a council chamber, law court and prison, as well as the residence of most of Venice's doges. The architects of this massive structure, with peach-and-white patternings in its distinctive brick facade, achieved an incredible delicacy by balancing the bulk of the building above two floors of Istrian stone arcades.

Grand Canal (Canal Grande): A trip along the Grand Canal, Venice's fabulous highway, is an unforgettable experience. Along certain sections of the canal the gondolas still function as *traghetti* (ferries), and, from the station to St Mark's Square, the banks are lined with ornate palaces and grand houses, mostly built between the 14th and 18th centuries. While some have been restored, others have a neglected air, awaiting their turn for renovation. Must-sees include the Ca'Grande, the Ca'Foscari, the Ca'd'Oro and the Guggenheim. As well as providing a cavalcade of pageantry, the canal offers a slice of local daily life, welcoming simpler craft such as gondolas and rubbish barges.

The Accademia: Housed in a former convent since 1807, the Accademia gallery displays the most complete collection of 14th- to 18th-century Venetian painting in existence. This outstanding gallery is arranged chronologically in 24 rooms, and includes works by Titian, Canaletto, Bellini and Carpaccio. Jacopo Tintoretto's dazzling St Mark's paintings, notably the haunting *Transport of the Body of St Mark*, are also here.

San Rocco: The area of San Polo that lies within the bend of the Grand Canal is home to the Scuola Grande di San Rocco, famous for its paintings by Jacopo Tintoretto. His magnificent works adorn every surface: the images are larger than life, full of chiaroscuro effects and floating, plunging figures in dramatic poses. One of the best known is *The Glorification of St Roch*.

Scala del Bovolo: The Palazzo Contarini has an outstanding external spiral staircase in its interior courtyard, the Scala Contarini del Bovolo, a Lombardesque work dating from 1499. Bovolo translates as 'snailshell' in Venetian dialect.

Ca D'Oro: The 15th-century Ca D'Oro is the city's most magnificent Gothic palace. On the facade, the friezes of interlaced foliage and mythological beasts were originally picked out in gold. The restored and modernised interior now features the Galleria Franchetti, which houses numerous Renaissance bronzes and sculptures.

The Frari: Officially known as Santa Maria Gloriosa dei Frari, this austere Franciscan centre is the largest and greatest of all the Venetian Gothic churches, founded in the 13th century and rebuilt in the 14th and 15th centuries. The adjoining cloisters house the state archives. The church's greatest treasure is Titian's *Assumption*, his masterpiece, hanging above the high altar. The great painter is buried here.

ST MARK'S LION

The winged lion represents St Mark, the patron saint of Venice, and adorns buildings, bridges and doorways. Whereas the seated lion represents the majesty of state, the walking lion symbolises sovereignty over its dominions. A golden winged lion of St Mark still adorns the city standard, and remains the symbol of the Veneto.

River Douro

The picturesque scenery of the Douro Valley in northern Portugal makes it a glorious cruise destination. The journey is a round trip from Porto, taking in country estates and port wine institutes.

The Phoenicians and Romans mined gold in the Baixo Douro region and used the river to transport the ore to the coast – hence the name, which means 'of gold', although some poetically say that the name also derives from the golden sheen of the river as it reflects the sunlight, and the sand-coloured hills through which it flows.

The Douro region itself lies north of the river, while to its south is Biero Alto. The river starts with small beginnings in the high hills of the Picos de Urbion, in Spain's Soria Province, to the north of Madrid (the river is called 'Duero' by the Spanish). It then flows west across to the border with Portugal, before turning southwest and delineating the border for approximately 97km (60 miles). It then flows west again, meandering though some enchanting countryside en route, including sleepy villages, castles and vineyards that have remained remarkably unchanged and pastoral for hundreds of years, before hitting the Atlantic at Portugal's second city, Porto (Oporto).

Sailing through Porto.

The river serves as a transportation route for wine products of Portugal's Paiz do Vinho region, and also supports a fishing industry. The river is navigable within Portugal, although there are rapids and occasional flooding in its lower reaches. Only vessels with a very shallow draft can enter the river due to sandbars at its mouth.

From Porto, you cruise 'upstream' and cross several dams, including the Crestuma-Lever and the Pachino. Excursions are made by motor coach to various *quintas* (country estates) and establishments that produce the region's favourite tipple – port.

A series of dams were constructed along the Douro in the 1980s for flood control and for the generation of electricity and hydroelectric power. Fortunately, the planners had the foresight to include locks within the dams, and these have enabled navigation right through Portugal and into Spain. The once fast-flowing river is now like a series of connected tranquil lakes with spectacular scenery.

In addition to the city highlights en route, the other attractions of a Douro cruise include the Portuguese cuisine, which is simple but full of taste. Fresh fish and seafood play an important part, as do ham and chicken, and fresh vegetables that are typically grown by small farms that do not use pesticides. Locally produced wines are plentiful, of good quality, and usually enjoyed with lunch and dinner. Events might include a *fado* (literally, fate) evening, a great chance to sample this unique Portuguese form of music that always tells a sad story.

DID YOU KNOW?

...that the best time to visit the Douro Valley is during the *vindima*, in late September and early October, when the grapes are being collected?
...that wine has been produced in the Douro Valley for around 2,000 years? It is also one of the world's oldest designated wine-producing regions – its demarcation dates to the mid-18th century.
...that the Douro is the third-longest river on the Iberian Peninsula, after the Tagus and the Ebro?
...that the *Spirit of Chartwell*, which cruises on the River Douro, was chosen by Queen Elizabeth II as the royal barge to lead the 1,000-strong flotilla during the celebrations and Diamond Jubilee Pageant in London on 3 June 2012?
... that nine dams have been built along the Douro's length?

Note that cruises along the Douro often offer a bus excursion from the border town of Vega de Terrón to the historic Spanish university city of Salamanca.

HIGHLIGHTS ON A CRUISE FROM PORTO

Only a handful of river cruise companies operate on the Douro, usually offering seven-night itineraries starting and finishing in Porto. Typical stops include Peso da Régua, Pinhão and Vega de Terrón (a jumping-off point for Salamanca, across the border in Spain). Apart from the joy of cruising the river as it carves its way through the steep hills, most of the excursions are a coach journey away from the various stops. Each itinerary crosses several dams, including the Crestuma-Lever and the Pachino. Cruises can be combined with a stay in Lisbon and Coimbra, Portugal's former medieval capital and still an important university town.

Rabelo boats once transported port down from the vineyards.

Porto

Located on the Douro, Porto (Oporto) is Portugal's second largest city, the heart of the port-wine trade and one of the most attractive cities on the Iberian Peninsula. It dominates the hillsides above the Douro, tumbling down the side of a gorge carved from granite by the fast-flowing water. The gorge is spanned by several graceful bridges, leading to Vila Nova de Gaia on the opposite bank, where all the great port lodges are located, including Cockburns and Sandeman – their English names reminders of the fact that British merchants controlled the industry from its inception. Cruise boats moor up in the heart of the city on the Vila Nova side, within easy reach on foot of the medieval town, the Ribeira district. On the banks of the river you'll see the colourful *rabelo* boats that were once used to transport port down from the vineyards.

The historic city has Unesco World Heritage status and was designated a European City of Culture in 2001. The city centre is a chaotic mix of medieval alleys, the old fisherman's quarter and a skyline of ornate Baroque towers, all crowned by a magnificent cathedral. Highlights include the Ponte Dom Luis I (the iron bridge), an impressive steel railway bridge that looms over the vividly painted houses of the Ribeira district and spans the river to the south bank. Built in 1886, the bridge has two decks, the upper one for the metro, and leads directly to port cellars in Vila Nova de Gaia.

There's also the cathedral, Sé, which crowns the highest point of the granite rock on which much of the old town stands. It was built as a defensive fortification in the 12th century, and despite extensive alterations it has retained its fortress-like appearance. The 18th-century Torre dos Clérigos is the tallest granite tower in Portugal and has become the emblem of Porto. Unless you really have no head for heights it is worth climbing the endless spiral staircase with 225 or so steps for the dazzling view over the city, the river Douro and its estuary. Another notable church is Santo Ildefonso, built in the 18th century and decorated with *azulejos* (glazed tiles) depicting scenes from the life of St Ildefonso and allegories of the Eucharist. Look out, too, for the Stock

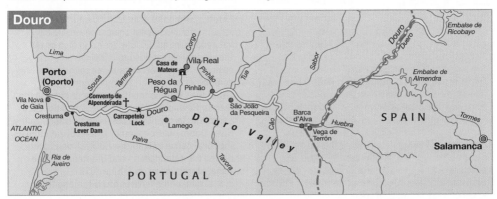

Casa de Mateus.

Exchange, built on the site of a convent, which burnt down in 1832. It is noted for its opulent neo-Moorish reception hall. Finally, across the Ponte Dom Luis I, are the port-wine lodges of Vila Nova de Gaia. Many of the larger ones welcome weekday visitors to tour the installations and taste their wines. Most prominent is Sandeman, whose distinctive silhouette rises on the skyline.

Peso da Régua

From Porto the Douro snakes eastwards to Peso da Régua past wooded valleys, fields of almond trees and quiet villages. Shortly after leaving Porto, the rivership passes through the floodgates of the Crestuma Lever Dam, one of several built over the last few decades to tame the river, which was previously difficult to navigate. Some cruises stop for the evening at Bitetos, with an excursion to the nearby 11th-century Convento de Alpendorada, which overlooks the river. The monastery hosts medieval-style banquets and wine-tastings, and provides an atmospheric setting for dinner. The Carrapetelo Lock, with a maximum

lift/drop of 35m/yds, is also a highlight of this stretch of the river.

The port region proper begins at Peso da Régua. At this point, the river suddenly enters a region of steep hills covered with green vineyards, and the occasional lavish manor house set back from the river. Giant lettering on the hillsides denotes each grower's name. Peso da Régua is the home of the Port Wine Institute, and almost all its inhabitants have some connection with the port-wine trade; in the past, this was the starting point for the *rabelo* boats, laden with barrels, on their long and treacherous journey to Vila Nova de Gaia on the coast.

For river cruise passengers it's now a departure point for coach tours to Vila Real, 25km (16 miles) to the north, and notable as home to the Casa de Mateus.

Pinhão

This small, rustic Douro town, located at the end of the wine trail, is known for its picturesque setting and its proximity to the *quintas*, the country seats of the big names in port production. The railway station has some beautiful *azulejos* on the walls, depicting local scenes and culture. The town also has a bridge by the French architect Gustave Eiffel (of tower fame). Riverships stop here to run excursions to the wine-growing estates, where visitors learn about grape crushing, fermentation and blending. Even if you don't drink port, it is worth the visit simply to admire the beauty of the estates, some of them with lavish gardens on the river banks.

Vila Real (Casa de Mateus)

The magnificent 18th-century Baroque house and gardens of Casa de Mateus (daily June–Sept 9am–7.30pm; Mar–May & Oct 9am–1pm, 2–6pm; Nov–Feb 10am–1pm, 2–5pm) lies 3km (2 miles) outside the busy town of Vila Real. It belonged to the counts of Vila Real, and was the birthplace of the navigator Diego Cão, who discovered the mouth of the Congo River in central Africa. The estate has beautifully cool, shady formal gardens and a fine *allée* of cedar

PORTUGUESE CUISINE

Food in Portugal conjures up images of empire, with influences from its erstwhile colonies Brazil, Angola, Mozambique, Goa and Macau much to the fore. The voyages of the explorer Vasco da Gama brought back cinnamon and curry powder, and both are still important flavourings in Portuguese cuisine. Common ingredients include fresh fish and seafood, ham, chicken, and fresh vegetables that are typically grown on small, organic farms. It is the quality of the produce that delights many visitors, whether the nutty, earthy potatoes or the juicy tomatoes that taste like an explosion of flavour to those accustomed to bland supermarket varieties. Pork is the dominant

meat, and the wonderful charcuterie features in many soups and stews.

Some local specialities in Porto include tripe of veal with beans. The story goes that altruistic locals donated all their meat to the ships departing to conquer the New World, leaving only the tripe for their own consumption. More palatable are the local salt cod (*bacalhau*), succulent roast lamb and the famous *caldo verde* – a soup of potatoes, cabbage and olive oil. Between spring and early autumn, sardines can be found as street food, cooked on small terracotta braziers. Sweet, egg-based puddings are also popular and go well with a glass of port.

Lamego's Nossa Senhora dos Remédios.

trees. The area is famous for its Mateus Rosé wine, and an image of the house appears on all Mateus Rosé bottles. Vila Real itself has little of interest, although it is the largest town in the region, and is on the edge of a dramatic gorge carved by the River Corgo (a tributary of the Douro).

Barca d'Alva

This is a gentle spot that was once the upper navigation limit on the Douro. It is the closest point to the Spanish border (less than 2km/1.2 miles away), and sits among almond and olive groves. The town itself, usually just a stopping-off place for the night, is only a few hundred yards from the Spanish border, inside the Douro International Natural Park.

São João da Pesqueira

São João, usually offered as an excursion from Pinhão or Ferradosa (the latter is northeast of the Douro), is a sprawling wine-growing village famed for its town hall, which has stunning tiled murals depicting port-wine-making scenes. It is surrounded by port *quintas* on a plateau that overlooks the valleys and vineyards of the Douro in a delightful, picture-postcard setting.

Lamego

Lamego, 12km (7.5 miles) south of the river and usually offered as a half-day tour from Peso da Régua on the return journey to Porto, is an important pilgrimage site, overlooked by the the Sanctuary Church of Nossa Senhora dos Remédios (Our Lady of the Remedies). A superb Baroque-style staircase of some 600 steps reaches the church, by which point most visitors are in need of a blessing from the saint. The view from the top, though, is worth it – it is absolutely stunning. In September, thousands of pilgrims flock to the town.

Lamego was once the trading post of the Moors who journeyed across from Spain. They left their legacy in the 12th-century castle with an unusual vaulted cistern. The town's museum houses an impressive collection of furniture, paintings, 16th-century Flemish tapestries, sculpture and jewellery from the Bishop's Palace within which it is situated.

Vega de Terrón (for Salamanca, 128km/80 miles away)

Across the Spanish border, riverships berth for the day at Vega de Terrón, while their passengers visit Salamanca, a university town since the 13th century. The Plaza Mayor, a huge, elegant square surrounded by gracious sandstone buildings, is one of the most impressive and beautiful in Europe. The twin cathedrals, Catedral Nueva (16th-century Gothic) and Catedral Vieja (12th-century Romanesque), the latter with its spectacular silver Byzantine dome, are also well worth seeing.

Barge cruising

A barge holiday offers a wonderful opportunity to sample life in the (very) slow lane in beautiful surroundings, both on board and off. This chapter covers all the essentials.

In this chapter, we answer some of the basic burning questions potential barge cruise customers might ask.

Why go barge cruising?

Quite simply because barges let you de-stress completely. They provide an antidote to the pressures of life in a fast-paced world, with their calming, slow speed. They allow you to holiday in surroundings that are comfortable but not pretentious, plus you can expect fine food and, hopefully, enjoyable company. Barges are like little bed-and-breakfast places tucked away in some forgotten corner. There are typically no computers and no telephones, which should also help you to disconnect from all the usual concerns of everyday life.

In addition, of course, they provide a wonderful way to experience and explore new surroundings – effortless discovery, if you like.

Tell me more

As with riverships, there are no casinos, bingo or horse racing or other potentially unappealing parlour games, or art auctions or other revenue-generating events that are for many a negative aspect of the ocean-cruise experience. And once on board, you only have to unpack once, convenient when compared with touring by road or train and constantly having to pack and unpack, as you change hotels.

What's the difference between a river cruise and a barge cruise?

The main difference is that cruise barges travel much slower (up to 6kph/3.75mph) than riverships (up to 18kph/11mph). They are also smaller and typically cater to a maximum of 12 persons, as opposed to riverships, which can carry up to 200.

Are meals included?

They certainly are, as are wonderful cooks. Full board is included in the cruise fare, and everything is cooked to order. The chef purchases their own food in local shops and markets, so it's really fresh.

What about drinks?

All drinks (both alcoholic and non-alcoholic), including Champagne and wines with dinner, are included.

Won't I get bored?

Hardly! There is always something to see on the canals – it's like live armchair travel.

Apart from totally unwinding, you can also be active if you wish. There are always lots of excursions and activities on offer. You can walk (probably faster than the barge can chug along), go bicycling (almost all barges have bicycles), hill climb, go hot-air ballooning, go horse riding or play golf or tennis. You can also

Cruising on the Canal du Midi, southern France.

DID YOU KNOW...?

...that the Canal du Midi in the South of France was the incredible work of one man? It was the work of 17th-century engineer Pierre-Paul Riquet, who sacrificed a fortune to finance his dream of creating a waterway linking the Atlantic with the Mediterranean. The mammoth project took 14 years to complete, using 12,000 workers; it was finally finished in in 1681. There have been relatively few modifications since the canal was constructed, although the original wooden lock gates have been replaced with steel ones. The canal offers 386km (240 miles) of navigable waterway, skirting the sun-bathed shores of the Mediterranean and winding its way up towards the wine regions of Bordeaux.

go food shopping with the chef or learn some cooking tips from him or her. Or you could simply head into the nearest village for a baguette or two, or sample some local cheese or charcuterie.

How about dining?
It's casual. With so few passengers, everyone eats at the same time. There are no assigned tables, which hopefully provides an opportunity to make new friends.

What about special diets?
If you are on a special diet, let your travel provider know when you book. The chef will be pleased to accommodate you, if possible. Some fresh foods will be purchased daily, which should mean that any special diets can be taken into account. Note that the galley on a barge is extremely compact, with little storage space for seldom-used items, so there won't be a big stash of unusual dietary items.

What's the best season for a barge cruise?
Late spring or early autumn (fall) are when you'll get the best weather for a cruise of this kind, although each season brings its own attractions. Note that cruise barges do not operate in winter.

Is barge cruising for solo travellers?
The world of cruising is made for couples. Solo travellers are an expensive afterthought, and few barges have dedicated cabins for them. You can occupy a double cabin on your own, of course, but you will have to pay higher fares.

Are barge cruises for honeymooners?
Possibly! Barge cruises in France provide an utterly romantic setting. Most arrangements will have been taken care of before you sail, so all you have to do is show up. Some cruise barges have accommodation in double-, or queen-sized beds, but, in general, cabins are small when compared to those in a typical hotel room.

If the budget is not a problem, the ultimate experience would be to charter a whole cruise barge (perhaps one of the smaller ones, for 4 to 6 passengers). You could sleep in different cabins each night and have a wonderful, indulgent, exclusive honeymoon.

Is barge cruising for families with children?
More families are discovering the joys of chartering a whole barge – most of them accommodate between 4 and 12 people, which could cover one or two average-sized families, or one such family plus friends. Meals and excursions can also be tailored for all tastes and age ranges. Well-respected operators such as Abercrombie & Kent specialise in holidays of this kind. Parents will, of course, need to be extremely vigilant about young children falling overboard when clambering around the deck.

Cycling alongside the Canal du Midi.

Are barge cruises suitable for disabled passengers?
Unfortunately, they are too small and not well equipped for passengers with disabilities. Cruise barge cabins are not the only problem, but getting from shore to vessel and vessel to shore can prove extremely difficult. My advice is to try a larger rivership, rather than a cruise barge, as these are much better equipped (more have lifts as well as larger cabins/suites that can better accommodate wheelchairs).

Are tips included?
In general, tips are not included. As a guideline, you should allow €8–10 (£6–8) per person, per day for gratuities. You give these to the barge master on the morning of disembarkation, and they will be shared among the crew.

Is airfare included?
Generally, airfare is not included, although it may be included in packages available through specialist operators.

Is insurance included?
No. To summarise briefly, for health cover, travellers from within the EU are covered to some degree with EHICs, but you are well advised to take out travel insurance with full medical cover (including repatriation by air ambulance) before travelling. Visitors from the US will need to take out full medical cover.

Is there a difference between cruise barges?
The appointments and interior decor range from rustic but comfortable to pure unabashed luxury, with prices to match.

What is the electric current?
Almost all cruise barge cabins have 220-volt electrical outlets. Take an adapter for any electrical appliance you use (hairdryers are usually provided).

How about motion sickness?

No. The movement of water on the rivers and canals is so slight that it is extremely unlikely that anyone would suffer from motion sickness.

Are there medical facilities on board?

No. First-aid kits are carried, cruise barges are always close to land, and any necessary arrangements in the event of a medical problem can be made relatively quickly.

I'm pregnant. Can I still cruise?

Typically most barge cruise companies will not allow a mother-to-be on a cruise past her 28th week of pregnancy. You may be required to produce a doctor's certificate in order to be allowed to travel. Fortunately, you'll never be far from shore, where medical help can be summoned.

Can I smoke on board?

Smoking on barges is usually restricted to the open deck area (as on riverships).

What about security?

Barges do not have key cards, generally speaking. Most have locking cabin doors, but the house-party atmosphere is supposed to engender an element of trust between passengers. The barge should always be locked if all passengers and crew are ashore.

WHAT IS A BARGE CRUISE?

It's about life in the very slow lane. Remember Simon & Garfunkel's 1966 song, *Feelin' Groovy*? The lyrics 'Slow down, you move too fast' are perfectly apt here.

There are just two speeds to a cruise barge: dead slow, and stop. So, slow down – way, way down – and simply pootle on your way. It is called the 'CD' approach – chug and drift, as you wind your way through some of the most tranquil landscapes in Europe.

Although there are some variations, a 'standard' canal barge cruise is six days long, with each cruise barge operating on fixed itineraries. (The seventh day can then be spent in cleaning and preparing the vessel again for the next set of passengers.)

Every cruise starts in a civilised manner with a glass of Champagne and moves gently through picture-postcard countryside. One of the first things to notice is the assortment of flowers and flower boxes that litter the uppermost deck – barge owners delight in trying to outdo each other.

There's nothing quite like pastoral countryside to take you back in time. Going more slowly than a person would on foot, cruise barges travel along the canal systems as well as the rivers. They cover very little in terms of distance but offer more time to get to know the countryside. You really can experience the colours of the blackberry bushes that overhang the path instead of speeding by them, as on a typical river cruise.

Taking a barge cruise is one of the very best ways to experience a country in small doses. In Europe, barge cruises can be taken in Belgium, France, Germany, the Netherlands and the UK, although the most popular country is undoubtedly France, where barge cruising has been carefully packaged and practised for many years.

Cruise barges (the French word for barge is *peniche*, although the French also call it *la maison qui marche* – 'the house that walks') chug along slowly in the daytime and moor early each evening, giving you time to

Auxerre is the centre of barging in France.

pay a visit to a local village, and get a restful night's sleep (no late nights or noisy overnight travelling).

The inland waterways of Europe all adhere to the CEVNI regulations (Code Européen des Voies de la Navigation Intérieure), which is a UN instrument with international authority and relevance.

French cruise barges have a reputation for excellent food and wine, and good conversation (no doubt the latter is to some degree the direct result of the former). As is typical in France, meals on cruise barges tend to be slow, sociable occasions. Locally grown fresh foods are usually purchased and prepared each day, allowing you to live well and feel like a houseguest. There is no mass dining here.

And you need to be as good at socialising as you are at eating when you join a barge cruise on your own (or as a couple), as you will be living in close quarters with a handful of others (most likely total strangers). A good sense of humour and an international outlook on life helps. Note, however, that most cruise barges can also be chartered exclusively, so you can just take your family and friends.

Design and layout

Many cruise barges have been skilfully converted from cargo- or munitions-carrying barges, most of which were built in either the Netherlands or Scotland (*L'Art du Vivre* is an example of a Scottish-built barge), while a handful of new ones have been constructed expressly for holidaying in the past few years. Most have the timeless appeal of a tiny country house.

Cruise barges are typically between 30 and 50m (100–166ft) in length, with a beam (maximum width) of between 5 and 7.3m (16.5–24ft), although their actual size depends on the area of operation and the ability to manoeuvre in the many locks that line the canals.

A cruise barge almost always has a steel hull, with a flat bottom, and (with a few exceptions) will have been converted from a cargo-carrying vessel. Their cruising speed is generally up to 6kph (3.75mph). Most carry a maximum of 12 passengers (although a few carry up to 24 passengers), and they tend to be beautifully fitted out with rich wood panelling, full carpeting, custom-built furniture and fine fabrics. Each barge has a dining salon/lounge-bar. Barge captains are often owner/operators, typically taking great pride in their vessel.

Some have air conditioning, and most have some form of heating. Most also have some kind of canopied sun deck. Cruise barge interiors always have plenty of cosy cushions on lounge seats and armchairs. Most cruise barges carry bicycles for your use; others may have a minibus that tootles alongside, ready to take you on excursions, all of which are included in the cruise fare.

Many cruise barges that carry fewer than 12 passengers have their own idiosyncrasies and niceties. Most are immaculately kept by their very proud own-

The cruise barge *Anjodi* in Languedoc.

ers, who lavish time and money on maintaining them to a high level.

Cabins and suites: Cabins tend to be rather small, but homely, although the overall look does tend to depend on the owner's preference in terms of decor. While most cruise barges are strictly for couples (with queen, double or twin beds), some barges also have single cabins. The size of cabins varies considerably – while there is no average cabin size, they measure from a tiny 6 sq m (64.5 sq ft) to a luxurious 24 sq m (258 sq ft). All cabins aboard *La Nouvelle Etoile* measure 18.5 sq m (200 sq ft).

Many cruise barges have suites measuring about 15 sq m (161.5 sq ft). The 'Monet Suite' aboard *L'Impressioniste* measures 15.77 sq m (169.8 sq ft), for example, and the 'Nuits-St-Georges' Suite aboard *La Belle Epoque* measures 15.36 sq m (165.3 sq ft). Further down the scale, the three twin-bedded cabins (often erroneously called 'staterooms' by enterprising marketeers) aboard *Nymphea* measure 6.25 sq m (67.2 sq ft).

If you want more space in your 'bedroom', you'll need to check the details carefully with your cruise barge booking agent or the owner, if you book direct (not recommended). The *Saint Louis* (available for whole vessel charter only) has cabins with a decent size of 11.7 sq m (127 sq ft).

Bathrooms: Cabins usually have en suites, with at least a toilet, basin and shower.

Luxury cruise barge crossing the Loire on the aqueduct at Briare.

Design specifics: Let's look at some of the details that make cruise barges so distinctive. What makes one cruise barge more luxurious than the next – apart from the size of the cabins – is the use of space and the quality of its decor, cabinetry and furnishings (in addition to the specialised local knowledge of the captain and crew, plus the quality of the cuisine).

Anjodi has a hot tub and a skylight in the salon. *Anacolouthe* has a baby grand piano in its lounge, which has rich wood panelling and a red colour scheme. *Elisabeth* has a split-level dining room with oak beamed ceiling. *Fleur de Lys* has a grand piano in its lounge and some rare vintage wines in the cellar, while bathrooms have two washbasins, as well as romantic canopied beds.

Fleur de Lys is also the only cruise barge I know of with a lounge decorated with fine antiques and a grand piano, plus a heated (decent-sized) plunge pool on deck. *Horizon II* is a split-level design with beautifully panelled interiors. *L'Impressioniste* has an exercise room and spa tub. *La Belle Epoque* also has richly panelled interiors, a fitness studio, hot tub and even a sauna. *La Nouvelle Etoile* has internet access in all cabins, tiled bathrooms and a lift (the only cruise barge to have one). *Napoleon* has one bedroom with a large, marble-clad bathroom – reminiscent of some of the bathrooms in the legendary Hotel Danieli in Venice – plus a sun deck measuring a spacious 75 sq m (800 sq ft).

Princess, built in 1973 by Daniel Ludwig, international shipping magnate and founder of Princess Hotels, has a canopied sun deck and cabin bathrooms with windows that open. *Quiétude* has an open fireplace. *Saroche* has a wood-burning stove in its split-level lounge, beautiful panelled interiors, satellite television and even its own washer/dryer (most unusual for a cruise barge). Meanwhile, *Sérénité* has lovely scrolled armrests on the dining room chairs, plus a very roomy dining room, with large, wood-trimmed picture windows.

Cuisine

The biggest event (indeed, it's the entertainment) of any barge cruise is the food. How you dine will depend on which cruise barge you choose. Dining ranges from homely cooking to outstanding nouvelle cuisine with all the trimmings. Tables are set with fine linen and china, and dinner is usually a leisurely candlelit affair, accompanied by rather good wines, some of which would be almost impossible to find outside the local producing region. Often, the owner of the barge, or his/her partner, is also the cook, and you can be assured that the ingredients are all fresh, and purchased almost daily.

BARGE CRUISING IN FRANCE

There are about 8,500km (5,280 miles) of navigable canals and waterways in France, and operators place their vessels in the best stretches, both for scenic beauty and architectural interest, as well as for ease of getting to and from your chosen cruise.

Locks

A barge cruise in France means going through a succession of locks, and nowhere is this more enjoyable and entertaining than on the Canal du Midi, with its numerous locks along the canal's 240km (149-mile) length or in Burgundy, where, between Dijon and Mâcon, a cruise barge can negotiate as many as 54 locks during a six-day journey. Lock hours of operation are civilised – between 8.30am and 6.30pm, with an hour off for lunch. If locks are of the hand-cranked type, you can lend a hand to open or close the lock gates – it's good exercise, and you get to talk to the lock keepers. Some lock keepers have a stock of vegetables to sell to the cruise barges.

Sights

Medieval walled towns, sleepy villages, towering cathedrals and cloistered abbeys, wine châteaux, chic shops, summer festivals and romantic hamlets all await you in France, dependent, of course, on the region in which you are cruising. In general, cruise barge companies split the country into several regions, and barges usually operate regular itineraries for the complete season (with few exceptions).

The key regions include Burgundy, home to the Canal de Bourgogne, Canal du Centre and the River Saône, and renowned for its fine wines and excellent cuisine. Highlights of the Canal de Bourgogne include the elegant historic city of Beaune, the vineyards of Meursault, Nuits-St-Georges, Santenay and Savigny, and the Unesco-protected Basilica of Vézelay and Abbey of Fontenay. Other attractions in the region include Auxerre, the centre of barging in France, and Chablis, another wine-tasting hotspot. Popular barge cruises include Dijon to Pont Royal (from big city to tiny hamlet) along the Canal de Bourgogne or from Dijon to Lyon along the Saône – a trip that is particularly good for wine lovers, who can visit all five appellations in one cruise.

Then there's the Loire Valley, also great wine country, where attractions along the Canal Latéral à la Loire include crossing Gustav Eiffel's 19th-century aqueduct at Briare (it crosses the River Loire, and so does your barge with you on board), the longest canal bridge in the world. Other highlights in the Loire include a visit to Montargis, often dubbed the 'Venice of France'.

An eastern France barge cruise would include Franche-Comté, east of Burgundy, as well as Alsace-Lorraine, which borders Germany, while southwestern France is another popular region, with Bordeaux and the Dordogne the highlights here. Provence is another great region for barge cruising in France, with a plethora of attractions including the great Roman cities of Avignon and Arles, the Roman aqueduct at the Pont du Gard and cowboys of the Camargue.

The cost

Rates typically range from €600 to more than €2,200 (£500–£1,850) per person for a six-day cruise, varying according to the season, with those in the spring and autumn being the least expensive and those in the peak summer season the most expensive. I do not recommend taking children under the age of 16, unless you charter the whole barge exclusively for family and friends. Rates include a Champagne reception, a cabin with private facilities, all meals, good wine with lunch and dinner, beverages (including an open bar), use of bicycles, side trips and airport/railway transfers. Other activities, such as horse riding, golf, tennis or hot-air ballooning, can be arranged at extra cost.

At the beginning and end of the season (around April and November), the weather can be unreliable, so it's best to take clothing that can be layered, including sweaters, plus a waterproof windbreaker.

Arrival

If you are travelling by train, note that many European stations do not have porters, so travel light and use luggage with wheels. Note that not all stations have lifts, and at some you might have to cross a footbridge with lots of stairs to reach the exit, so make sure, too, that you can manage to carry your own luggage up the stairs.

Chartering a private cruise barge

Private 'whole barge' charters (often with special themes, such as a fine French 'dégustation' cuisine cruise) are the way to go if you want to travel with a few select friends or as a large family, although you'll certainly have to pay for the privilege. You can even arrange a 'tandem' cruise, with two barges on identical itineraries. The cost for a private charter of a six- or eight-person luxury cruise barge is between around €18,000 and €55,000 (£15,000–45,000) for one week.

FRENCH WATERWAY TERMS
barge un péniche
beam une largeur
embankment une digue
distance marker un point kilométrique
dock une darse
downstream aval
(lock) gates les portes
length la longueur
lock une écluse
lock keeper un éclusier
port (left side) bâbord
propeller une hélice
rudder un gouvernail
starboard (right side) tribord
towpath un chemin de halage
upstream amont
wheelhouse une timonerie

Emerald Star approaching Durnstein, Austria.

River cruise companies

This list of the main river cruise providers includes background information on each company, including whether it owns or charters riverships, plus essential characteristics of its cruises.

When you are choosing a river cruise, it can be useful to know a little about the companies that own and operate them. Here is a summary of the main providers, with background information and details of key features of their cruises.

Other companies that market and sell river cruises, but either charter, or part-charter, or sell into riverships of other owners and operators (such as UK-based Newmarket Travel, Riviera Travel and Shearings, and US-based companies including Abercrombie & Kent), are not listed here. The financial investment companies that own riverships and charter them to tour operators (often for language-specific markets) are not included here either, but their riverships may be found in the listings section of this book.

A-ROSA Cruises

German company A-ROSA Cruises (established in 1969 as Seetours, when it was one of the first com-

A-ROSA Stella at Chalon-sur-Saône, France.

panies to charter riverships – in Russia) began operating its own river cruises in 2002. Seetours was founded by (the late) Alf Pollak with financial backing from Holland America Line, for whom Pollak was the general sales agent in Germany. The company – which became A-ROSA Cruises in 2003 – is based in Rostock, Germany. It also operates spa resorts in Austria and Germany.

The onboard dining concept is different to most, in that there is no formal meal service – instead, meals are provided in a self-service buffet (without tablecloths). Extra-cost 'all-inclusive' drinks packages are available.

However, aboard the riverships operated by A-ROSA Cruises exclusively for the English-speaking market – predominantly in North America – waiter service is provided for dinner, and other items are included, but this comes at a higher price point.

AmaWaterways

Founded in 2002 by modern river cruise industry pioneer Rudi Schreiner, cruise industry executive Kristin Karst and the late former owner of Brendan Worldwide Vacations, Jimmy Murphy as Amadeus Waterways (the company changed its name in 2008), AmaWaterways has helped to redefine European river cruising. The company fully owns, operates and markets its own riverships, all of which are newbuilds (not refits or renamed older vessels).

The company's riverships have spacious cabins, 82 percent of which have French balconies. Each passenger is provided with a large pocket-sized travel guide, with detailed information on the route, highlights, sights and historical information. There is also plenty of information for individual excursions. AmaWaterways spends considerably more on highquality food ingredients and wine and on hotel crew service training than any other river cruise company. The company is also known to offer the highest levels of customer care and friendliness in the river cruise industry.

APT (Australian Pacific Touring)

Founded in Melbourne, Australia, in the 1920s by Bill McGeary, APT River Cruises is part of the APT Group. Still a family-owned company, run by Rob and Lou McGeary, it added European river cruises to its portfolio for its mainly Australasian clients in the 1990s, although its offering has really taken off in the last few years or so. APT is a partner of AMA Waterways, some of whose riverships are used for its European river cruise programmes, and it maintains the same very high standards. APT may also purchase space on the riverships of other companies (in which case, the overall quality may be different). APT also owns the lower-priced brand 'Travelmarvel by APT'.

Avalon Waterways

Originally founded in 1928 by Antonio Mantegazza, who used his rowing boat to take passengers across Lake Lugano in Switzerland, the company became Avalon Waterways in 2003, under the umbrella of privately held company Group Voyages Inc., and it was run from Colorado. Now based in California, the company includes well-known tour operator brands Globus and Cosmos (the group consists of more than 30 tourism and aviation businesses).

Avalon operates, but does not own, its own vessels. Over half of all the riverships in the Avalon fleet have beds that face the river. Gratuities and all drinks (except premium brands) are included in the cruise price, but there is a strong emphasis on extra onboard revenue generated by selling optional excursions and premium-brand drinks.

CroisiEurope

CroisiEurope was founded in France in 1976 by the late Gérard Schmitter as Alsace Croisières and originally ran lunch and dinner cruises (river cruising proper started in 1982). Alsace Croisières became CroisiEurope in 1997, in order to reaffirm its commitment to Europe. The company, which is presently run by Gérard Schmitter's four offspring, has its headquarters in Strasbourg, France; other offices are in Lyon (France), Brussels (Belgium) and Ft Lauderdale (US). The fleet consists of more than three dozen riverships, most of which are owned, with a few chartered.

The company specialises in river cruising, mainly for French-speaking passengers, but now markets to more international passengers. Most of its riverships have the same layout, cabin sizes, features and facilities in two grades: 'Prestige' and 'Excellency' (equivalent to 'standard' and 'standard-plus'). Negatives include the deck lounge chairs, which are white plastic patio-style ones and not particularly elegant (stainless steel or aluminium ones are generally more comfortable and stable as well as smarter). The company also runs gastronomic theme cruises several times each year, including dinners ashore with notable French chefs. Excursions and gratuities are at extra cost.

Crystal River Cruises

A new entrant into river cruising, Crystal River Cruises is owned by well-known and respected parent company Crystal Cruises (founded originally in 1998 by NYK Line, but owned since 2015 by Genting Hong Kong), which operates two excel-

Avalon Artistry II interior.

lent mid-size ocean-going cruise ships and one boutique-size ship.

The new river cruse divison purchased the unusual, double-width, 1987-built Mozart, completely refitted it to Crystal River Cruises's upscale standards and renamed it Crystal Mozart. The company also ordered four new riverships to start operating in 2017. These are: Crystal Bach, Crystal Mahler (each accommodates 110 passengers; both are scheduled for the Danube, Main and Rhine rivers), Crystal Debussy, and Crystal Ravel (each accommodates 84 passengers; both are scheduled for the French rivers).

Emerald Waterways

This company, which debuted in 2014 with two brand new riverships, is a division of Scenic. It is a lower-priced alternative to its parent company (about 20 percent lower, but with fewer choices included), and is aimed at a younger audience, with excursions that are more active. The company's riverships each feature an indoor pool, which can be covered and converted into a cinema at night.

Grand Circle Cruise Line

Grand Circle Travel was founded in New York in 1958 by Ethel Andrus, a retired schoolteacher. She founded the American Association of Retired Persons (AARP – today an extremely large organisation for retirees and senior citizens) and served its members until 1982. Grand Circle Travel was purchased in 1985 by Alan Lewis, who moved the company to Boston. Its first privately owned rivership was River Symphony in 1998. The company was sold in 2007 to private equity firm Court Square Capital Travel.

THE VIKING 'LONGSHIPS'

Each of the many Viking 'Longships' is named after a Norse god. All the riverships in this series have been intelligently designed and have an identical number of cabins. However, some small modifications have been made to the decor and design as the series has progressed.

A solar panel-topped skylight sits above an uncluttered two-deck-high atrium lobby, and natural light floods in through floor-to-ceiling windows. The 'Longships' are full of natural light, which makes them feel wonderfully open. Between the two decks is a central glass-and-wood stairway. An elevator provides accessibility for mobility-limited passengers, except to the open Sun Deck.

The forward observation (main) lounge is both contemporary and comfortable, with a bar and bar stools in the back section and an indoor-outdoor Aquavit Terrace at the front. Two 24-hour self-help beverage stations are located at the entrance to the lounge. Although the lounge seating includes large armchairs and sofa seating, it unfortunately can't accommodate everyone at once (for talks, for example) when the vessel is full, and thick pillars make it feel cramped.

An indoor-outdoor 'Aquavit Terrace' occupies the front third of the lounge. The outdoor section has around 10 tables, with chairs for three or four.

Wooden railings adorn the exterior Sun Deck, together with fold-down canopies and chairs, shuffleboard court and herb garden, tended to by the chef.

Accommodation

Viking 'Longships' feature a patented off-centre hallway through the Upper and Middle Decks. The interior hallways are positioned off-centre. This arrangement allows for full balcony cabins on one side and narrower cabins (some as suites with separate sleeping and living areas) on the other. There's an ice machine in each hallway.

Aft are two large suites (with separate bedrooms), measuring approximately 41 sq m (445 sq ft). These each feature a wrap-around outdoor balcony and large wet room. Meanwhile, the double-sized suites have both a full and a French balcony.

There are 93 cabins in three categories, including 25 cabins without balconies. Intelligently designed and highly functional, the cabins have square-edged limewood cabinetry and soft-close drawers. A sliding glass door leads to a full or French balcony (windows only on the lowest deck – by regulation). Full-balcony cabins feature both a proper balcony (with two small mesh chairs and small drinks table), plus a French balcony.

The decor includes Nordic wood, earth tones and fabric-covered walls. The generously sized beds (200 x 160cm/79 x 63ins) are very comfortable, with room underneath to store luggage. Faux suede or silky headboards, excellent mattresses and chic white duvets complete the picture.

Facilities include flat-panel Sony TVs and infotainment systems, mini-fridges, hairdryers and ice buckets. Fresh fruit and bottled water are provided daily. There are 110v and 220v electrical sockets, light switches on both sides of the bed, as well as room dimmers – a lot of thought has gone into the lighting. Sliding-door cupboards have wooden hangers, plus there's a personal safe.

The bathrooms are tiled, have heated floors and mirrors, washbasins and generously proportioned glazed shower enclosures. Bathrobes are available on request, and towels are of a good size. Low-flush, environmentally friendly toilets mean that you may have to flush twice. The space for the toilet is very tight. L'Occitane products are provided.

Depending on the vessel, the sliding bathroom doors are either wood or frosted glass – the latter is a neat idea, but it's not particularly practical, because, when the bathroom light is switched on during the night, brightness floods into the cabin and can disturb anyone who is asleep. Aboard *Viking Freya* and *Viking Njord* the glass walls of the shower enclosures can be 'crystallised'.

Restaurant and food

The restaurant has floor-to-ceiling windows that let in abundant natural light and it's tastefully decorated. Many of the dining chairs do not have armrests, however.

The food is quite tasty, and there's a decent variety of dishes (typically three main courses). It's unfussy, simple fare rather than fancy cuisine, and it is not of a particularly high standard, especially the vegetarian food. Wines supplied during lunch and dinner are very young. Breakfast buffets are rather repetitive.

Alternatively, there's the Aquavit Terrace, an indoor-outdoor area, with retractable sliding glass doors and around nine tables outside. Breakfast and snacks/casual light lunches are available here, as is a fixed bistro-style set menu at dinner. Weather-permitting, eating outside here can be delightful.

Overall

Viking River Cruises appeals to its mainly North American and British clientele, to whom it caters extremely well. Even with the high density of 190 passengers, the 'Longships' don't feel crowded, except perhaps in the main lounge. The constant background music played – including on the open decks, hallways and in the restaurant – is irritating and unnecessary. Although port charges are included, gratuities are not; at time of printing, these were 'suggested' at €12 per person, per day.

Grand Circle Travel caters exclusively to North American retirees, with its own riverships in Europe under the Grand Circle Cruise Line brand. It also offers an extensive array of pre- and post-cruise optional stays and tours. The deck lounge chairs are inelegant white plastic ones, which spoil an otherwise decent product.

Lüftner Cruises

The Austrian family-owned company was founded over 30 years ago by Dr Wolfgang and Martina Lüftner (they are among the most respected pioneers of European river cruises). The company, based in Innsbruck, Austria, owns and operates its own fleet of modern riverships, many of which are chartered to other operators. The company organises cruises and provides high-quality food and elegant, restrained and tasteful interior decor combined with superior-quality furnishings and fabrics aboard its riverships. Drinks and gratuities are at extra cost.

Nicko Cruises

Based in Stuttgart, Germany, this company was founded in 1992 by Eckkehard Beller to market and operate river cruises with chartered riverships. It first started with cruises in Russia, but added ones on the Rhine in 2002. In 2005 it launched the first 'twin-cruise' rivership (*Flamenco*), with French balconies for each cabin. Switzerland-based financial investment company Capvik became a major investor in February 2013.

In 2015, however, Nicko Tours declared insolvency. The company, including its riverships, was purchased by Portuguese company Douro Azul. The brand continues to operate as before, under the Nicko Cruises name, principally for the German-speaking market. Premium-brand drinks, optional excursions and gratuities are available at extra cost.

Scenic

Founded in Newcastle, Australia, in 1986 by Glen Moroney, Scenic Tours began by operating coach tours throughout Australia. In 2008, the company began its European river cruise operations, marketing primarily to passengers from Australian and New Zealand. Growing rapidly, the company expanded by making its cruises available to British passengers. The company, which is still Australian owned, changed its name to Scenic in 2015. It now owns and operates several riverships in Europe, all of which feature 'butler'-style service.

The company provides very good information about the included excursions, and each passenger gets an excellent GPS-based 'Tailor-Made' information system, which includes self-guided city tours. Also provided in each cabin are Nordic walking sticks, umbrellas, good bedside reading lights, and under-bed space for storing luggage. The river

Passengers returning to Belvedere.

cruises are fully inclusive, including gratuities and all onboard drinks.

See also Emerald Waterways (see page 113), a sister company that operates river cruises at a lower price point, but without some of the included items of Scenic.

Tauck

Based in Connecticut, US, this company was founded in 1925 by Arthur Tauck as a tour packager and operator to take participants on life-enriching tours. The company charters its riverships from Swiss company Scylla but operate under the Tauck brand name. Tauck is known for its attention to its care of clients and provides more staff from the US (at least four per rivership) aboard its vessels than most other river cruise operators, to the benefit of its mainly North American clientele. On excursions, sightseers are split into three or four smaller groups, using the 'Quietvox' system (where you wear an earpiece into which information is conveyed) for guided tours. In 2017, Tauck plans to increase its family cruising capacity.

Travelmarvel River Cruises

A division of APT, this company has a small fleet of chartered riverships (but not from AMA Waterways) for 'all-inclusive' river cruising at reduced prices for its mainly youthful, active Australasian passengers. The cabins (particularly the bathrooms) are small. The food is quite decent, but you won't find much in the way of between-meal snacks, and any premium drinks cost extra, as do most excursions.

Uniworld Boutique River Cruises

Uniworld was founded by Yugoslavian travel entrepreneur Serba Ilich in 1976. The company started offering river cruises in Europe in 1994 and was one of the first companies to charter Russian riverships exclusively for American passengers.

Based in Encino, California, Uniworld has its own European river cruise line, Global River Cruises (which itself owns 75 percent of Holland River Line – established as a Swiss-owned company and based in Basel, Switzerland). While most of its riverships in Europe are nearly new, some features are a little basic – the plastic chairs on deck, for example. Also, dining room chairs typically have no armrests. The company's passengers are typically all English speakers.

In 2004 Uniworld was purchased by The Travel Corporation (founded by South Africa-born Stanley Tollman), the parent company of Trafalgar Tours, Contiki Tours and several others, including Red Carnation Hotels. Some of Uniworld's riverships are owned, while some are chartered from other owners.

Vantage Deluxe River Cruises

Vantage Deluxe World Travel was founded in 1983 by Gordon Lewis (river cruises started in 1999), whose son, Hank, is the present president (his brother Alan Lewis is president of Grand Circle Cruise Lines – a competitor – although some operational details are actually shared). The company headquarters are in Boston, US. The fleet presently consists of several owned and chartered riverships.

The company sells direct (via e-brochures) instead of marketing via travel agents. It caters exclusively to North Americans and specialises in trips for solo travellers. Dining is in an open-seating arrangement. Smoking is not allowed inside any of the riverships – only outside on the open decks.

Vantage provides self-serve buffet breakfasts and lunches, while dinner is served. Low-salt, low-fat, gluten-free and diabetic menu selections are available. However, the food is quite average, with little choice of main courses (entrées) for dinner and a limited choice of breads, pastry items and cheeses.

The deck lounge chairs are white plastic ones. Gratuities and drinks (except for a Captain's Dinner evening) are not included, but some excursions are.

Viking River Cruises

Viking River Cruises is perhaps the world's best-known river cruise company. It was founded by a Scandinavian and Dutch consortium and headed by Torstein Hagen (formerly connected with the long-defunct ocean-going Royal Viking Line) and Christer Salen (formerly of Salen Lindblad Cruising – the ocean-going expedition cruise company now called Quark Expeditions). The company has grown fast from small beginnings in 1997 when it chartered a single Russian rivership. The company then purchased Aqua Viva, a French operator, with two vessels.

In 2000, in a brilliant coup in European river cruising, Viking purchased KD River Cruises, Europe's oldest established rivership operator, with the landing stages (a valuable asset) included in the purchase. The UK's Travel Renaissance, founded in 1977 by Graham Clubb (for many years Viking's UK general sales agent) was purchased by Viking in 2005.

Some riverships cater exclusively to North Americans; others cater to European and international passengers. An ambitious new-build programme saw several new vessels constructed specifically for North American passengers and introduced in a period of just two years.

The company deservedly prides itself on the consistently high standard of its product, cuisine and service. Pluses include, aboard the newest riverships, smart, comfortable deck lounge chairs made of stainless steel or aluminium, and pocket-sized travel guides, with information on the route, for each passenger. Gratuities and most drinks cost extra.

How we evaluate the riverships

To help you differentiate between riverships, we have rated each one according to our quality criteria. This section explains the ratings and Berlitz star system.

Just as I have been evaluating and rating ocean-going cruise ships professionally since 1980, I have also been travelling extensively aboard Europe's riverships to construct an independent Berlitz rating system for the 300-plus vessels in service.

In our rating system each rivership is graded out of a total of 500 points across five areas: hardware/facilities, accommodation, cuisine, service/hospitality plus any 'other' components, with a maximum of 100 points in each category. In each area, the little things – the extra touches that improve the quality of the overall experience – mean the addition or deduction of points on the great scorecard.

The 500 points have then been divided into ranges, to create our independent Berlitz star ratings from 1 to 5. So any vessel awarded between 251 and 300 points is classed as a 3-star rivership; one gaining between 301 and 350 points is a 3-star plus rivership (I have quoted double categories for all except 5-star vessels to help differentiate within categories); and a rivership with a total of between 351 and 400 points is classed as 4-star, etc.

In creating criteria for evaluating riverships, the qualitative differences, conveniences and comfort factors, together with the operating and product delivery standards are taken into account. The resulting scoring system is fair and equitable for all, as in the Berlitz Cruising and Cruise Ships guide (in continuous publication for over 30 years).

Note that many riverships are of the same size and configuration. The subtle differences are in the onboard product, and, most notably, the food and service. It's all about the details (the size of wine glasses, towels and personal amenities, for example), staff training, service and presentation.

Scores also take into account nationality-specific factors, because some are dedicated to a single national market audience, such as Australia, Germany, North America, etc.

Ultimately, there really is no world's best river cruise line or river ship – despite what the brochures might claim (they are, after all, written by marketing departments), only the vessel and cruise that is right for you. Hopefully our ratings will go a long way towards helping you find your ideal match.

Note that sometimes, companies change vessels between different areas, for operational or other reasons. So, although we list the riverships and the rivers they sail on at the time of going to press, always check with the cruise company in case there has been a change.

CRITERIA

Hardware: This includes the general profile and condition of the vessel, its age, maintenance, decking material, pool and hot tub, deck furniture (such as deck lounge chairs – whether hardwood, stainless steel, or plastic, and are with or without cushioned pads). It also covers interior cleanliness – eg the public bathrooms, lift (elevator), floor and wall coverings, stairways, passageways and doorways.

The score also reflects the quality of the facilities, public rooms (including the main lounge, library and shop), ceiling height, pillars, lobby, stairways, hallways, lifts, wellness facilities, public restrooms, lighting, air conditioning and ventilation systems, floor coverings, decor and any artwork. It covers dining-room facilities including windows, chairs (with or without armrests), lighting and tableware including china, cutlery, linen and centrepieces (flowers).

Accommodation: For suites/superior grades, this includes the design and layout of all suites, balconies, lighting, beds/berths, furniture (placement,

Alongside *My Story*.

S.S. Antoinette bedroom.

and mattress quality), hanging space (including whether wooden or plastic hangers are provided), drawer space, bedside tables, vanity desks, lighting, mirrors, air conditioning and ventilation, artworks, soundproofing, soft furnishings, written information, tea- and coffee-making equipment, flowers, fruit, bathrobes and slippers (if any).

It reflects the bathroom facilities, notably the shower unit, washbasin, cabinets, storage for toiletries, and the size and quality of the towels.

NB: suites should not be designated as such, unless the bedroom is completely separate from the living area.

For standard cabins this includes the design and layout, furniture and fittings, clothes storage space, bedside tables, vanity unit, lighting, air conditioning and ventilation, artwork, insulation and noise levels. It also covers soft furnishings and details such as the in-cabin information folder (list of services), flowers, fruit, slippers (if any), towels and bed linen, plus bathroom facilities, notably the shower unit, washbasin, cabinets, storage for toiletries and the towels.

Note that balconies can be described as 'full' (a full balcony, just wide enough to sit down) or 'French' (floor-to-ceiling glass doors opening on to railings, with just room enough to stick your toes out). Some vessels have both. Others have windows only, which may or may not open. Cabins on the lowest deck almost always have 'panoramic' windows instead (because they are too close to the water line).

Cuisine: The score covers the restaurant, informal dining/buffets, the ingredients used and tea/coffee/bar snacks. Under 'restaurant' we have included menus (variety and presentation), culinary creativity, the appeal, taste, texture, freshness, colour and balance of the food, plus garnishes, fresh fruit and wine list and wine prices.

Informal dining/buffets covers the hardware (eg hot and cold display units, sneeze guards, tongs and other serving utensils) plus presentation, food tem-

peratures and food labelling, the quality and consistency of the ingredients, plus portion size.

Tea/coffee/bar snacks covers the quality and variety of tea and coffee provided. This includes afternoon tea, cakes and sandwiches, whether mugs or cups and saucers are provided, whether cream and milk is provided, and bar snacks.

Service: In the restaurant this includes the staff (serving, taking from the correct side, etc), wine waiters, communication skills, approach, uniform and finesse.

In bars and lounges, this covers the ambience, communication skills (between bartenders, service staff and passengers), attitude, personality, flair and finesse, plus the glasses used.

With relation to cabins, it includes housekeeping, cleanliness, in-cabin food service (if there is any), linen and bathrobe changes, and communication skills.

Miscellaneous: This category embraces a range of elements that do not easily fall into the ones above. It includes such miscellaneous areas as the accuracy of the information in the brochure/cruise provider's website, any information on the itinerary and on destinations visited en route, airport/train station transfers and the standard of any excursions. It also covers lecturers, any entertainment provided and in-cabin infotainment systems.

THE STAR RATINGS

Points are then converted into star ratings, as follows:

★★★★★ = 451–500 points
★★★★+ = 401–450 points
★★★★ = 351–400 points
★★★+ = 301–350 points
★★★ = 251–300 points
★★+ = 201–250 points
★★ = 151–200 points
★+ = 101–150 points
★ = 1–100 points

The five star categories are broken down below. Note that riverships that have a plus sign (+) next to their rating are a little better than the number of stars awarded.

5 Stars (★★★★★)

The vessel must have finely appointed, excellently designed interiors and be spotlessly maintained. As for accommodation, suites (minimum size expected 25 sq m/270 sq ft) and large cabins (minimum 16 sq m/172 sq ft) should have the highest-quality fittings and furnishings. A choice of bed linen and pillows (regular goose down pillows or the non-allergenic type) should be provided, as should bathrobes for all passengers, plus high-quality personal toiletries. The cuisine must be the best dining available in a rivership, with at least three choices of main courses for dinner, plus pasta dishes for lunch. A full sit-down service must be provided by staff schooled in the art of service and hospitality. All extras on a rivership of this kind (lectures, entertainment, audiovisual equipment, etc) would be expected to be of an extremely high standard. This is as good as it gets for a rivership.

4 Stars (★★★★)

To reach this level, a vessel must have well-appointed, well-fitted interiors and be well maintained. In terms of accommodation, suites (minimum size expected 22 sq m/236 sq ft) and cabins (minimum 14 sq m/150 sq ft) must have practical, high-quality fittings. A very good dining experience must be provided, and there must be at least three choices of main course (entrée) for dinner. Vegetarian options must also be available. A full, sit-down service must be provided by staff with professional food and drink service skills. Any components sitting within our 'other' category should be of a high standard.

3 Stars (★★★)

The vessel must have nicely appointed interiors, although the style, finish or layout will be less elegant, refined or sophisticated than on higher-rated riverships. The level of cleanliness must be of a standard well above basic. As for accommodation, suites (minimum size expected 20 sq m/215 sq ft) and cabins (minimum 11 sq m/118 sq ft) must be of a good standard and very comfortable. Under cuisine, there will be a choice of main courses for dinner, and vegetarian options should be available for all meals. Ser-

vice should be provided by staff with a good knowledge of serving food and drinks professionally. Any components relating to our 'other' category should be well above the minimum required.

2 Stars (★★)

The vessel must have interiors that are decent, although they may well be made from average-quality materials (more basic than those of a higher star rating). Overall levels of cleanliness will be above basic. Suites (minimum size expected 18 sq m/193 sq ft) and cabins will be practical (minimum size 9 sq m/96 sq ft) but less luxurious and well equipped than higher-rated vessels. In terms of cuisine, there will typically be little or no choice. Breakfast and lunch will be self-service buffet-style meals. Waiters and waitresses will provide an acceptable level of service, with training a weak point. Miscellaneous items covered under our 'other' category may be acceptable, although not sparkling.

1 Star (★)

At this level, the hardware will include extremely utilitarian interiors that could do with improvement. The accommodation will typically be tiny and simply equipped, and with poor soundproofing. The cuisine will be at the most basic end of the scale, with little choice and lower-quality produce used. As for service, the staff is unlikely to have been trained in its art. Miscellaneous 'other' items may well be at the most basic level.

Queen Isabel restaurant.

ALEMANNIA ★★★+

A RIVERSHIP FOR THE DESTINATIONS, NOT THE ACCOMMODATION OR FOOD.

Operator ....Crucemundo River Cruises	**Passenger beds**.. 184
Built 1971	**Sit outside (real) balcony** .... No
Registry .... Switzerland	**French (open-air) balcony** .... No
Identification number ....ENI 07001703	**Approximate cabin size (sq m)** 12–24
Length (m) 110.0	**Lift (elevator)**.. Yes
Number of decks (excluding sun deck)......3	**Rivers sailed**.. Rhine

BERLITZ'S RATINGS		
	Possible	Achieved
Hardware	100	46
Accommodation	100	41
Cuisine	100	51
Service	100	48
Miscellaneous	100	50
OVERALL SCORE 236 points out of 500		

ALINA ★★★★

CHOOSE THIS STYLISH RIVERSHIP FOR A HIGH-QUALITY CRUISE EXPERIENCE.

Operator .... Phoenix Cruises	**Passenger beds**..216
Built 2011	**Sit outside (real) balcony** .... No
Registry .... Switzerland	**French (open-air) balcony** .... Yes
Identification number ....ENI 07001934	**Approximate cabin size (sq m)** 14–16
Length (m) 135.0	**Lift (elevator)**.. No
Number of decks (excluding sun deck)......3	**Rivers sailed**............... Danube, Rhine, Main

BERLITZ'S RATINGS		
	Possible	Achieved
Hardware	100	78
Accommodation	100	77
Cuisine	100	80
Service	100	75
Miscellaneous	100	78
OVERALL SCORE 388 points out of 500		

ALLEGRA I ★★★+
THIS SMART-LOOKING VESSEL PROVIDES A GOOD-VALUE EXPERIENCE.

Operator .... Phoenix Cruises	**Passenger beds**.. 178
Built 2011	**Sit outside (real) balcony** .... No
Registry ....Malta	**French (open-air) balcony** .... Yes
Identification number ....ENI 04809190	**Approximate cabin size (sq m)** 12–15
Length (m) 135.0	**Lift (elevator)**... No
Number of decks (excluding sun deck)......3	**Rivers sailed**................ Rhine, Main, Danube

BERLITZ'S RATINGS

	Possible	Achieved
Hardware	100	76
Accommodation	100	68
Cuisine	100	71
Service	100	64
Miscellaneous	100	74

OVERALL SCORE 353 points out of 500

ALLEGRO ★★★
A RIVERSHIP FOR A BASIC, BUT ACCEPTABLE, NO-FRILLS RIVER CRUISE.

Operator .... Kras Reizen	**Passenger beds**.. 150
Built 1990	**Sit outside (real) balcony** .... No
Registry .... Netherlands	**French (open-air) balcony** .... No
Identification number ....ENI 02326758	**Approximate cabin size (sq m)** 10–12
Length (m) 105.0	**Lift (elevator)**.. Yes
Number of decks (excluding sun deck)......2	**Rivers sailed**.. Rhine

BERLITZ'S RATINGS

	Possible	Achieved
Hardware	100	52
Accommodation	100	44
Cuisine	100	54
Service	100	52
Miscellaneous	100	60

OVERALL SCORE 262 points out of 500

AMABELLA ★★★★+

A TIP-TOP CONTEMPORARY RIVERSHIP KNOWN FOR ITS HIGH-QUALITY CUISINE.

Operator ....AMA Waterways	**Passenger beds**.......................................161
Built 2010	**Sit outside (real) balcony**......................... No
Registry .... Switzerland	**French (open-air) balcony** .... Yes
Identification number ....ENI 02332082	**Approximate cabin size (sq m)** 13–32.5
Length (m) 135	**Lift (elevator)**... Yes
Number of decks (excluding sun deck)......3	**Rivers sailed**............... Danube, Main, Rhine

BERLITZ'S RATINGS		
	Possible	Achieved
Hardware	100	80
Accommodation	100	83
Cuisine	100	85
Service	100	80
Miscellaneous	100	85
OVERALL SCORE 413 points out of 500		

AMACELLO ★★★★+

HIGH STANDARDS AND OUTSTANDING CUISINE ABOARD THIS EXCELLENT RIVERSHIP.

Operator ....AMA Waterways	**Passenger beds**.......................................150
Built 2008	**Sit outside (real) balcony**......................... No
Registry .... Switzerland	**French (open-air) balcony** .... Yes
Identification number ....ENI 07001862	**Approximate cabin size (sq m)** 13–23.5
Length (m) 110.0	**Lift (elevator)**... Yes
Number of decks (excluding sun deck)......3	**Rivers sailed**........................... Rhône, Saône

BERLITZ'S RATINGS		
	Possible	Achieved
Hardware	100	76
Accommodation	100	83
Cuisine	100	85
Service	100	79
Miscellaneous	100	84
OVERALL SCORE 407 points out of 500		

AMACERTO ★★★★+

THIS SUPERB CONTEMPORARY RIVERSHIP IS PRAISED FOR ITS HIGH-QUALITY CUISINE.

Operator ....AMA Waterways	**Passenger beds**...164
Built 2012	**Sit outside (real) balcony**.......................... No
Registry .... Switzerland	**French (open-air) balcony** .... Yes
Identification number ....ENI 07001949	**Approximate cabin size (sq m)** 15–32.5
Length (m) 135.0	**Lift (elevator)**... Yes
Number of decks (excluding sun deck)......3	**Rivers sailed**............... Danube, Main, Rhine

BERLITZ'S RATINGS		
	Possible	Achieved
Hardware	100	81
Accommodation	100	83
Cuisine	100	85
Service	100	80
Miscellaneous	100	85
OVERALL SCORE 414 points out of 500		

AMADANTE ★★★★+

THIS VERY COMFORTABLE RIVERSHIP DELIVERS A HIGH STANDARD AND EXCELLENT CUISINE.

Operator ....AMA Waterways	**Passenger beds**...150
Built 2008	**Sit outside (real) balcony**.......................... No
Registry .... Switzerland	**French (open-air) balcony** .... Yes
Identification number ....ENI 07001864	**Approximate cabin size (sq m)** 13–23.5
Length (m) 110.0	**Lift (elevator)**... Yes
Number of decks (excluding sun deck)......3	**Rivers sailed**............... Danube, Main, Rhine

BERLITZ'S RATINGS		
	Possible	Achieved
Hardware	100	78
Accommodation	100	83
Cuisine	100	85
Service	100	81
Miscellaneous	100	85
OVERALL SCORE 412 points out of 500		

AMADESSA NYR
CHOOSE THIS CHIC VESSEL FOR A TOP-NOTCH RIVER CRUISE.

Operator ....AMA Waterways	Passenger beds..164
Built 2016	Sit outside (real) balcony......................... Yes
Registry .... Switzerland	French (open-air) balcony .... Yes
Identification number ....N/A	Approximate cabin size (sq m) 15–32.5
Length (m) 135.0	Lift (elevator)... Yes
Number of decks (excluding sun deck)......3	Rivers sailed..N/A

NEW RIVERSHIP

BERLITZ'S RATINGS		
	Possible	Achieved
Hardware	100	NYR
Accommodation	100	NYR
Cuisine	100	NYR
Service	100	NYR
Miscellaneous	100	NYR
OVERALL SCORE NYR points out of 500		

AMADOLCE ★★★★+
A RIVERSHIP PRAISED FOR ITS OUTSTANDING CUISINE AND HIGH STANDARDS.

Operator ....AMA Waterways	Passenger beds..150
Built 2009	Sit outside (real) balcony......................... Yes
Registry .... Switzerland	French (open-air) balcony .... Yes
Identification number ....ENI 07001909	Approximate cabin size (sq m) 13–23.5
Length (m) 110.0	Lift (elevator)... Yes
Number of decks (excluding sun deck)......3	Rivers sailed.......................Bordeaux region

BERLITZ'S RATINGS		
	Possible	Achieved
Hardware	100	80
Accommodation	100	82
Cuisine	100	84
Service	100	80
Miscellaneous	100	85
OVERALL SCORE 411 points out of 500		

AMALYRA ★★★★+
OUTSTANDING CUISINE AND GOOD SERVICE ON A CONTEMPORARY RIVERSHIP.

Operator ....AMA Waterways		
Built 2009		
Registry .... Switzerland		
Identification number ....ENI 07001908		
Length (m) 110.0		
Number of decks (excluding sun deck)......3		

Passenger beds... 150	
Sit outside (real) balcony .... No	
French (open-air) balcony .... Yes	
Approximate cabin size (sq m) 13–23.5	
Lift (elevator)... Yes	
Rivers sailed................ Rhine, Main, Danube	

BERLITZ'S RATINGS

	Possible	Achieved
Hardware	100	80
Accommodation	100	82
Cuisine	100	85
Service	100	81
Miscellaneous	100	85
OVERALL SCORE 413 points out of 500		

AMAPRIMA ★★★★+
OUTSTANDING CUISINE AND HIGH STANDARDS CHARACTERISE THIS COMFORTABLE RIVERSHIP.

Operator ....AMA Waterways		
Built 2013		
Registry .... Switzerland		
Identification number ....ENI 07001958		
Length (m) 135.0		
Number of decks (excluding sun deck)......3		

Passenger beds... 164	
Sit outside (real) balcony .... No	
French (open-air) balcony .... Yes	
Approximate cabin size (sq m) 15–32.5	
Lift (elevator)... Yes	
Rivers sailed................ Rhine, Main, Danube	

BERLITZ'S RATINGS

	Possible	Achieved
Hardware	100	85
Accommodation	100	83
Cuisine	100	86
Service	100	83
Miscellaneous	100	86
OVERALL SCORE 423 points out of 500		

AMAREINA ★★★★+

AN ABSOLUTELY FIRST-CLASS RIVERSHIP OFFERING FINE FOOD AND SERVICE.

Operator ....AMA Waterways	**Passenger beds**.. 164
Built 2014	**Sit outside (real) balcony**......................... No
Registry .... Switzerland	**French (open-air) balcony** .... Yes
Identification number ....ENI 02336818	**Approximate cabin size (sq m)** 15–32.5
Length (m) 135.0	**Lift (elevator)**... Yes
Number of decks (excluding sun deck)......3	**Rivers sailed**.. Rhine

BERLITZ'S RATINGS		
	Possible	Achieved
Hardware	100	85
Accommodation	100	83
Cuisine	100	86
Service	100	83
Miscellaneous	100	86
OVERALL SCORE 423 points out of 500		

AMASERENA ★★★★+

THIS VESSEL HAS REAL BALCONIES AND EXCELLENT FOOD AND SERVICE.

Operator ....AMA Waterways	**Passenger beds**.. 164
Built 2015	**Sit outside (real) balcony**......................... No
Registry .... Switzerland	**French (open-air) balcony** .... Yes
Identification number .... MMSI 269057524	**Approximate cabin size (sq m)** 15–32.5
Length (m) 135.0	**Lift (elevator)**... Yes
Number of decks (excluding sun deck)......3	**Rivers sailed**................ Rhine, Main, Danube

BERLITZ'S RATINGS		
	Possible	Achieved
Hardware	100	85
Accommodation	100	83
Cuisine	100	86
Service	100	83
Miscellaneous	100	86
OVERALL SCORE 423 points out of 500		

AMASONATA ★★★★+

EXCELLENT CUISINE AND GOOD SERVICE IN A STYLISH, CONTEMPORARY RIVERSHIP.

Operator ....AMA Waterways	**Passenger beds**..164
Built 2014	**Sit outside (real) balcony** ....No
Registry .... Switzerland	**French (open-air) balcony** ....Yes
Identification number ....ENI 07001981	**Approximate cabin size (sq m)** 15–32.5
Length (m) 135.0	**Lift (elevator)**.......................................Yes
Number of decks (excluding sun deck)......3	**Rivers sailed**................................... Danube

BERLITZ'S RATINGS		
	Possible	Achieved
Hardware	100	85
Accommodation	100	83
Cuisine	100	86
Service	100	82
Miscellaneous	100	86
OVERALL SCORE 422 points out of 500		

AMASTELLA NYR

A FAMILY-FRIENDLY RIVERSHIP WITH STYLE AND REALLY FINE CUISINE.

Operator ....AMA Waterways	**Passenger beds**..158
Built 2016	**Sit outside (real) balcony** ....Yes
Registry .... Switzerland	**French (open-air) balcony** ....Yes
Identification number ....N/A	**Approximate cabin size (sq m)** 15–32.5
Length (m) 135.0	**Lift (elevator)**.......................................Yes
Number of decks (excluding sun deck)......3	**Rivers sailed**............... Rhine, Main, Danube

NEW RIVERSHIP

BERLITZ'S RATINGS		
	Possible	Achieved
Hardware	100	NYR
Accommodation	100	NYR
Cuisine	100	NYR
Service	100	NYR
Miscellaneous	100	NYR
OVERALL SCORE NYR points out of 500		

AMAVENITA ★★★★+
THIS RIVERSHIP IS AN EXCELLENT CHOICE FOR AUSTRALASIANS.

Operator ....APT Touring	**Passenger beds**...164
Built 2016	**Sit outside (real) balcony**.........................Yes
Registry .... Switzerland	**French (open-air) balcony** ....Yes
Identification number .... MMSI 269057515	**Approximate cabin size (sq m)** 15–32.5
Length (m) 135.0	**Lift (elevator)**..Yes
Number of decks (excluding sun deck)......3	**Rivers sailed**...............Rhine, Main, Danube

BERLITZ'S RATINGS

	Possible	Achieved
Hardware	100	85
Accommodation	100	83
Cuisine	100	85
Service	100	82
Miscellaneous	100	84

OVERALL SCORE 419 points out of 500

AMAVERDE ★★★★+
THIS EXCELLENT CONTEMPORARY RIVERSHIP IS KNOWN FOR ITS HIGH-QUALITY CUISINE.

Operator ....APT Touring	**Passenger beds**...161
Built 2011	**Sit outside (real) balcony**.........................Yes
Registry .... Switzerland	**French (open-air) balcony** ....Yes
Identification number ....ENI 07001725	**Approximate cabin size (sq m)** 13–32.5
Length (m) 135.0	**Lift (elevator)**..Yes
Number of decks (excluding sun deck)......3	**Rivers sailed**...................................... Danube

BERLITZ'S RATINGS

	Possible	Achieved
Hardware	100	84
Accommodation	100	82
Cuisine	100	86
Service	100	82
Miscellaneous	100	86

OVERALL SCORE 420 points out of 500

AMAVIDA ★★★★+

A RIVERSHIP HIGHLY PRAISED FOR ITS FINE REGIONAL CUISINE AND TOP STANDARDS.

Operator ....AMA Waterways	**Passenger beds**....................................... 106
Built 2013	**Sit outside (real) balcony** .... No
Registry ....Portugal	**French (open-air) balcony** .... Yes
Identification number ....N/A	**Approximate cabin size (sq m)** 15–30.0
Length (m) 79.5	**Lift (elevator)**... Yes
Number of decks (excluding sun deck)......3	**Rivers sailed**.......................................Douro

BERLITZ'S RATINGS		
	Possible	Achieved
Hardware	100	85
Accommodation	100	83
Cuisine	100	86
Service	100	81
Miscellaneous	100	86
OVERALL SCORE 421 points out of 500		

AMAVIOLA ᴺʸᴿ

STYLISHLY DESIGNED FOR FAMILIES, THIS RIVERSHIP HAS IT ALL.

Operator ....AMA Waterways	**Passenger beds**....................................... 158
Built 2016	**Sit outside (real) balcony** .... Yes
Registry .... Switzerland	**French (open-air) balcony** .... Yes
Identification number ....N/A	**Approximate cabin size (sq m)** 15–33.0
Length (m) 135.0	**Lift (elevator)**... Yes
Number of decks (excluding sun deck)......3	**Rivers sailed**...............Rhine, Main, Danube

NEW RIVERSHIP

BERLITZ'S RATINGS		
	Possible	Achieved
Hardware	100	NYR
Accommodation	100	NYR
Cuisine	100	NYR
Service	100	NYR
Miscellaneous	100	NYR
OVERALL SCORE NYR points out of 500		

AMADEUS BRILLIANT ★★★★
A GOOD CHOICE FOR A FIRST-RATE CRUISE IN COMFORTABLE SURROUNDINGS.

Operator .... Luftner Cruises	**Passenger beds**....................................... 150
Built 2011	**Sit outside (real) balcony**......................... No
Registry .... Germany	**French (open-air) balcony** .... Yes
Identification number ....ENI 04809350	**Approximate cabin size (sq m)** 10–22.0
Length (m) 110.0	**Lift (elevator)**.. Yes
Number of decks (excluding sun deck) 3	**Rivers sailed**............... Danube, Rhine, Main

BERLITZ'S RATINGS

	Possible	Achieved
Hardware	100	79
Accommodation	100	78
Cuisine	100	74
Service	100	74
Miscellaneous	100	76
OVERALL SCORE 381 points out of 500		

AMADEUS CLASSIC ★★★★
A GOOD-LOOKING RIVERSHIP BUT DATED WHEN COMPARED TO NEWER VESSELS.

Operator .... Luftner Cruises	**Passenger beds**....................................... 146
Built 2001	**Sit outside (real) balcony**......................... No
Registry .... Germany	**French (open-air) balcony** .... Yes
Identification number ....ENI 04801620	**Approximate cabin size (sq m)** 15–22.0
Length (m) 110.0	**Lift (elevator)**... No
Number of decks (excluding sun deck) 3	**Rivers sailed**............... Danube, Rhine, Main

BERLITZ'S RATINGS

	Possible	Achieved
Hardware	100	73
Accommodation	100	73
Cuisine	100	72
Service	100	72
Miscellaneous	100	76
OVERALL SCORE 366 points out of 500		

AMADEUS DIAMOND ★★★★
THIS FIRST-CLASS RIVERSHIP COMBINES STYLE WITH GOOD FOOD AND HOSPITALITY.

Operator .... Luftner Cruises	**Passenger beds**.. 146
Built 2009	**Sit outside (real) balcony** .... No
Registry .... Germany	**French (open-air) balcony** .... Yes
Identification number ....ENI 04807380	**Approximate cabin size (sq m)** 10–22.0
Length (m) 110.0	**Lift (elevator)**... No
Number of decks (excluding sun deck)......3	**Rivers sailed**..Seine

BERLITZ'S RATINGS		
	Possible	Achieved
Hardware	100	78
Accommodation	100	77
Cuisine	100	81
Service	100	78
Miscellaneous	100	81
OVERALL SCORE 395 points out of 500		

AMADEUS ELEGANT ★★★★
A FINE-LOOKING RIVERSHIP WITH EXCELLENT ITINERARIES, FOOD AND WINE.

Operator .... Luftner Cruises	**Passenger beds**.. 150
Built 2010	**Sit outside (real) balcony** .... No
Registry .... Germany	**French (open-air) balcony** .... Yes
Identification number ....ENI 04808350	**Approximate cabin size (sq m)** 10–22.0
Length (m) 110.0	**Lift (elevator)**.. Yes
Number of decks (excluding sun deck)......3	**Rivers sailed**...............Danube, Rhine, Main

BERLITZ'S RATINGS		
	Possible	Achieved
Hardware	100	79
Accommodation	100	77
Cuisine	100	81
Service	100	79
Miscellaneous	100	81
OVERALL SCORE 397 points out of 500		

AMADEUS PRINCESS ★★★★
THIS RIVERSHIP HAS ELEGANT DECOR AND PROVIDES A DECENT STANDARD.

Operator .... Luftner Cruises	Passenger beds......................... 160
Built 2006	Sit outside (real) balcony .... No
Registry .... Germany	French (open-air) balcony .... Yes
Identification number ....ENI 04804710	Approximate cabin size (sq m) 15–22.0
Length (m) 110.0	Lift (elevator)................................... Yes
Number of decks (excluding sun deck)......3	Rivers sailed............... Danube, Rhine, Main

BERLITZ'S RATINGS

	Possible	Achieved
Hardware	100	74
Accommodation	100	73
Cuisine	100	74
Service	100	75
Miscellaneous	100	76

OVERALL SCORE 372 points out of 500

AMADEUS ROYAL ★★★★
CHOOSE THIS RIVERSHIP FOR A VERY COMFORTABLE, WELL-ROUNDED CRUISE.

Operator .... Luftner Cruises	Passenger beds......................... 144
Built 2005	Sit outside (real) balcony .... No
Registry .... Germany	French (open-air) balcony .... Yes
Identification number ....ENI 04803670	Approximate cabin size (sq m) 15–24.0
Length (m) 110.0	Lift (elevator)................................... Yes
Number of decks (excluding sun deck)......3	Rivers sailed.......................... Rhône, Saône

BERLITZ'S RATINGS

	Possible	Achieved
Hardware	100	77
Accommodation	100	75
Cuisine	100	73
Service	100	73
Miscellaneous	100	80

OVERALL SCORE 378 points out of 500

AMADEUS SILVER ★★★★
THIS EXTREMELY COMFORTABLE RIVERSHIP DELIVERS A FIRST-CLASS RIVER CRUISE.

Operator	Luftner Cruises	**Passenger beds**	180
Built	2013	**Sit outside (real) balcony**	No
Registry	Netherlands	**French (open-air) balcony**	Yes
Identification number	ENI 02335475	**Approximate cabin size (sq m)**	16–24.0
Length (m)	135.0	**Lift (elevator)**	No
Number of decks (excluding sun deck)	3	**Rivers sailed**	Rhine, Main, Danube

BERLITZ'S RATINGS		
	Possible	Achieved
Hardware	100	81
Accommodation	100	81
Cuisine	100	75
Service	100	75
Miscellaneous	100	82
OVERALL SCORE 394 points out of 500		

AMADEUS SILVER II ᴺʸᴿ
THIS IS A GOOD CHOICE FOR A STYLISH, FIRST-RATE RIVER CRUISE.

Operator	Luftner Cruises	**Passenger beds**	168
Built	2015	**Sit outside (real) balcony**	No
Registry	Germany	**French (open-air) balcony**	Yes
Identification number	MMSI 211682330	**Approximate cabin size (sq m)**	17.5–26.5
Length (m)	135.0	**Lift (elevator)**	Yes
Number of decks (excluding sun deck)	3	**Rivers sailed**	Rhine, Main, Danube

BERLITZ'S RATINGS		
	Possible	Achieved
Hardware	100	NYR
Accommodation	100	NYR
Cuisine	100	NYR
Service	100	NYR
Miscellaneous	100	NYR
OVERALL SCORE NYR points out of 500		

AMADEUS SILVER III ^{NYR}
AN EXCELLENT CHOICE FOR A STYLISH, WELL-ORCHESTRATED CRUISE.

Operator .... Luftner Cruises	**Passenger beds** 168
Built 2016	**Sit outside (real) balcony** .... No
Registry .... Germany	**French (open-air) balcony** .... Yes
Identification number ....N/A	**Approximate cabin size (sq m)** 17.5–26.5
Length (m) 135.0	**Lift (elevator)** .... Yes
Number of decks (excluding sun deck) 3	**Rivers sailed** .... Rhine, Main, Danube

NEW RIVERSHIP

BERLITZ'S RATINGS

	Possible	Achieved
Hardware	100	NYR
Accommodation	100	NYR
Cuisine	100	NYR
Service	100	NYR
Miscellaneous	100	NYR

OVERALL SCORE NYR points out of 500

AMADEUS SYMPHONY ★★★★
A FIRST-CLASS RIVERSHIP COMBINING STYLE, GREAT FOOD AND GOOD HOSPITALITY.

Operator .... Luftner Cruises	**Passenger beds** 146
Built 2003	**Sit outside (real) balcony** .... No
Registry .... Germany	**French (open-air) balcony** .... Yes
Identification number .... ENI 04802330	**Approximate cabin size (sq m)** 15–22.0
Length (m) 110.0	**Lift (elevator)** .... No
Number of decks (excluding sun deck) 3	**Rivers sailed** .... Rhône, Saône

BERLITZ'S RATINGS

	Possible	Achieved
Hardware	100	74
Accommodation	100	73
Cuisine	100	74
Service	100	76
Miscellaneous	100	74

OVERALL SCORE 371 points out of 500

AMELIA ★★★★

THIS RIVERSHIP PROVIDES GOOD FOOD AND SERVICE IN A CONTEMPORARY SETTING.

Operator .... Phoenix Cruises	**Passenger beds** 216
Built 2012	**Sit outside (real) balcony** .... No
Registry .... Malta	**French (open-air) balcony** .... Yes
Identification number .... ENI 07001948	**Approximate cabin size (sq m)** 14–16.0
Length (m) 135.0	**Lift (elevator)** .... Yes
Number of decks (excluding sun deck) 3	**Rivers sailed** .... Danube, Rhine, Main

BERLITZ'S RATINGS		
	Possible	Achieved
Hardware	100	79
Accommodation	100	78
Cuisine	100	80
Service	100	76
Miscellaneous	100	76
OVERALL SCORE 389 points out of 500		

AMSTERDAM ★★

A VINTAGE RIVERSHIP OFFERING A BASIC, NO-FRILLS, BUDGET CRUISE.

Operator .... Feenstra Rhine Line	**Passenger beds** 100
Built 1948	**Sit outside (real) balcony** .... No
Registry .... Netherlands	**French (open-air) balcony** .... No
Identification number .... ENI 02325952	**Approximate cabin size (sq m)** 6
Length (m) 78.0	**Lift (elevator)** .... No
Number of decks (excluding sun deck) 2	**Rivers sailed** .... Rhine

BERLITZ'S RATINGS		
	Possible	Achieved
Hardware	100	33
Accommodation	100	32
Cuisine	100	40
Service	100	42
Miscellaneous	100	41
OVERALL SCORE 188 points out of 500		

ANDANTE ★★

THIS RIVERSHIP WILL PROVIDE YOU WITH A BASIC NO-FRILLS RIVER CRUISE.

Operator .... Kras Reizen	Passenger beds.. 92
Built 1959	Sit outside (real) balcony......................... No
Registry .... Netherlands	French (open-air) balcony .... No
Identification number ....ENI 02325292	Approximate cabin size (sq m) 9
Length (m) 74.4	Lift (elevator)... No
Number of decks (excluding sun deck)...... 2	Rivers sailed....................................... Rhine

BERLITZ'S RATINGS

	Possible	Achieved
Hardware	100	35
Accommodation	100	33
Cuisine	100	40
Service	100	41
Miscellaneous	100	41

OVERALL SCORE 190 points out of 500

ANESHA ᴺʸᴿ

CHOOSE THIS HANDSOME RIVERSHIP FOR A DELIGHTFUL CRUISE EXPERIENCE.

Operator .... Phoenix Cruises	Passenger beds...................................... 180
Built .... Yes	Sit outside (real) balcony......................... No
Registry .... Switzerland	French (open-air) balcony .... Yes
Identification number .... MMSI 269057529	Approximate cabin size (sq m) 17–18.5
Length (m) 135	Lift (elevator)... Yes
Number of decks (excluding sun deck)...... 3	Rivers sailed............... Rhine, Danube, Main

BERLITZ'S RATINGS

	Possible	Achieved
Hardware	100	NYR
Accommodation	100	NYR
Cuisine	100	NYR
Service	100	NYR
Miscellaneous	100	NYR

OVERALL SCORE NYR points out of 500

ANTONIO BELLUCCI ★★★+

A SMART, CONTEMPORARY VESSEL THAT DELIVERS A GOOD ALL-ROUND CRUISE EXPERIENCE.

Operator ....Feenstra Rhine Line	**Passenger beds**..140
Built 2012	**Sit outside (real) balcony**.........................No
Registry .... Switzerland	**French (open-air) balcony** ....Yes
Identification number ....ENI 02334599	**Approximate cabin size (sq m)** 13–32.0
Length (m) 110.0	**Lift (elevator)**...Yes
Number of decks (excluding sun deck)......3	**Rivers sailed**...............Rhine, Main, Danube

BERLITZ'S RATINGS

	Possible	Achieved
Hardware	100	77
Accommodation	100	71
Cuisine	100	63
Service	100	64
Miscellaneous	100	73
OVERALL SCORE 348 points out of 500		

ARIANA ★★★+

THIS MODERN RIVERSHIP PROVIDES A MODEST BUT GOOD-VALUE CRUISE EXPERIENCE.

Operator .... Phoenix Cruises	**Passenger beds**..162
Built 2012	**Sit outside (real) balcony**.........................No
Registry ....Bulgaria	**French (open-air) balcony** ....Yes
Identification number ....ENI 02334084	**Approximate cabin size (sq m)** 12–14
Length (m) 110.0	**Lift (elevator)**...Yes
Number of decks (excluding sun deck)......3	**Rivers sailed**....................................Danube

BERLITZ'S RATINGS

	Possible	Achieved
Hardware	100	77
Accommodation	100	72
Cuisine	100	63
Service	100	64
Miscellaneous	100	72
OVERALL SCORE 348 points out of 500		

ARLENE ★★★
CHOOSE THIS SMALL, DATED VESSEL FOR A LOW-BUDGET, NO-FRILLS CRUISE.

Operator ....Feenstra Rhine Line	**Passenger beds**..........................106
Built 1986	**Sit outside (real) balcony**.........................No
Registry .... Netherlands	**French (open-air) balcony** ....No
Identification number ....ENI 02326752	**Approximate cabin size (sq m)** 8–10.0
Length (m) 91.2	**Lift (elevator)**................................No
Number of decks (excluding sun deck)......2	**Rivers sailed**.................................... Rhine

BERLITZ'S RATINGS		
	Possible	Achieved
Hardware	100	54
Accommodation	100	52
Cuisine	100	51
Service	100	59
Miscellaneous	100	60
OVERALL SCORE 276 points out of 500		

A-ROSA AQUA ★★★+
MODERN HOTEL-STYLE RIVERSHIP WITH EXCELLENT FEATURES FOR A GOOD CRUISE.

Operator ....A-ROSA River Cruises	**Passenger beds**..........................198
Built 2009	**Sit outside (real) balcony**.........................No
Registry ....Germany	**French (open-air) balcony** ....Yes
Identification number ....ENI 04807500	**Approximate cabin size (sq m)** 14.5
Length (m) 135.0	**Lift (elevator)**................................No
Number of decks (excluding sun deck)......3	**Rivers sailed**.................................... Rhine

BERLITZ'S RATINGS		
	Possible	Achieved
Hardware	100	72
Accommodation	100	65
Cuisine	100	65
Service	100	68
Miscellaneous	100	72
OVERALL SCORE 342 points out of 500		

A-ROSA BELLA ★★★+
A POPULAR MODERN RIVERSHIP IDEAL FOR YOUTHFUL, ACTIVE TYPES.

Operator	A-ROSA River Cruises	Passenger beds	202
Built	2002	Sit outside (real) balcony	No
Registry	Germany	French (open-air) balcony	Yes
Identification number	ENI 40801170	Approximate cabin size (sq m)	14.5–16.5
Length (m)	124.5	Lift (elevator)	No
Number of decks (excluding sun deck)	3	Rivers sailed	Danube

BERLITZ'S RATINGS		
	Possible	Achieved
Hardware	100	70
Accommodation	100	65
Cuisine	100	65
Service	100	65
Miscellaneous	100	71
OVERALL SCORE 336 points out of 500		

A-ROSA BRAVA ★★★+
A WELL-RUN, CONTEMPORARY-STYLE RIVERSHIP FOR YOUTHFUL, ACTIVE TYPES.

Operator	A-ROSA River Cruises	Passenger beds	202
Built	2011	Sit outside (real) balcony	No
Registry	Germany	French (open-air) balcony	Yes
Identification number	ENI 04809910	Approximate cabin size (sq m)	14.5
Length (m)	135.0	Lift (elevator)	No
Number of decks (excluding sun deck)	3	Rivers sailed	Rhône, Saône

BERLITZ'S RATINGS		
	Possible	Achieved
Hardware	100	72
Accommodation	100	68
Cuisine	100	65
Service	100	68
Miscellaneous	100	72
OVERALL SCORE 345 points out of 500		

A-ROSA DONNA ★★★+
UPBEAT DECOR AND MINIMALIST STYLE ARE THE FEATURES OF THIS WELL-RUN RIVERSHIP.

Operator ....A-ROSA River Cruises
Built 2002
Registry .... Germany
Identification number ....ENI 04801180
Length (m) 124.5
Number of decks (excluding sun deck)......3

Passenger beds... 200
Sit outside (real) balcony......................... No
French (open-air) balcony .... Yes
Approximate cabin size (sq m) 14.5–16.5
Lift (elevator)... No
Rivers sailed .... Danube

BERLITZ'S RATINGS

	Possible	Achieved
Hardware	100	70
Accommodation	100	65
Cuisine	100	65
Service	100	66
Miscellaneous	100	72

OVERALL SCORE 338 points out of 500

A-ROSA FLORA ★★★+
THIS FUNKY RIVERSHIP IS AIMED AT AN ACTIVE, YOUTHFUL CLIENTELE.

Operator ....A-ROSA River Cruises
Built 2014
Registry .... Germany
Identification number ....ENI 04820970
Length (m) 135.0
Number of decks (excluding sun deck)......3

Passenger beds... 166
Sit outside (real) balcony......................... No
French (open-air) balcony .... Yes
Approximate cabin size (sq m) 14.5–29.0
Lift (elevator)... No
Rivers sailed ....Danube, Rhine, Main

BERLITZ'S RATINGS

	Possible	Achieved
Hardware	100	74
Accommodation	100	66
Cuisine	100	65
Service	100	68
Miscellaneous	100	75

OVERALL SCORE 348 points out of 500

A-ROSA LUNA ★★★+
A SMART, CONTEMPORARY RIVERSHIP WELL SUITED TO ACTIVE TYPES.

Operator ....A-ROSA River Cruises	**Passenger beds**...174
Built 2004	**Sit outside (real) balcony**..........................No
Registry ....Germany	**French (open-air) balcony** ....Yes
Identification number ....ENI 04803520	**Approximate cabin size (sq m)** 14.5
Length (m) 125.8	**Lift (elevator)**..No
Number of decks (excluding sun deck)......3	**Rivers sailed**..........................Rhône, Saône

BERLITZ'S RATINGS

	Possible	Achieved
Hardware	100	70
Accommodation	100	65
Cuisine	100	65
Service	100	65
Miscellaneous	100	72
OVERALL SCORE 337 points out of 500		

A-ROSA MIA ★★★+
UPBEAT DECOR AND MINIMALIST STYLE FOR CRUISING FOR ACTIVE TYPES.

Operator ....A-ROSA River Cruises	**Passenger beds**...200
Built 2003	**Sit outside (real) balcony**..........................No
Registry ....Germany	**French (open-air) balcony** ....Yes
Identification number ....ENI 04801870	**Approximate cabin size (sq m)** 14.5–16.5
Length (m) 124.5	**Lift (elevator)**..No
Number of decks (excluding sun deck)......3	**Rivers sailed**......................................Danube

BERLITZ'S RATINGS

	Possible	Achieved
Hardware	100	70
Accommodation	100	65
Cuisine	100	65
Service	100	65
Miscellaneous	100	72
OVERALL SCORE 337 points out of 500		

A-ROSA RIVA ★★★+

PROVIDES AN UPBEAT, YOUTHFUL SETTING FOR AN AGREEABLE RIVER CRUISE.

Operator	A-ROSA River Cruises
Built	2004
Registry	Germany
Identification number	ENI 04802780
Length (m)	124.5
Number of decks (excluding sun deck)	3

Passenger beds	200
Sit outside (real) balcony	No
French (open-air) balcony	Yes
Approximate cabin size (sq m)	14.5–16.5
Lift (elevator)	No
Rivers sailed	Danube

BERLITZ'S RATINGS

	Possible	Achieved
Hardware	100	70
Accommodation	100	65
Cuisine	100	65
Service	100	65
Miscellaneous	100	72

OVERALL SCORE 337 points out of 500

A-ROSA SILVA ★★★+

A WELL-RUN, TRENDY RIVERSHIP AIMED AT THE YOUNGER END OF THE MARKET.

Operator	A-ROSA River Cruises
Built	2012
Registry	Germany
Identification number	ENI 04810230
Length (m)	135.0
Number of decks (excluding sun deck)	3

Passenger beds	186
Sit outside (real) balcony	No
French (open-air) balcony	Yes
Approximate cabin size (sq m)	14.5–29
Lift (elevator)	No
Rivers sailed	Danube, Rhine, Main

BERLITZ'S RATINGS

	Possible	Achieved
Hardware	100	74
Accommodation	100	68
Cuisine	100	66
Service	100	68
Miscellaneous	100	72

OVERALL SCORE 348 points out of 500

A-ROSA STELLA ★★★+
THIS CONTEMPORARY RIVERSHIP IS A GOOD OPTION FOR ACTIVE TYPES.

Operator	A-ROSA River Cruises	Passenger beds	174
Built	2005	Sit outside (real) balcony	No
Registry	Germany	French (open-air) balcony	Yes
Identification number	ENI 04803530	Approximate cabin size (sq m)	14.5
Length (m)	125.8	Lift (elevator)	No
Number of decks (excluding sun deck)	3	Rivers sailed	Rhône, Saône

BERLITZ'S RATINGS		
	Possible	Achieved
Hardware	100	72
Accommodation	100	64
Cuisine	100	66
Service	100	67
Miscellaneous	100	72
OVERALL SCORE 341 points out of 500		

A-ROSA VIVA ★★★+
A WELL-RUN RIVERSHIP AIMED AT A YOUTHFUL, ACTIVE CLIENTELE.

Operator	A-ROSA River Cruises	Passenger beds	202
Built	2010	Sit outside (real) balcony	No
Registry	Germany	French (open-air) balcony	Yes
Identification number	ENI 04808030	Approximate cabin size (sq m)	14.5
Length (m)	135.0	Lift (elevator)	No
Number of decks (excluding sun deck)	3	Rivers sailed	Rhine

BERLITZ'S RATINGS		
	Possible	Achieved
Hardware	100	73
Accommodation	100	69
Cuisine	100	67
Service	100	67
Miscellaneous	100	72
OVERALL SCORE 348 points out of 500		

AURELIA ★★★★

AURELIA PROVIDES GOOD FOOD AND SERVICE IN A CONTEMPORARY SETTING.

Operator .... Phoenix Cruises	Passenger beds.. 154
Built 2006	Sit outside (real) balcony......................... No
Registry .... Switzerland	French (open-air) balcony .... Yes
Identification number ....ENI 07001841	Approximate cabin size (sq m) 10–14.0
Length (m) 110.0	Lift (elevator)... No
Number of decks (excluding sun deck)......3	Rivers sailed............... Danube, Rhine, Main

BERLITZ'S RATINGS

	Possible	Achieved
Hardware	100	76
Accommodation	100	68
Cuisine	100	78
Service	100	68
Miscellaneous	100	74
OVERALL SCORE 364 points out of 500		

AVALON AFFINITY ★★★+

A PLEASANT, SPACIOUS RIVERSHIP WITH DECENT FACILITIES AND FOOD.

Operator .... Avalon Waterways	Passenger beds.. 138
Built 2009	Sit outside (real) balcony......................... No
Registry .... Germany	French (open-air) balcony .... Yes
Identification number ....ENI 02330846	Approximate cabin size (sq m) 16–24
Length (m) 110.0	Lift (elevator)... Yes
Number of decks (excluding sun deck)......3	Rivers sailed.......................... Rhône, Saône

BERLITZ'S RATINGS

	Possible	Achieved
Hardware	100	73
Accommodation	100	72
Cuisine	100	63
Service	100	63
Miscellaneous	100	72
OVERALL SCORE 343 points out of 500		

AVALON ARTISTRY II ★★★★
THIS RIVERSHIP HAS VERY GOOD FACILITIES, SMART DECOR AND REASONABLE CUISINE.

Operator .... Avalon Waterways	**Passenger beds**... 138
Built 2013	**Sit outside (real) balcony** .... No
Registry .... Germany	**French (open-air) balcony** .... Yes
Identification number ....ENI 02334737	**Approximate cabin size (sq m)** 16–28
Length (m) 110.0	**Lift (elevator)**... Yes
Number of decks (excluding sun deck)......3	**Rivers sailed** .... Rhine, Main, Danube

BERLITZ'S RATINGS		
	Possible	Achieved
Hardware	100	77
Accommodation	100	75
Cuisine	100	64
Service	100	65
Miscellaneous	100	74
OVERALL SCORE 355 points out of 500		

AVALON CREATIVITY ★★★+
THIS COMFORTABLE, CONTEMPORARY RIVERSHIP DELIVERS A MODERATELY GOOD CRUISE.

Operator .... Avalon Waterways	**Passenger beds**... 140
Built 2009	**Sit outside (real) balcony** .... No
Registry .... Germany	**French (open-air) balcony** .... Yes
Identification number ....ENI 02331194	**Approximate cabin size (sq m)** 16–24
Length (m) 110.0	**Lift (elevator)**... Yes
Number of decks (excluding sun deck)......3	**Rivers sailed** ....Seine

BERLITZ'S RATINGS		
	Possible	Achieved
Hardware	100	72
Accommodation	100	72
Cuisine	100	63
Service	100	64
Miscellaneous	100	71
OVERALL SCORE 342 points out of 500		

AVALON EXPRESSION ★★★★

A CONTEMPORARY RIVERSHIP DELIVERING A GOOD CRUISE EXPERIENCE.

Operator .... Avalon Waterways	**Passenger beds**....................................... 166
Built 2013	**Sit outside (real) balcony**......................... No
Registry .... Germany	**French (open-air) balcony** .... Yes
Identification number ....ENI 02334920	**Approximate cabin size (sq m)** 16–28
Length (m) 135.0	**Lift (elevator)**... Yes
Number of decks (excluding sun deck)...... 3	**Rivers sailed**............... Danube, Rhine, Main

BERLITZ'S RATINGS

	Possible	Achieved
Hardware	100	81
Accommodation	100	80
Cuisine	100	77
Service	100	74
Miscellaneous	100	80
OVERALL SCORE 392 points out of 500		

AVALON FELICITY ★★★+

THIS COMFORTABLE, CONTEMPORARY RIVERSHIP DELIVERS A MODERATELY GOOD CRUISE.

Operator .... Avalon Waterways	**Passenger beds**....................................... 138
Built 2010	**Sit outside (real) balcony**......................... No
Registry .... Germany	**French (open-air) balcony** .... Yes
Identification number ....ENI 02332007	**Approximate cabin size (sq m)** 16–24
Length (m) 110.0	**Lift (elevator)**... Yes
Number of decks (excluding sun deck)...... 3	**Rivers sailed**....................................... Rhine

BERLITZ'S RATINGS

	Possible	Achieved
Hardware	100	75
Accommodation	100	76
Cuisine	100	74
Service	100	63
Miscellaneous	100	76
OVERALL SCORE 364 points out of 500		

AVALON ILLUMINATION ★★★★
THIS CONTEMPORARY RIVERSHIP DELIVERS A DECENT OVERALL CRUISE.

Operator .... Avalon Waterways	**Passenger beds** 166
Built 2014	**Sit outside (real) balcony** .... No
Registry .... Switzerland	**French (open-air) balcony** .... Yes
Identification number ....ENI 02335487	**Approximate cabin size (sq m)** 16–28
Length (m) 135.0	**Lift (elevator)** .... Yes
Number of decks (excluding sun deck) 3	**Rivers sailed** .... Danube, Rhine, Main

BERLITZ'S RATINGS

	Possible	Achieved
Hardware	100	81
Accommodation	100	80
Cuisine	100	77
Service	100	75
Miscellaneous	100	80

OVERALL SCORE 393 points out of 500

AVALON IMAGERY II ᴺʸᴿ
A CONTEMPORARY VESSEL WITH A HIGH COMFORT FACTOR.

Operator .... Avalon Waterways	**Passenger beds** 128
Built 2016	**Sit outside (real) balcony** .... No
Registry .... Switzerland	**French (open-air) balcony** .... Yes
Identification number .... MMSI 269057454	**Approximate cabin size (sq m)** 16–28
Length (m) 110.0	**Lift (elevator)** .... Yes
Number of decks (excluding sun deck) 3	**Rivers sailed** .... Rhine

BERLITZ'S RATINGS

	Possible	Achieved
Hardware	100	NYR
Accommodation	100	NYR
Cuisine	100	NYR
Service	100	NYR
Miscellaneous	100	NYR

OVERALL SCORE NYR points out of 500

AVALON LUMINARY ★★★+

THIS SPACIOUS RIVERSHIP HAS SOME NOTABLE FEATURES BUT DISAPPOINTING CUISINE.

Operator .... Avalon Waterways
Built 2010
Registry .... Germany
Identification number .... ENI 02332637
Length (m) 110.0
Number of decks (excluding sun deck) 3

Passenger beds 138
Sit outside (real) balcony .... No
French (open-air) balcony .... Yes
Approximate cabin size (sq m) 16–24
Lift (elevator) .... Yes
Rivers sailed .... Danube, Rhine, Main

BERLITZ'S RATINGS		
	Possible	Achieved
Hardware	100	75
Accommodation	100	73
Cuisine	100	63
Service	100	63
Miscellaneous	100	72
OVERALL SCORE 346 points out of 500		

AVALON PANORAMA ★★★+

THIS STYLISH CONTEMPORARY RIVERSHIP DELIVERS A GOOD ALL-ROUND CRUISE.

Operator .... Avalon Waterways
Built 2011
Registry .... Switzerland
Identification number .... ENI 02333460
Length (m) 135.0
Number of decks (excluding sun deck) 3

Passenger beds 166
Sit outside (real) balcony .... No
French (open-air) balcony .... Yes
Approximate cabin size (sq m) 16–28
Lift (elevator) .... Yes
Rivers sailed .... Danube, Rhine, Main

BERLITZ'S RATINGS		
	Possible	Achieved
Hardware	100	75
Accommodation	100	73
Cuisine	100	63
Service	100	64
Miscellaneous	100	72
OVERALL SCORE 347 points out of 500		

AVALON PASSION ^NYR
A CONTEMPORARY VESSEL WITH A HIGH COMFORT FACTOR.

Operator .... Avalon Waterways	**Passenger beds** 168
Built 2016	**Sit outside (real) balcony** .... No
Registry .... Switzerland	**French (open-air) balcony** .... Yes
Identification number ....N/A	**Approximate cabin size (sq m)** 16–28
Length (m) 135.0	**Lift (elevator)** .... Yes
Number of decks (excluding sun deck) 3	**Rivers sailed** .... Rhine, Main, Danube

NEW RIVERSHIP

BERLITZ'S RATINGS		
	Possible	Achieved
Hardware	100	NYR
Accommodation	100	NYR
Cuisine	100	NYR
Service	100	NYR
Miscellaneous	100	NYR
OVERALL SCORE NYR points out of 500		

AVALON POETRY II ★★★★
THIS SUPER-CONTEMPORARY RIVERSHIP PROVIDES A FINE CRUISE EXPERIENCE.

Operator .... Avalon Waterways	**Passenger beds** 168
Built 2014	**Sit outside (real) balcony** .... No
Registry .... Switzerland	**French (open-air) balcony** .... Yes
Identification number .... ENI 02335229	**Approximate cabin size (sq m)** 16–28
Length (m) 110.0	**Lift (elevator)** .... Yes
Number of decks (excluding sun deck) 3	**Rivers sailed** .... Rhine, Main, Danube

BERLITZ'S RATINGS		
	Possible	Achieved
Hardware	100	77
Accommodation	100	77
Cuisine	100	71
Service	100	70
Miscellaneous	100	76
OVERALL SCORE 371 points out of 500		

AVALON TAPESTRY II ★★★★
A GOOD CHOICE FOR A WELL-ORGANISED CRUISE EXPERIENCE.

Operator .... Avalon Waterways	**Passenger beds**... 140
Built 2015	**Sit outside (real) balcony** .... No
Registry .... Switzerland	**French (open-air) balcony** .... Yes
Identification number ....ENI 02335808	**Approximate cabin size (sq m)** 16–28
Length (m) 135.0	**Lift (elevator)**... Yes
Number of decks (excluding sun deck)......3	**Rivers sailed**........................... Rhône, Saône

BERLITZ'S RATINGS

	Possible	Achieved
Hardware	100	78
Accommodation	100	77
Cuisine	100	71
Service	100	70
Miscellaneous	100	77
OVERALL SCORE 373 points out of 500		

AVALON TRANQUILITY II ★★★★
THIS IS A GOOD CHOICE FOR A STYLISH, WELL-ORGANISED CRUISE.

Operator .... Avalon Waterways	**Passenger beds**... 128
Built 2015	**Sit outside (real) balcony** .... No
Registry .... Switzerland	**French (open-air) balcony** .... Yes
Identification number ....ENI 02335906	**Approximate cabin size (sq m)** 16–28
Length (m) 110.0	**Lift (elevator)**... Yes
Number of decks (excluding sun deck)......3	**Rivers sailed**....................................... Rhine

BERLITZ'S RATINGS

	Possible	Achieved
Hardware	100	79
Accommodation	100	77
Cuisine	100	71
Service	100	71
Miscellaneous	100	77
OVERALL SCORE 375 points out of 500		

AVALON VISIONARY ★★★★

THIS RIVERSHIP DELIVERS A SOLID CRUISE EXPERIENCE, BUT DISAPPOINTING FOOD.

Operator .... Avalon Waterways	**Passenger beds**.. 138
Built 2012	**Sit outside (real) balcony** .... No
Registry .... Germany	**French (open-air) balcony** .... Yes
Identification number ....ENI 02334430	**Approximate cabin size (sq m)** 16–28
Length (m) 135.0	**Lift (elevator)**... Yes
Number of decks (excluding sun deck)......3	**Rivers sailed**............... Danube, Rhine, Main

BERLITZ'S RATINGS		
	Possible	Achieved
Hardware	100	76
Accommodation	100	73
Cuisine	100	64
Service	100	66
Miscellaneous	100	74
OVERALL SCORE 353 points out of 500		

AVALON VISTA ★★★★

CHOOSE THIS CONTEMPORARY RIVERSHIP FOR THE ITINERARY BUT NOT FOR THE FOOD.

Operator .... Avalon Waterways	**Passenger beds**.. 166
Built 2012	**Sit outside (real) balcony** .... No
Registry .... Germany	**French (open-air) balcony** .... Yes
Identification number ....ENI 02333954	**Approximate cabin size (sq m)** 16–28
Length (m) 135.0	**Lift (elevator)**... Yes
Number of decks (excluding sun deck)......3	**Rivers sailed**............... Rhine, Main, Danube

BERLITZ'S RATINGS		
	Possible	Achieved
Hardware	100	76
Accommodation	100	75
Cuisine	100	64
Service	100	66
Miscellaneous	100	74
OVERALL SCORE 355 points out of 500		

AZOLLA ★★+

A VINTAGE RIVERSHIP APPEALING FOR ITS NO-FRILLS, OLD-WORLD AMBIENCE AND STYLE.

Operator ....Feenstra Rhine Line	**Passenger beds**..90
Built 1965	**Sit outside (real) balcony** .... No
Registry .... Netherlands	**French (open-air) balcony** .... No
Identification number ....ENI 02311625	**Approximate cabin size (sq m)** 6–9
Length (m) 76.5	**Lift (elevator)**... No
Number of decks (excluding sun deck)......2	**Rivers sailed** .... Rhine

BERLITZ'S RATINGS		
	Possible	Achieved
Hardware	100	38
Accommodation	100	35
Cuisine	100	40
Service	100	44
Miscellaneous	100	46
OVERALL SCORE 203 points out of 500		

BEETHOVEN ★★★

THIS FUSS-FREE FRENCH RIVERSHIP IS COMFORTABLE BUT DATED.

Operator ....CroisiEurope	**Passenger beds**...................................... 180
Built 2004	**Sit outside (real) balcony** .... No
Registry ....France	**French (open-air) balcony** .... No
Identification number ....ENI 01823122	**Approximate cabin size (sq m)** 13
Length (m) 110.0	**Lift (elevator)**... No
Number of decks (excluding sun deck)......3	**Rivers sailed** .... Danube, Rhine, Main

BERLITZ'S RATINGS		
	Possible	Achieved
Hardware	100	60
Accommodation	100	62
Cuisine	100	60
Service	100	60
Miscellaneous	100	62
OVERALL SCORE 304 points out of 500		

BELLEFLEUR ★★★+
THIS COMFORTABLE OLDER RIVERSHIP OFFERS A LOW-COST CRUISE WITH FRENCH AMBIENCE.

Operator .... APT	**Passenger beds** 150
Built 2001	**Sit outside (real) balcony** .... No
Registry .... Germany	**French (open-air) balcony** .... No
Identification number ....ENI 04800250	**Approximate cabin size (sq m)** 11–15.5
Length (m) 114.3	**Lift (elevator)** .... No
Number of decks (excluding sun deck) 3	**Rivers sailed** .... Rhône, Saône

BERLITZ'S RATINGS		
	Possible	Achieved
Hardware	100	61
Accommodation	100	62
Cuisine	100	61
Service	100	60
Miscellaneous	100	64
OVERALL SCORE 308 points out of 500		

BELLEJOUR ★★★+
THIS VESSEL IS GOOD FOR A COMFORTABLE, VALUE CRUISE.

Operator .... Various tour operators	**Passenger beds** 180
Built 2004	**Sit outside (real) balcony** .... No
Registry .... Malta	**French (open-air) balcony** .... Yes
Identification number ....ENI 09948006	**Approximate cabin size (sq m)** 16
Length (m) 126.7	**Lift (elevator)** .... No
Number of decks (excluding sun deck) 3	**Rivers sailed** .... Rhine, Main, Danube

BERLITZ'S RATINGS		
	Possible	Achieved
Hardware	100	61
Accommodation	100	64
Cuisine	100	58
Service	100	60
Miscellaneous	100	67
OVERALL SCORE 310 points out of 500		

BELLEVUE ★★★+
A STYLISH GLASS-FRONTED CONTEMPORARY RIVERSHIP DELIVERING A GOOD CRUISE EXPERIENCE.

Operator .... Transocean Flussreisen	**Passenger beds** 201
Built 2006	**Sit outside (real) balcony** .... No
Registry .... Malta	**French (open-air) balcony** .... Yes
Identification number .... ENI 09948013	**Approximate cabin size (sq m)** 13
Length (m) 135.0	**Lift (elevator)** .... No
Number of decks (excluding sun deck) 3	**Rivers sailed** .... Danube, Rhine, Main

BERLITZ'S RATINGS

	Possible	Achieved
Hardware	100	65
Accommodation	100	68
Cuisine	100	64
Service	100	65
Miscellaneous	100	68

OVERALL SCORE 330 points out of 500

BELLISSIMA ★★★+
GOOD FOR SAILING AROUND THE VENETIAN LAGOON ON A LOW BUDGET.

Operator .... Various tour operators	**Passenger beds** 142
Built 2004	**Sit outside (real) balcony** .... No
Registry .... Germany	**French (open-air) balcony** .... Yes
Identification number .... ENI 07001859	**Approximate cabin size (sq m)** 12–20
Length (m) 109.9	**Lift (elevator)** .... No
Number of decks (excluding sun deck) 2	**Rivers sailed** .... Po, Venetian Lagoon

BERLITZ'S RATINGS

	Possible	Achieved
Hardware	100	66
Accommodation	100	67
Cuisine	100	66
Service	100	62
Miscellaneous	100	66

OVERALL SCORE 327 points out of 500

BELLRIVA ★★★

AN ADEQUATE BUT VERY HIGH-DENSITY AND DATED RIVERSHIP FOR A LOW-COST CRUISE.

Operator	1A Vista Reisen	**Passenger beds**	186
Built	1971	**Sit outside (real) balcony**	No
Registry	Germany	**French (open-air) balcony**	No
Identification number	ENI 07001702	**Approximate cabin size (sq m)**	9–12
Length (m)	104.6	**Lift (elevator)**	No
Number of decks (excluding sun deck)	2	**Rivers sailed**	Rhine

BERLITZ'S RATINGS		
	Possible	Achieved
Hardware	100	50
Accommodation	100	51
Cuisine	100	51
Service	100	53
Miscellaneous	100	55
OVERALL SCORE 260 points out of 500		

BELVEDERE ★★★+

CHOOSE THIS FAIRLY STYLISH RIVERSHIP FOR A GOOD-QUALITY RIVER CRUISE EXPERIENCE.

Operator	Transocean Flussreisen	**Passenger beds**	176
Built	2006	**Sit outside (real) balcony**	No
Registry	Malta	**French (open-air) balcony**	Yes
Identification number	ENI 09948010	**Approximate cabin size (sq m)**	16–22
Length (m)	126.0	**Lift (elevator)**	No
Number of decks (excluding sun deck)	3	**Rivers sailed**	Danube

BERLITZ'S RATINGS		
	Possible	Achieved
Hardware	100	66
Accommodation	100	68
Cuisine	100	65
Service	100	65
Miscellaneous	100	67
OVERALL SCORE 331 points out of 500		

BIJOU ★★★

AN ATTRACTIVE, WELL-APPOINTED RIVERSHIP FOR FRENCH RIVER CRUISING.

Operator .... Various tour operators	**Passenger beds** 153
Built 2000	**Sit outside (real) balcony** .... No
Registry .... Malta	**French (open-air) balcony** .... No
Identification number .... ENI 04802070	**Approximate cabin size (sq m)** 11–14
Length (m) 110.0	**Lift (elevator)** .... Yes
Number of decks (excluding sun deck) 2	**Rivers sailed** .... Rhône, Saône

BERLITZ'S RATINGS

	Possible	Achieved
Hardware	100	58
Accommodation	100	57
Cuisine	100	60
Service	100	58
Miscellaneous	100	62

OVERALL SCORE 295 points out of 500

BIZET ★★★

CHOOSE THIS RIVERSHIP FOR THE ITINERARY AND DESTINATIONS, NOT THE FOOD.

Operator .... Grand Circle Cruise Line	**Passenger beds** 120
Built 2002	**Sit outside (real) balcony** .... No
Registry .... Malta	**French (open-air) balcony** .... Yes
Identification number .... ENI 07001815	**Approximate cabin size (sq m)** 12
Length (m) 110.0	**Lift (elevator)** .... Yes
Number of decks (excluding sun deck) 2	**Rivers sailed** .... Seine

BERLITZ'S RATINGS

	Possible	Achieved
Hardware	100	58
Accommodation	100	58
Cuisine	100	61
Service	100	57
Miscellaneous	100	63

OVERALL SCORE 297 points out of 500

BOLERO ★★★
A CONSISTENT MIDDLE-OF-THE-ROAD RIVERSHIP THAT LACKS PANACHE.

Operator .... Lippstadter Tours	**Passenger beds** 180
Built 2003	**Sit outside (real) balcony** .... No
Registry .... Germany	**French (open-air) balcony** .... Yes
Identification number .... ENI 09948004	**Approximate cabin size (sq m)** 15
Length (m) 126.7	**Lift (elevator)** .... No
Number of decks (excluding sun deck) 3	**Rivers sailed** .... Danube

BERLITZ'S RATINGS		
	Possible	Achieved
Hardware	100	58
Accommodation	100	58
Cuisine	100	58
Service	100	57
Miscellaneous	100	61
OVERALL SCORE 292 points out of 500		

BOTTICELLI ★★★+
A CONSISTENT, STANDARD-QUALITY RIVER CRUISE FOR FRANCOPHILES ON A BUDGET.

Operator .... CroisiEurope	**Passenger beds** 154
Built 2004	**Sit outside (real) balcony** .... No
Registry .... France	**French (open-air) balcony** .... No
Identification number .... ENI 01823123	**Approximate cabin size (sq m)** 11
Length (m) 110.0	**Lift (elevator)** .... No
Number of decks (excluding sun deck) 2	**Rivers sailed** .... Seine

BERLITZ'S RATINGS		
	Possible	Achieved
Hardware	100	61
Accommodation	100	61
Cuisine	100	64
Service	100	56
Miscellaneous	100	61
OVERALL SCORE 303 points out of 500		

CALYPSO ★★★
THIS RIVERSHIP IS BEST CHOSEN FOR THE ITINERARY AND DESTINATIONS, NOT THE FOOD.

Operator .... Phoenix Cruises	Passenger beds..96
Built 1978	Sit outside (real) balcony......................... No
Registry .... Netherlands	French (open-air) balcony .... No
Identification number .... ENI 2321970	Approximate cabin size (sq m) 11–12
Length (m) 75.6	Lift (elevator)... No
Number of decks (excluding sun deck)......2	Rivers sailed.. Rhine

BERLITZ'S RATINGS

	Possible	Achieved
Hardware	100	50
Accommodation	100	49
Cuisine	100	55
Service	100	56
Miscellaneous	100	59

OVERALL SCORE 269 points out of 500

CAMARGUE ★★★+
THIS SMART YET CASUAL RIVERSHIP IS QUITE COMFORTABLE.

Operator .... CroisiEurope	Passenger beds... 104
Built 1995	Sit outside (real) balcony......................... No
Registry ....France	French (open-air) balcony .... Yes
Identification number ....ENI 01822739	Approximate cabin size (sq m) 15.8
Length (m) 110.0	Lift (elevator)... No
Number of decks (excluding sun deck)......2	Rivers sailed.......................... Rhône, Saône

BERLITZ'S RATINGS

	Possible	Achieved
Hardware	100	63
Accommodation	100	64
Cuisine	100	58
Service	100	55
Miscellaneous	100	63

OVERALL SCORE 303 points out of 500

CASANOVA ★★★
THIS RIVERSHIP HAS ELEGANT DECOR AND PROVIDES A DECENT OVERALL EXPERIENCE.

Operator .... Various tour operators	**Passenger beds**..96
Built 2001	**Sit outside (real) balcony**........................ No
Registry .... Switzerland	**French (open-air) balcony** .... Yes
Identification number ....ENI 04800110	**Approximate cabin size (sq m)** 12–16
Length (m) 103.0	**Lift (elevator)**... No
Number of decks (excluding sun deck)......2	**Rivers sailed**..........Various European rivers

BERLITZ'S RATINGS

	Possible	Achieved
Hardware	100	58
Accommodation	100	57
Cuisine	100	55
Service	100	56
Miscellaneous	100	58

OVERALL SCORE 284 points out of 500

CEZANNE ★★★
THIS OLDER RIVERSHIP WILL PROVIDE A FAIRLY BASIC RIVER CRUISE EXPERIENCE.

Operator .... Various tour operators	**Passenger beds**..102
Built 1993	**Sit outside (real) balcony**........................ No
Registry .... Switzerland	**French (open-air) balcony** .... No
Identification number ....ENI 05117120	**Approximate cabin size (sq m)** 15
Length (m) 118.0	**Lift (elevator)**... No
Number of decks (excluding sun deck)......2	**Rivers sailed**..Seine

BERLITZ'S RATINGS

	Possible	Achieved
Hardware	100	56
Accommodation	100	57
Cuisine	100	58
Service	100	56
Miscellaneous	100	60

OVERALL SCORE 287 points out of 500

CHARDONNAY ★★★
ALTHOUGH IT IS QUITE DATED, THIS COMFORTABLE SMALL RIVERSHIP HAS ITS CHARM.

Operator ....Grand Circle Cruise Line	**Passenger beds**..50
Built 1999	**Sit outside (real) balcony**.........................No
Registry ....Switzerland	**French (open-air) balcony**......................Yes
Identification number ....N/A	**Approximate cabin size (sq m)** ....N/A
Length (m) 89.0	**Lift (elevator)**..No
Number of decks (excluding sun deck)......2	**Rivers sailed**...........................Rhône, Saône

BERLITZ'S RATINGS

	Possible	Achieved
Hardware	100	47
Accommodation	100	45
Cuisine	100	50
Service	100	58
Miscellaneous	100	58
OVERALL SCORE 258 points out of 500		

CHARLES DICKENS NYR
ANGLOPHILES WILL LOVE THE TRADITIONAL BRITISH STYLE AND AMBIENCE.

Operator ....Riviera Travel	**Passenger beds**.......................................140
Built 2015	**Sit outside (real) balcony**.......................Yes
Registry .... Netherlands	**French (open-air) balcony**......................Yes
Identification number .... MMSI 244860500	**Approximate cabin size (sq m)** 14–22.8
Length (m) 110.0	**Lift (elevator)**..Yes
Number of decks (excluding sun deck)......3	**Rivers sailed**...............Rhine, Main, Danube

BERLITZ'S RATINGS

	Possible	Achieved
Hardware	100	NYR
Accommodation	100	NYR
Cuisine	100	NYR
Service	100	NYR
Miscellaneous	100	NYR
OVERALL SCORE NYR points out of 500		

CLASSICA ★★★
THIS COMFORTABLE MODERN RIVERSHIP HAS A GOOD AMBIENCE.

Operator .... Various tour operators	**Passenger beds** 157
Built 2000	**Sit outside (real) balcony** .... No
Registry .... Malta	**French (open-air) balcony** .... No
Identification number .... ENI 09948009	**Approximate cabin size (sq m)** 12–15
Length (m) 111.2	**Lift (elevator)** .... Yes
Number of decks (excluding sun deck) 2	**Rivers sailed** .... Danube

BERLITZ'S RATINGS		
	Possible	Achieved
Hardware	100	58
Accommodation	100	58
Cuisine	100	60
Service	100	60
Miscellaneous	100	61
OVERALL SCORE 297 points out of 500		

COUNTESS ★★★+
THIS COMFORTABLE RIVERSHIP DELIVERS A DECENT ALL-ROUND CRUISE.

Operator .... Riviera Travel	**Passenger beds** 138
Built 2008	**Sit outside (real) balcony** .... No
Registry .... Germany	**French (open-air) balcony** .... Yes
Identification number .... ENI 02329477	**Approximate cabin size (sq m)** 16–24
Length (m) 110.0	**Lift (elevator)** .... Yes
Number of decks (excluding sun deck) 3	**Rivers sailed** .... Rhône, Saône

BERLITZ'S RATINGS		
	Possible	Achieved
Hardware	100	67
Accommodation	100	70
Cuisine	100	63
Service	100	62
Miscellaneous	100	68
OVERALL SCORE 330 points out of 500		

CRYSTAL MOZART NYR

THIS DOUBLE-WIDE RIVERSHIP EXUDES AN ABUNDANCE OF SPACE AND MODERN STYLE.

Operator ....Dertour Cruises	Passenger beds.. 160
Built 1987	Sit outside (real) balcony........................ No
Registry ....Malta	French (open-air) balcony .... Yes
Identification number ....ENI 04805980	Approximate cabin size (sq m) 20–80
Length (m) 120.6	Lift (elevator)... No
Number of decks (excluding sun deck)......3	Rivers sailed.................................. Danube

BERLITZ'S RATINGS

	Possible	Achieved
Hardware	100	NYR
Accommodation	100	NYR
Cuisine	100	NYR
Service	100	NYR
Miscellaneous	100	NYR
OVERALL SCORE NYR points out of 500		

CYRANO DE BERGERAC ★★★+

THIS SMART-LOOKING RIVERSHIP HAS GOOD FEATURES, AND A FRENCH AMBIENCE.

Operator ....CroisiEurope	Passenger beds.. 150
Built 2013	Sit outside (real) balcony........................ No
Registry ....France	French (open-air) balcony .... Yes
Identification number ....ENI 01831891	Approximate cabin size (sq m) 12
Length (m) 110.0	Lift (elevator)... No
Number of decks (excluding sun deck)......3	Rivers sailed.......................Bordeaux region

BERLITZ'S RATINGS

	Possible	Achieved
Hardware	100	74
Accommodation	100	71
Cuisine	100	63
Service	100	64
Miscellaneous	100	65
OVERALL SCORE 337 points out of 500		

DCS AMETHYST ★★★
A FAIRLY ATTRACTIVE RIVERSHIP OFFERING A GOOD-QUALITY CRUISE EXPERIENCE.

Operator ....DCS	**Passenger beds**................................178
Built 2004	**Sit outside (real) balcony**..........................No
Registry ....Malta	**French (open-air) balcony** .... Yes
Identification number ....ENI 09948007	**Approximate cabin size (sq m)** 15–22
Length (m) 126.7	**Lift (elevator)**...No
Number of decks (excluding sun deck)......3	**Rivers sailed**................................... Danube

BERLITZ'S RATINGS

	Possible	Achieved
Hardware	100	61
Accommodation	100	60
Cuisine	100	58
Service	100	58
Miscellaneous	100	61
OVERALL SCORE 298 points out of 500		

DA VINCI ★★★
THIS PLEASANT IF SLIGHTLY TIRED RIVERSHIP IS DECENT FOR A LOW-COST CRUISE.

Operator .... Shearings Holidays	**Passenger beds**..110
Built 1995	**Sit outside (real) balcony**......................... No
Registry .... Switzerland	**French (open-air) balcony** .... No
Identification number ....ENI 07001839	**Approximate cabin size (sq m)** 11–12
Length (m) 104.5	**Lift (elevator)**.. Yes
Number of decks (excluding sun deck)......2	**Rivers sailed**..........Various European rivers

BERLITZ'S RATINGS

	Possible	Achieved
Hardware	100	59
Accommodation	100	55
Cuisine	100	57
Service	100	57
Miscellaneous	100	60
OVERALL SCORE 288 points out of 500		

DANUBIA ★★+
THIS OLDER-STYLE RIVERSHIP OFFERS MODESTLY PRICED CRUISES.

Operator ....Polster & Pohl	**Passenger beds**..154
Built 1980	**Sit outside (real) balcony**...........................No
Registry ....Romania	**French (open-air) balcony**.........................No
Identification number ....ENI 46000113	**Approximate cabin size (sq m)** 10
Length (m) 102.0	**Lift (elevator)**...No
Number of decks (excluding sun deck)......2	**Rivers sailed**....................................Danube

BERLITZ'S RATINGS		
	Possible	Achieved
Hardware	100	45
Accommodation	100	46
Cuisine	100	46
Service	100	48
Miscellaneous	100	51
OVERALL SCORE 236 points out of 500		

DER KLEINE PRINZ ★★+
AN OLDER, INTIMATE, BUDGET RIVERSHIP WITH SOMBRE DECOR BUT GOOD ARTWORKS.

Operator ....Quality Tours	**Passenger beds**..90
Built 1992	**Sit outside (real) balcony**...........................No
Registry ....Germany	**French (open-air) balcony**.........................No
Identification number ....ENI 04803150	**Approximate cabin size (sq m)** 16
Length (m) 93.3	**Lift (elevator)**..Yes
Number of decks (excluding sun deck)......2	**Rivers sailed**....................................Danube

BERLITZ'S RATINGS		
	Possible	Achieved
Hardware	100	41
Accommodation	100	38
Cuisine	100	44
Service	100	46
Miscellaneous	100	51
OVERALL SCORE 220 points out of 500		

DERTOUR AMADEUS ★★★
A GOOD CHOICE FOR A WELL-ROUNDED MEDIUM-BUDGET RIVER CRUISE.

Operator ....Dertour Cruises	**Passenger beds**.. 146
Built 1997	**Sit outside (real) balcony**......................... No
Registry ....Germany	**French (open-air) balcony** .... No
Identification number ....ENI 08848003	**Approximate cabin size (sq m)** 15
Length (m) 110.0	**Lift (elevator)**... No
Number of decks (excluding sun deck)......3	**Rivers sailed**.................................... Danube

BERLITZ'S RATINGS

	Possible	Achieved
Hardware	100	62
Accommodation	100	60
Cuisine	100	57
Service	100	58
Miscellaneous	100	61

OVERALL SCORE 298 points out of 500

DIANA ★★
A VINTAGE RIVERSHIP OFFERING NO-FRILLS CRUISES TO BUDGET TRAVELLERS.

Operator ....Various tour operators	**Passenger beds**..78
Built 1964	**Sit outside (real) balcony**......................... No
Registry .... Netherlands	**French (open-air) balcony** .... No
Identification number ....ENI 02325126	**Approximate cabin size (sq m)** 9
Length (m) 78.0	**Lift (elevator)**... No
Number of decks (excluding sun deck)......2	**Rivers sailed**..........Various European rivers

BERLITZ'S RATINGS

	Possible	Achieved
Hardware	100	35
Accommodation	100	34
Cuisine	100	38
Service	100	41
Miscellaneous	100	42

OVERALL SCORE 190 points out of 500

DOUCE FRANCE ★★★

THIS MIDDLE-OF-THE-ROAD RIVERSHIP IS DATED BUT COMFORTABLE.

Operator ....CroisiEurope	Passenger beds.. 164
Built 1997	Sit outside (real) balcony .... No
Registry ....France	French (open-air) balcony .... No
Identification number ....ENI 01822845	Approximate cabin size (sq m) 12
Length (m) 110.0	Lift (elevator).. No
Number of decks (excluding sun deck)...... 2	Rivers sailed .... Rhine, Main, Danube

BERLITZ'S RATINGS		
	Possible	Achieved
Hardware	100	58
Accommodation	100	58
Cuisine	100	60
Service	100	57
Miscellaneous	100	61
OVERALL SCORE 294 points out of 500		

DOURO CRUISER ★★★+

THIS SMALL, HIGH-DENSITY RIVERSHIP IS MODESTLY COMFORTABLE.

Operator ....Douro Azul	Passenger beds.. 130
Built 2005	Sit outside (real) balcony .... No
Registry ....Portugal	French (open-air) balcony .... Yes
Identification number .... MMSI 255804680	Approximate cabin size (sq m) 15
Length (m) 78.1	Lift (elevator).. No
Number of decks (excluding sun deck)......3	Rivers sailed ....Douro

BERLITZ'S RATINGS		
	Possible	Achieved
Hardware	100	60
Accommodation	100	59
Cuisine	100	61
Service	100	62
Miscellaneous	100	63
OVERALL SCORE 305 points out of 500		

DOURO QUEEN ★★★+

A SMART RIVERSHIP WITH GOOD FEATURES FOR BUSY DOURO CRUISES.

Operator	Douro Azul	**Passenger beds**	130
Built	2005	**Sit outside (real) balcony**	No
Registry	Portugal	**French (open-air) balcony**	Yes
Identification number	MMSI 263751340	**Approximate cabin size (sq m)**	15
Length (m)	77.4	**Lift (elevator)**	No
Number of decks (excluding sun deck)	2	**Rivers sailed**	Douro

BERLITZ'S RATINGS		
	Possible	Achieved
Hardware	100	61
Accommodation	100	61
Cuisine	100	62
Service	100	63
Miscellaneous	100	65
OVERALL SCORE 312 points out of 500		

DOURO SPIRIT ★★★+

THIS STYLISH RIVERSHIP OFFERS A FAIRLY DECENT DOURO CRUISE.

Operator	Various tour operators	**Passenger beds**	130
Built	2011	**Sit outside (real) balcony**	No
Registry	Portugal	**French (open-air) balcony**	Yes
Identification number	N/A	**Approximate cabin size (sq m)**	15–22.2
Length (m)	79.5	**Lift (elevator)**	Yes
Number of decks (excluding sun deck)	3	**Rivers sailed**	Douro

BERLITZ'S RATINGS		
	Possible	Achieved
Hardware	100	68
Accommodation	100	64
Cuisine	100	63
Service	100	64
Miscellaneous	100	68
OVERALL SCORE 327 points out of 500		

EDELWEISS ★★★★
A HIGH-QUALITY CONTEMPORARY RIVERSHIP FOR A FIRST-CLASS CRUISE.

Operator ....Mittelthurgau Travel	**Passenger beds**...180
Built 2013	**Sit outside (real) balcony**........................ Yes
Registry .... Switzerland	**French (open-air) balcony** .... Yes
Identification number ....ENI 07001964	**Approximate cabin size (sq m)** ....N/A
Length (m) 110.0	**Lift (elevator)**.. Yes
Number of decks (excluding sun deck)......3	**Rivers sailed**................ Rhine, Main, Danube

BERLITZ'S RATINGS

	Possible	Achieved
Hardware	100	76
Accommodation	100	77
Cuisine	100	73
Service	100	72
Miscellaneous	100	74

OVERALL SCORE 372 points out of 500

ELBE PRINCESSE NYR
THIS CUSTOM-BUILT VESSEL FOR THE ELBE IS INNOVATIVE AND CHIC.

Operator ....CroisiEurope	**Passenger beds**...80
Built 2016	**Sit outside (real) balcony**........................ No
Registry ....France	**French (open-air) balcony** .... Yes
Identification number ....N/A	**Approximate cabin size (sq m)** 11–14.5
Length (m) 95.0	**Lift (elevator)**... No
Number of decks (excluding sun deck)......2	**Rivers sailed**.....................Elbe–Havel–Oder

NEW RIVERSHIP

BERLITZ'S RATINGS

	Possible	Achieved
Hardware	100	NYR
Accommodation	100	NYR
Cuisine	100	NYR
Service	100	NYR
Miscellaneous	100	NYR

OVERALL SCORE NYR points out of 500

ELEGANT LADY ★★★

A SMART-LOOKING RIVERSHIP THAT PROVIDES A GOOD-VALUE RIVER CRUISE.

Operator .... Plantours Cruises	**Passenger beds**.. 128
Built 2002	**Sit outside (real) balcony** .... No
Registry .... Bulgaria	**French (open-air) balcony** .... No
Identification number ....ENI 08923003	**Approximate cabin size (sq m)** 14
Length (m) 110.0	**Lift (elevator)**... No
Number of decks (excluding sun deck)...... 2	**Rivers sailed**............... Rhine, Danube, Main

BERLITZ'S RATINGS		
	Possible	Achieved
Hardware	100	61
Accommodation	100	56
Cuisine	100	57
Service	100	57
Miscellaneous	100	60
OVERALL SCORE 291 points out of 500		

EMERALD BELLE ᴺʸᴿ

A WELL-DEFINED CRUISE EXPERIENCE WITH DECENT FOOD AND SERVICE.

Operator .... Emerald Waterways	**Passenger beds**.. 182
Built 2016	**Sit outside (real) balcony** .... No
Registry .... Malta	**French (open-air) balcony** .... Yes
Identification number ....N/A	**Approximate cabin size (sq m)** 12–29
Length (m) 135.0	**Lift (elevator)**... Yes
Number of decks (excluding sun deck)...... 3	**Rivers sailed**............... Rhine, Main, Danube

NEW RIVERSHIP

BERLITZ'S RATINGS		
	Possible	Achieved
Hardware	100	NYR
Accommodation	100	NYR
Cuisine	100	NYR
Service	100	NYR
Miscellaneous	100	NYR
OVERALL SCORE NYR points out of 500		

EMERALD DAWN ★★★★

EXCELLENT VALUE AND MODERN STYLE ABOARD THIS FINE VESSEL.

Operator .... Emerald Waterways	**Passenger beds**... 182
Built 2015	**Sit outside (real) balcony**.......................... No
Registry ....Malta	**French (open-air) balcony** .... Yes
Identification number .... MMSI 256403000	**Approximate cabin size (sq m)** 12–29
Length (m) 135.0	**Lift (elevator)**... Yes
Number of decks (excluding sun deck)......3	**Rivers sailed** .... Rhine, Main, Danube

BERLITZ'S RATINGS		
	Possible	Achieved
Hardware	100	83
Accommodation	100	80
Cuisine	100	76
Service	100	78
Miscellaneous	100	81
OVERALL SCORE 398 points out of 500		

EMERALD SKY ★★★★

THIS SMART RIVERSHIP HAS STATE-OF-THE-ART FEATURES AND STYLISH CABINS.

Operator .... Emerald Waterways	**Passenger beds**... 182
Built 2014	**Sit outside (real) balcony**.......................... No
Registry ....Malta	**French (open-air) balcony** .... Yes
Identification number ....ENI 02336545	**Approximate cabin size (sq m)** 16–29
Length (m) 135.0	**Lift (elevator)**... Yes
Number of decks (excluding sun deck)......3	**Rivers sailed** .... Rhine, Main, Danube

BERLITZ'S RATINGS		
	Possible	Achieved
Hardware	100	82
Accommodation	100	80
Cuisine	100	75
Service	100	78
Miscellaneous	100	81
OVERALL SCORE 396 points out of 500		

EMERALD STAR ★★★★

THIS SMART, CONTEMPORARY RIVERSHIP IS DESIGNED FOR THE YOUTHFUL TRAVELLER.

Operator .... Emerald Waterways	**Passenger beds**.. 182
Built 2014	**Sit outside (real) balcony** .... No
Registry .... Malta	**French (open-air) balcony** .... Yes
Identification number .... ENI 02336546	**Approximate cabin size (sq m)** 16–29
Length (m) 135.0	**Lift (elevator)**.. Yes
Number of decks (excluding sun deck)......3	**Rivers sailed** .... Rhine, Main, Danube

BERLITZ'S RATINGS

	Possible	Achieved
Hardware	100	82
Accommodation	100	80
Cuisine	100	75
Service	100	78
Miscellaneous	100	81

OVERALL SCORE 396 points out of 500

EMERALD SUN ★★★★

THIS SMART RIVERSHIP PROVIDES A HIGH-QUALITY, HIGH-VALUE CRUISE.

Operator .... Emerald Waterways	**Passenger beds**.. 182
Built 2015	**Sit outside (real) balcony** .... No
Registry .... Malta	**French (open-air) balcony** .... Yes
Identification number .... MMSI 256404000	**Approximate cabin size (sq m)** 12–29
Length (m) 135.0	**Lift (elevator)**.. Yes
Number of decks (excluding sun deck)......3	**Rivers sailed** .... Rhine, Main, Danube

BERLITZ'S RATINGS

	Possible	Achieved
Hardware	100	83
Accommodation	100	80
Cuisine	100	76
Service	100	78
Miscellaneous	100	81

OVERALL SCORE 398 points out of 500

ESMERALDA ★★★
THIS OLDER VESSEL PROVIDES THE BASICS FOR NO-FRILLS CRUISING.

Operator .... Various tour operators	**Passenger beds**.. 126
Built 1995	**Sit outside (real) balcony** .... No
Registry .... Netherlands	**French (open-air) balcony** .... No
Identification number .... ENI 02315764	**Approximate cabin size (sq m)** 11
Length (m) 90.0	**Lift (elevator)**... Yes
Number of decks (excluding sun deck) 2	**Rivers sailed** .... Rhine

BERLITZ'S RATINGS

	Possible	Achieved
Hardware	100	58
Accommodation	100	56
Cuisine	100	57
Service	100	56
Miscellaneous	100	56

OVERALL SCORE 283 points out of 500

ESPRIT ★★★★
CHOOSE THIS VESSEL FOR A HIGH-QUALITY CRUISE EXPERIENCE.

Operator .... Tauck	**Passenger beds**.. 118
Built 2010	**Sit outside (real) balcony** .... No
Registry .... Switzerland	**French (open-air) balcony** .... Yes
Identification number .... ENI 07001923	**Approximate cabin size (sq m)** 14–28
Length (m) 110.0	**Lift (elevator)**... Yes
Number of decks (excluding sun deck) 3	**Rivers sailed** .... Rhine, Main, Danube

BERLITZ'S RATINGS

	Possible	Achieved
Hardware	100	73
Accommodation	100	73
Cuisine	100	65
Service	100	67
Miscellaneous	100	74

OVERALL SCORE 352 points out of 500

EXCELLENCE CORAL ★★★
A CHARMING, COMPACT RIVERSHIP OFFERING A BASIC YET DECENT CRUISE.

Operator ....Swiss Excellence	**Passenger beds**..87
Built 1998	**Sit outside (real) balcony**..........................No
Registry ....Switzerland	**French (open-air) balcony**.......................No
Identification number ....ENI 07001711	**Approximate cabin size (sq m)** 10–13
Length (m) 82.0	**Lift (elevator)**...No
Number of decks (excluding sun deck)......2	**Rivers sailed**......................Elbe, Havel, Oder

BERLITZ'S RATINGS		
	Possible	Achieved
Hardware	100	55
Accommodation	100	55
Cuisine	100	58
Service	100	58
Miscellaneous	100	65
OVERALL SCORE 291 points out of 500		

EXCELLENCE PRINCESS ★★★★
THIS WELL-APPOINTED RIVERSHIP DELIVERS A FINE QUALITY CRUISE EXPERIENCE.

Operator ....Swiss Excellence	**Passenger beds**..186
Built 2014	**Sit outside (real) balcony**..........................No
Registry ....Switzerland	**French (open-air) balcony**.....................Yes
Identification number ....ENI 02335839	**Approximate cabin size (sq m)** 13–20
Length (m) 135.0	**Lift (elevator)**...Yes
Number of decks (excluding sun deck)......3	**Rivers sailed**...................................Danube

BERLITZ'S RATINGS		
	Possible	Achieved
Hardware	100	80
Accommodation	100	78
Cuisine	100	67
Service	100	68
Miscellaneous	100	73
OVERALL SCORE 366 points out of 500		

EXCELLENCE QUEEN ★★★+
THIS CONTEMPORARY, ELEGANT RIVERSHIP DELIVERS A GOOD-QUALITY CRUISE EXPERIENCE.

Operator ....Swiss Excellence	**Passenger beds**...................................142
Built 2010	**Sit outside (real) balcony**..........................No
Registry .... Switzerland	**French (open-air) balcony** ....Yes
Identification number ....ENI 02333632	**Approximate cabin size (sq m)** 13–30
Length (m) 110.0	**Lift (elevator)**..Yes
Number of decks (excluding sun deck) 3	**Rivers sailed**...............Rhine, Main, Danube

BERLITZ'S RATINGS		
	Possible	Achieved
Hardware	100	72
Accommodation	100	65
Cuisine	100	63
Service	100	64
Miscellaneous	100	70
OVERALL SCORE 334 points out of 500		

EXCELLENCE RHÔNE ★★★+
A MODERN RIVERSHIP THAT'S RELIABLE FOR A WELL-ROUNDED CRUISE.

Operator ....Swiss Excellence	**Passenger beds**...................................142
Built 2006	**Sit outside (real) balcony**..........................No
Registry .... Switzerland	**French (open-air) balcony** ....Yes
Identification number ....ENI 07001833	**Approximate cabin size (sq m)** 12–18
Length (m) 110.0	**Lift (elevator)**..No
Number of decks (excluding sun deck) 3	**Rivers sailed**...........................Rhône, Saône

BERLITZ'S RATINGS		
	Possible	Achieved
Hardware	100	66
Accommodation	100	63
Cuisine	100	60
Service	100	61
Miscellaneous	100	68
OVERALL SCORE 318 points out of 500		

EXCELLENCE ROYAL ★★★+
THIS CONTEMPORARY, ELEGANT RIVERSHIP DELIVERS A GOOD-QUALITY CRUISE EXPERIENCE.

Operator ....Swiss Excellence	**Passenger beds**.. 144
Built 2010	**Sit outside (real) balcony** .... No
Registry .... Switzerland	**French (open-air) balcony** .... Yes
Identification number ....ENI 02332815	**Approximate cabin size (sq m)** 13–17
Length (m) 110.0	**Lift (elevator)**.. No
Number of decks (excluding sun deck)......3	**Rivers sailed**..Seine

BERLITZ'S RATINGS

	Possible	Achieved
Hardware	100	72
Accommodation	100	64
Cuisine	100	63
Service	100	63
Miscellaneous	100	70

OVERALL SCORE 332 points out of 500

FERNÃO DE MAGALHÃES (MAGELLAN) ★★★
AN OLDER DOURO RIVERSHIP FOR A MIDDLE-OF-THE-ROAD RIVER CRUISE.

Operator ....Various tour operators	**Passenger beds**.. 142
Built 2003	**Sit outside (real) balcony** .... No
Registry ....France	**French (open-air) balcony** .... No
Identification number ....ENI 01823118	**Approximate cabin size (sq m)** 12–13
Length (m) 75.0	**Lift (elevator)**.. No
Number of decks (excluding sun deck)......3	**Rivers sailed**..Douro

BERLITZ'S RATINGS

	Possible	Achieved
Hardware	100	62
Accommodation	100	52
Cuisine	100	55
Service	100	57
Miscellaneous	100	58

OVERALL SCORE 284 points out of 500

FILIA RHENI ★★★+

THIS SMART-LOOKING RIVERSHIP DELIVERS FINE FOOD AND A QUALITY CRUISE.

Operator ....Saga Travel	**Passenger beds**.. 150
Built 2000	**Sit outside (real) balcony**......................... No
Registry .... Germany	**French (open-air) balcony** .... No
Identification number ....ENI 04608050	**Approximate cabin size (sq m)** 14
Length (m) 110.0	**Lift (elevator)**... No
Number of decks (excluding sun deck)......3	**Rivers sailed**.................................... Danube

BERLITZ'S RATINGS

	Possible	Achieved
Hardware	100	60
Accommodation	100	58
Cuisine	100	69
Service	100	65
Miscellaneous	100	65

OVERALL SCORE 317 points out of 500

FLAMENCO ★★★+

CONTEMPORARY AND CASUAL, THIS RIVERSHIP PROVIDES A GOOD-VALUE EXPERIENCE.

Operator .... Various tour operators	**Passenger beds**.. 200
Built 2005	**Sit outside (real) balcony**......................... No
Registry ....Malta	**French (open-air) balcony** .... Yes
Identification number ....ENI 09948011	**Approximate cabin size (sq m)** 13
Length (m) 135.0	**Lift (elevator)**... No
Number of decks (excluding sun deck)......3	**Rivers sailed**.................................... Danube

BERLITZ'S RATINGS

	Possible	Achieved
Hardware	100	72
Accommodation	100	71
Cuisine	100	61
Service	100	61
Miscellaneous	100	66

OVERALL SCORE 331 points out of 500

FLORENTINA ★★★+
THIS OLDER-STYLE RIVERSHIP MAY SUIT IF YOU'RE ON A TIGHT BUDGET.

Operator .... Various tour operators	**Passenger beds** 94
Built 1981	**Sit outside (real) balcony** .... No
Registry .... Czech Republic	**French (open-air) balcony** .... No
Identification number .... ENI 32108292	**Approximate cabin size (sq m)** 10
Length (m) 80.0	**Lift (elevator)** .... No
Number of decks (excluding sun deck) 2	**Rivers sailed** .... Elbe, Moldau

BERLITZ'S RATINGS		
	Possible	Achieved
Hardware	100	50
Accommodation	100	48
Cuisine	100	48
Service	100	50
Miscellaneous	100	52
OVERALL SCORE 248 points out of 500		

FRANCE ★★★
THIS CASUAL, STANDARD RIVERSHIP PROVIDES GOOD VALUE FOR MONEY CRUISES.

Operator .... CroisiEurope	**Passenger beds** 160
Built 2001	**Sit outside (real) balcony** .... No
Registry .... France	**French (open-air) balcony** .... No
Identification number .... ENI 01823029	**Approximate cabin size (sq m)** 12
Length (m) 110.0	**Lift (elevator)** .... No
Number of decks (excluding sun deck) 2	**Rivers sailed** .... Seine

BERLITZ'S RATINGS		
	Possible	Achieved
Hardware	100	60
Accommodation	100	57
Cuisine	100	60
Service	100	57
Miscellaneous	100	58
OVERALL SCORE 292 points out of 500		

FREDERIC CHOPIN ★★★

A SMALL BUT SMART-LOOKING RIVERSHIP, JUST ADEQUATE FOR A BASIC CRUISE.

Operator	Various tour operators	**Passenger beds**	79
Built	2002	**Sit outside (real) balcony**	No
Registry	Switzerland	**French (open-air) balcony**	No
Identification number	ENI 04801240	**Approximate cabin size (sq m)**	9–13
Length (m)	83.0	**Lift (elevator)**	No
Number of decks (excluding sun deck)	2	**Rivers sailed**	Elbe, Havel, Oder

BERLITZ'S RATINGS

	Possible	Achieved
Hardware	100	61
Accommodation	100	58
Cuisine	100	60
Service	100	56
Miscellaneous	100	60

OVERALL SCORE 295 points out of 500

GÉRARD SCHMITTER ★★★+

THIS SMART-LOOKING RIVERSHIP HAS GOOD FEATURES AND A FRENCH AMBIENCE.

Operator	CroisiEurope	**Passenger beds**	176
Built	2012	**Sit outside (real) balcony**	No
Registry	France	**French (open-air) balcony**	Yes
Identification number	ENI 01831335	**Approximate cabin size (sq m)**	12
Length (m)	110.0	**Lift (elevator)**	No
Number of decks (excluding sun deck)	3	**Rivers sailed**	Danube, Rhine, Main

BERLITZ'S RATINGS

	Possible	Achieved
Hardware	100	73
Accommodation	100	67
Cuisine	100	61
Service	100	64
Miscellaneous	100	66

OVERALL SCORE 331 points out of 500

GIL EANES ★★★+
DELIVERS AN ADEQUATE CRUISE EXPERIENCE, BUT THERE'S LITTLE FINESSE.

Operator ....CroisiEurope	Passenger beds.. 132
Built 2015	Sit outside (real) balcony ....No
Registry ....France	French (open-air) balcony ....Yes
Identification number .... MMSI 226010820	Approximate cabin size (sq m) 14
Length (m) 80.0	Lift (elevator)...Yes
Number of decks (excluding sun deck)......2	Rivers sailed......................................Douro

BERLITZ'S RATINGS

	Possible	Achieved
Hardware	100	74
Accommodation	100	68
Cuisine	100	62
Service	100	65
Miscellaneous	100	67

OVERALL SCORE 336 points out of 500

GRACE NYR
THIS IS A GOOD CHOICE FOR A STYLISH, FIRST-RATE RIVER CRUISE.

Operator .... Tauck	Passenger beds..142
Built 2016	Sit outside (real) balcony ....No
Registry .... Switzerland	French (open-air) balcony ....Yes
Identification number ....N/A	Approximate cabin size (sq m) 14–28
Length (m) 135.0	Lift (elevator)...Yes
Number of decks (excluding sun deck)......3	Rivers sailed......................................Rhine

NEW RIVERSHIP

BERLITZ'S RATINGS

	Possible	Achieved
Hardware	100	NYR
Accommodation	100	NYR
Cuisine	100	NYR
Service	100	NYR
Miscellaneous	100	NYR

OVERALL SCORE NYR points out of 500

HEIDELBERG ★★★
THIS MODERN RIVERSHIP WOULD BE A GOOD CHOICE FOR A WELL-ROUNDED CRUISE.

Operator .... Various tour operators	**Passenger beds**... 112
Built 2004	**Sit outside (real) balcony**.......................... No
Registry .... Switzerland	**French (open-air) balcony** .... Yes
Identification number ....ENI 04802890	**Approximate cabin size (sq m)** 13–18
Length (m) 110.0	**Lift (elevator)**... No
Number of decks (excluding sun deck)...... 2	**Rivers sailed**............................Mosel, Rhine

BERLITZ'S RATINGS

	Possible	Achieved
Hardware	100	58
Accommodation	100	57
Cuisine	100	57
Service	100	56
Miscellaneous	100	60

OVERALL SCORE 288 points out of 500

HEINRICH HEINE ★★★
THIS NOW-DATED RIVERSHIP HAS SOME GOOD FEATURES FOR A COMFORTABLE CRUISE.

Operator .... Various tour operators	**Passenger beds**... 110
Built 1991	**Sit outside (real) balcony**.......................... No
Registry .... Bulgaria	**French (open-air) balcony** .... No
Identification number ....ENI 08948008	**Approximate cabin size (sq m)** 12–17
Length (m) 106.6	**Lift (elevator)**... Yes
Number of decks (excluding sun deck)...... 2	**Rivers sailed**................................... Danube

BERLITZ'S RATINGS

	Possible	Achieved
Hardware	100	51
Accommodation	100	51
Cuisine	100	52
Service	100	53
Miscellaneous	100	58

OVERALL SCORE 265 points out of 500

HEMINGWAY ★★★

THIS RIVERSHIP IS DATED, BUT IS STILL MODESTLY COMFORTABLE.

Operator .... Papageno Touristik		**Passenger beds** 148	
Built 1994		**Sit outside (real) balcony** .... No	
Registry .... Switzerland		**French (open-air) balcony** .... No	
Identification number ....ENI 07001903		**Approximate cabin size (sq m)** 9–10	
Length (m) 105.0		**Lift (elevator)** .... No	
Number of decks (excluding sun deck) 2		**Rivers sailed** .... Rhine	

BERLITZ'S RATINGS

	Possible	Achieved
Hardware	100	52
Accommodation	100	51
Cuisine	100	60
Service	100	55
Miscellaneous	100	61

OVERALL SCORE 279 points out of 500

INFANTE DON HENRIQUE ★★★

EXPECT A COMFORTABLE, STANDARD CRUISE ON THIS SMALL DOURO RIVERSHIP.

Operator ....CroisiEurope		**Passenger beds** 142	
Built 2003		**Sit outside (real) balcony** .... No	
Registry ....France		**French (open-air) balcony** .... No	
Identification number ....ENI 01823121		**Approximate cabin size (sq m)** 12	
Length (m) 75.0		**Lift (elevator)** .... Yes	
Number of decks (excluding sun deck) 2		**Rivers sailed** ....Douro	

BERLITZ'S RATINGS

	Possible	Achieved
Hardware	100	57
Accommodation	100	55
Cuisine	100	58
Service	100	58
Miscellaneous	100	60

OVERALL SCORE 288 points out of 500

INSPIRE ★★★★
THIS SMART RIVERSHIP DELIVERS A HIGH-QUALITY CRUISE EXPERIENCE.

Operator .... Tauck	Passenger beds... 142
Built 2014	Sit outside (real) balcony......................... No
Registry ....Malta	French (open-air) balcony .... Yes
Identification number ....ENI 65000006	Approximate cabin size (sq m) 14–28
Length (m) 135.0	Lift (elevator)... Yes
Number of decks (excluding sun deck)......3	Rivers sailed .... Rhine

BERLITZ'S RATINGS		
	Possible	Achieved
Hardware	100	78
Accommodation	100	79
Cuisine	100	75
Service	100	75
Miscellaneous	100	75
OVERALL SCORE 382 points out of 500		

INVICTA ★★
A SMALL, OLDER DOURO RIVERSHIP FOR A BASIC, INEXPENSIVE CRUISE.

Operator .... Various tour operators	Passenger beds...80
Built 1963	Sit outside (real) balcony......................... No
Registry ....Portugal	French (open-air) balcony .... No
Identification number ....ENI 02315334	Approximate cabin size (sq m) 6–9
Length (m) 68.0	Lift (elevator).. No
Number of decks (excluding sun deck)......2	Rivers sailed .... Douro

BERLITZ'S RATINGS		
	Possible	Achieved
Hardware	100	38
Accommodation	100	36
Cuisine	100	40
Service	100	41
Miscellaneous	100	43
OVERALL SCORE 198 points out of 500		

JANE AUSTEN ★★★★

BLING IS ABSENT IN THIS VERY COMFORTABLE ENGLISH-STYLE RIVERSHIP.

Operator ....Riviera Travel	**Passenger beds**............................. 148
Built 2014	**Sit outside (real) balcony**.......................... No
Registry .... Switzerland	**French (open-air) balcony**...................... Yes
Identification number ....ENI 07001430	**Approximate cabin size (sq m)** 15–22.5
Length (m) 135.0	**Lift (elevator)**.. Yes
Number of decks (excluding sun deck)......3	**Rivers sailed**............... Rhine, Main, Danube

BERLITZ'S RATINGS		
	Possible	Achieved
Hardware	100	81
Accommodation	100	78
Cuisine	100	74
Service	100	74
Miscellaneous	100	78
OVERALL SCORE 385 points out of 500		

JOHANNES BRAHMS ★★★

A SHALLOW DRAUGHT VESSEL FOR BUDGET CRUISES ON THE ODER.

Operator .... Various tour operators	**Passenger beds**..80
Built 1998	**Sit outside (real) balcony**.......................... No
Registry .... Germany	**French (open-air) balcony**...................... No
Identification number ....ENI 04033510	**Approximate cabin size (sq m)** 11
Length (m) 81.9	**Lift (elevator)**.. No
Number of decks (excluding sun deck)......2	**Rivers sailed**..Oder

BERLITZ'S RATINGS		
	Possible	Achieved
Hardware	100	58
Accommodation	100	57
Cuisine	100	57
Service	100	58
Miscellaneous	100	60
OVERALL SCORE 290 points out of 500		

JOY NYR

A FINE CHOICE FOR A STYLISH, FIRST-RATE, WELL-ORGANISED CRUISE.

Operator .... Tauck	Passenger beds 142
Built 2016	Sit outside (real) balcony .... No
Registry .... Switzerland	French (open-air) balcony .... Yes
Identification number .... N/A	Approximate cabin size (sq m) 14–28
Length (m) 135.0	Lift (elevator) .... Yes
Number of decks (excluding sun deck) 3	Rivers sailed .... Danube

BERLITZ'S RATINGS

	Possible	Achieved
Hardware	100	NYR
Accommodation	100	NYR
Cuisine	100	NYR
Service	100	NYR
Miscellaneous	100	NYR
OVERALL SCORE NYR points out of 500		

KATHARINA VON BORA ★★★

THIS SMALL, SMART-LOOKING RIVERSHIP IS ADEQUATE FOR A BASIC CRUISE.

Operator .... Various tour operators	Passenger beds 80
Built 2000	Sit outside (real) balcony .... No
Registry .... Switzerland	French (open-air) balcony .... No
Identification number .... ENI 05803950	Approximate cabin size (sq m) 9–11
Length (m) 83.0	Lift (elevator) .... No
Number of decks (excluding sun deck) 2	Rivers sailed .... Various European rivers

BERLITZ'S RATINGS

	Possible	Achieved
Hardware	100	59
Accommodation	100	58
Cuisine	100	57
Service	100	58
Miscellaneous	100	60
OVERALL SCORE 292 points out of 500		

KOENIGSTEIN ★★+
THIS SMALL, STANDARD-QUALITY RIVERSHIP IS DATED BUT CHARACTERFUL.

Operator ....Konigstein River Cruises	**Passenger beds**..60
Built 1992	**Sit outside (real) balcony** ....No
Registry ....Germany	**French (open-air) balcony** ....No
Identification number ....ENI 05502420	**Approximate cabin size (sq m)** 11
Length (m) 68.0	**Lift (elevator)**..No
Number of decks (excluding sun deck)......2	**Rivers sailed**......Elbe, Havel, Moldau, Vltava

BERLITZ'S RATINGS

	Possible	Achieved
Hardware	100	48
Accommodation	100	45
Cuisine	100	51
Service	100	51
Miscellaneous	100	51
OVERALL SCORE 246 points out of 500		

L'EUROPE ★★★
A RELATIVELY COMFORTABLE RIVERSHIP OFFERING A DECENT FRENCH-STYLE CRUISE.

Operator ....CroisiEurope	**Passenger beds**..178
Built 2006	**Sit outside (real) balcony** ....No
Registry ....France	**French (open-air) balcony** ....No
Identification number ....ENI 01823178	**Approximate cabin size (sq m)** 12
Length (m) 110.0	**Lift (elevator)**..No
Number of decks (excluding sun deck)......3	**Rivers sailed**...............Danube, Rhine, Main

BERLITZ'S RATINGS

	Possible	Achieved
Hardware	100	62
Accommodation	100	62
Cuisine	100	60
Service	100	55
Miscellaneous	100	59
OVERALL SCORE 298 points out of 500		

LA BELLE DE CADIX ★★★

THIS HIGH-DENSITY RIVERSHIP PROVIDES A DECENT BUT HECTIC CRUISE EXPERIENCE.

Operator .... CroisiEurope	Passenger beds... 176
Built 2005	Sit outside (real) balcony .... No
Registry .... Belgium	French (open-air) balcony .... No
Identification number .... IMO 9068938	Approximate cabin size (sq m) 9-12
Length (m) 110.0	Lift (elevator)... No
Number of decks (excluding sun deck)...... 3	Rivers sailed .... Guadalquiver

BERLITZ'S RATINGS		
	Possible	Achieved
Hardware	100	64
Accommodation	100	57
Cuisine	100	60
Service	100	55
Miscellaneous	100	60
OVERALL SCORE 296 points out of 500		

LA BOHEME ★★★

THIS OLDER RIVERSHIP DELIVERS A STANDARD-QUALITY CRUISE EXPERIENCE.

Operator .... CroisiEurope	Passenger beds... 164
Built 1995	Sit outside (real) balcony .... No
Registry .... France	French (open-air) balcony .... No
Identification number .... ENI 01822744	Approximate cabin size (sq m) 12
Length (m) 110.0	Lift (elevator)... No
Number of decks (excluding sun deck)...... 2	Rivers sailed .... Danube, Rhine, Main

BERLITZ'S RATINGS		
	Possible	Achieved
Hardware	100	56
Accommodation	100	54
Cuisine	100	60
Service	100	55
Miscellaneous	100	57
OVERALL SCORE 282 points out of 500		

LADY ANNE ★★+
A TIRED GRANNY OF A RIVERSHIP FOR BUDGET, BUT COMFORTABLE, NO-FRILLS CRUISING.

Operator ....Feenstra Rhine Line	**Passenger beds**...106
Built 1963	**Sit outside (real) balcony**.........................No
Registry ....Netherlands	**French (open-air) balcony** ....No
Identification number ....ENI 02007059	**Approximate cabin size (sq m)** 6
Length (m) 70.0	**Lift (elevator)**..No
Number of decks (excluding sun deck)......2	**Rivers sailed**...Rhine

BERLITZ'S RATINGS

	Possible	Achieved
Hardware	100	38
Accommodation	100	38
Cuisine	100	57
Service	100	45
Miscellaneous	100	51
OVERALL SCORE 229 points out of 500		

LAFAYETTE ★★★+
THIS SMALL VESSEL PROVIDES A MODERATELY COMFORTABLE CRUISE.

Operator ....CroisiEurope	**Passenger beds**...84
Built 2014	**Sit outside (real) balcony**.........................No
Registry ....France	**French (open-air) balcony** ....No
Identification number ....ENI 01822624	**Approximate cabin size (sq m)** 16
Length (m) 90.0	**Lift (elevator)**..No
Number of decks (excluding sun deck)......2	**Rivers sailed**...............Rhine, Main, Danube

BERLITZ'S RATINGS

	Possible	Achieved
Hardware	100	72
Accommodation	100	66
Cuisine	100	64
Service	100	63
Miscellaneous	100	66
OVERALL SCORE 331 points out of 500		

LEONARDO DA VINCI ★★★
THIS FRENCH-STYLE RIVERSHIP DELIVERS A GOOD-VALUE, COMFORTABLE CRUISE.

Operator ....CroisiEurope	**Passenger beds**... 144
Built 2003	**Sit outside (real) balcony**........................ No
Registry ....France	**French (open-air) balcony** .... No
Identification number ....ENI 01823119	**Approximate cabin size (sq m)** 10–2
Length (m) 105.0	**Lift (elevator)**.. No
Number of decks (excluding sun deck)......2	**Rivers sailed**............... Danube, Rhine, Main

BERLITZ'S RATINGS		
	Possible	Achieved
Hardware	100	61
Accommodation	100	57
Cuisine	100	60
Service	100	56
Miscellaneous	100	57
OVERALL SCORE 291 points out of 500		

LOIRE PRINCESSE ★★★+
THIS VESSEL, CUSTOM-BUILT FOR THE LOIRE, IS INNOVATIVE AND CHIC.

Operator ....CroisiEurope	**Passenger beds**...96
Built 2015	**Sit outside (real) balcony**...................... Yes
Registry ....France	**French (open-air) balcony** .... No
Identification number .... MMSI 226010880	**Approximate cabin size (sq m)** 15
Length (m) 95.0	**Lift (elevator)**.. No
Number of decks (excluding sun deck)......2	**Rivers sailed**.. Loire

BERLITZ'S RATINGS		
	Possible	Achieved
Hardware	100	74
Accommodation	100	67
Cuisine	100	65
Service	100	65
Miscellaneous	100	71
OVERALL SCORE 342 points out of 500		

LORD BYRON ★★★★
A HIGH-QUALITY CONTEMPORARY RIVERSHIP FOR A FIRST-CLASS CRUISE EXPERIENCE.

Operator ....Riviera Travel	Passenger beds.. 140
Built 2012	Sit outside (real) balcony....................... No
Registry ....UK	French (open-air) balcony .... Yes
Identification number ....ENI 65000004	Approximate cabin size (sq m) 14–22
Length (m) 110.0	Lift (elevator).. No
Number of decks (excluding sun deck)......3	Rivers sailed................ Rhine, Main, Danube

BERLITZ'S RATINGS		
	Possible	Achieved
Hardware	100	78
Accommodation	100	76
Cuisine	100	76
Service	100	76
Miscellaneous	100	78
OVERALL SCORE 384 points out of 500		

MAXIMA 1 ★★★+
THIS MODERN RIVERSHIP PROVIDES DECENT CREATURE COMFORTS.

Operator .... Various tour operators	Passenger beds..136
Built 2003	Sit outside (real) balcony........................ Yes
Registry ....Malta	French (open-air) balcony .... Yes
Identification number ....ENI 09948005	Approximate cabin size (sq m) 16
Length (m) 126.7	Lift (elevator).. No
Number of decks (excluding sun deck)......3	Rivers sailed................ Rhine, Main, Danube

BERLITZ'S RATINGS		
	Possible	Achieved
Hardware	100	68
Accommodation	100	67
Cuisine	100	63
Service	100	64
Miscellaneous	100	332
OVERALL SCORE 332 points out of 500		

MELODIA ★★★+

THIS TRENDY, CONTEMPORARY, GLASS-FRONTED RIVERSHIP DELIVERS A GOOD CRUISE.

Operator	Premicon
Built	2011
Registry	Germany
Identification number	ENI 04809200
Length (m)	135.0
Number of decks (excluding sun deck)	3

Passenger beds	135
Sit outside (real) balcony	No
French (open-air) balcony	Yes
Approximate cabin size (sq m)	12–15
Lift (elevator)	No
Rivers sailed	Danube

BERLITZ'S RATINGS

	Possible	Achieved
Hardware	100	75
Accommodation	100	68
Cuisine	100	63
Service	100	65
Miscellaneous	100	71

OVERALL SCORE 342 points out of 500

MICHAELANGELO ★★★

CHOOSE THIS FRENCH RIVERSHIP FOR A MODERATELY COMFORTABLE EXPERIENCE.

Operator	CroisiEurope
Built	2000
Registry	France
Identification number	MMSI 211520770
Length (m)	110.0
Number of decks (excluding sun deck)	2

Passenger beds	160
Sit outside (real) balcony	No
French (open-air) balcony	No
Approximate cabin size (sq m)	10–12
Lift (elevator)	No
Rivers sailed	Po, Venetian Lagoon

BERLITZ'S RATINGS

	Possible	Achieved
Hardware	100	60
Accommodation	100	56
Cuisine	100	60
Service	100	56
Miscellaneous	100	60

OVERALL SCORE 292 points out of 500

MISTRAL ★★★

A DATED RIVERSHIP, BUT WITH SOME WELL-ORGANISED FRENCH CHIC.

Operator	CroisiEurope	Passenger beds	158
Built	1999	Sit outside (real) balcony	No
Registry	France	French (open-air) balcony	No
Identification number	MMSI 226001420	Approximate cabin size (sq m)	12
Length (m)	110.0	Lift (elevator)	No
Number of decks (excluding sun deck)	2	Rivers sailed	Rhône, Saône

BERLITZ'S RATINGS		
	Possible	Achieved
Hardware	100	59
Accommodation	100	56
Cuisine	100	60
Service	100	56
Miscellaneous	100	61
OVERALL SCORE 292 points out of 500		

MODIGLIANI ★★★

A CONSISTENT, STANDARD-QUALITY VENETIAN LAGOON CRUISE WITH FRENCH FOOD.

Operator	CroisiEurope	Passenger beds	160
Built	2001	Sit outside (real) balcony	No
Registry	France	French (open-air) balcony	No
Identification number	ENI 01823030	Approximate cabin size (sq m)	12
Length (m)	110.0	Lift (elevator)	No
Number of decks (excluding sun deck)	2	Rivers sailed	Danube, Rhine, Main

BERLITZ'S RATINGS		
	Possible	Achieved
Hardware	100	58
Accommodation	100	57
Cuisine	100	60
Service	100	56
Miscellaneous	100	60
OVERALL SCORE 291 points out of 500		

MONA LISA ★★★

DISAPPOINTINGLY SMALL, PLAIN CABINS, BUT GOOD FRENCH AMBIENCE AND FOOD.

Operator ....CroisiEurope	Passenger beds..100
Built 2000	Sit outside (real) balcony .... No
Registry ....France	French (open-air) balcony .... No
Identification number ....ENI 01822875	Approximate cabin size (sq m) 12
Length (m) 82.5	Lift (elevator).. No
Number of decks (excluding sun deck)......2	Rivers sailed................ Danube, Rhine, Main

BERLITZ'S RATINGS

	Possible	Achieved
Hardware	100	60
Accommodation	100	57
Cuisine	100	60
Service	100	56
Miscellaneous	100	60
OVERALL SCORE 293 points out of 500		

MONET ★★★

THIS COMFORTABLE, BUT NOW DATED, RIVERSHIP HAS A LITTLE FRENCH FLAIR.

Operator ....CroisiEurope	Passenger beds..160
Built 1999	Sit outside (real) balcony .... No
Registry ....France	French (open-air) balcony .... No
Identification number ....ENI 01822874	Approximate cabin size (sq m) 12
Length (m) 110.0	Lift (elevator).. No
Number of decks (excluding sun deck)......2	Rivers sailed................ Danube, Rhine, Main

BERLITZ'S RATINGS

	Possible	Achieved
Hardware	100	58
Accommodation	100	57
Cuisine	100	60
Service	100	56
Miscellaneous	100	58
OVERALL SCORE 289 points out of 500		

MY STORY ★★+
A RIVERSHIP FOR THE ITINERARY AND DESTINATIONS BUT NOT THE FOOD.

Operator .... Transocean Flussreisen	**Passenger beds**.. 100
Built 1971	**Sit outside (real) balcony**......................... No
Registry .... Netherlands	**French (open-air) balcony** .... No
Identification number ....ENI 07001704	**Approximate cabin size (sq m)** 9
Length (m) 105.0	**Lift (elevator)**.. Yes
Number of decks (excluding sun deck) 2	**Rivers sailed**...........Various European rivers

BERLITZ'S RATINGS

	Possible	Achieved
Hardware	100	48
Accommodation	100	47
Cuisine	100	48
Service	100	51
Miscellaneous	100	54
OVERALL SCORE 248 points out of 500		

NESTROY ★★★+
THIS STYLISH, MODERN RIVERSHIP DELIVERS A STANDARD CRUISE EXPERIENCE.

Operator .... Various tour operators	**Passenger beds**... 226
Built 2007	**Sit outside (real) balcony** .... No
Registry .... Switzerland	**French (open-air) balcony** .... Yes
Identification number ....ENI 08001848	**Approximate cabin size (sq m)** 12–17
Length (m) 124.8	**Lift (elevator)**.. Yes
Number of decks (excluding sun deck) 3	**Rivers sailed**.................................... Danube

BERLITZ'S RATINGS

	Possible	Achieved
Hardware	100	67
Accommodation	100	62
Cuisine	100	58
Service	100	57
Miscellaneous	100	62
OVERALL SCORE 306 points out of 500		

NORMANDIE ★★★

CHOOSE THIS FRENCH RIVERSHIP FOR A STANDARD BUT CONSISTENT EXPERIENCE.

Operator .... Various tour operators	**Passenger beds** 100
Built 1989	**Sit outside (real) balcony** .... No
Registry .... Netherlands	**French (open-air) balcony** .... No
Identification number .... ENI 02327268	**Approximate cabin size (sq m)** 7–11
Length (m) 91.2	**Lift (elevator)** .... No
Number of decks (excluding sun deck) 2	**Rivers sailed** .... Danube

BERLITZ'S RATINGS

	Possible	Achieved
Hardware	100	55
Accommodation	100	52
Cuisine	100	53
Service	100	55
Miscellaneous	100	56

OVERALL SCORE 273 points out of 500

OLYMPIA ★★+

THIS SMALL, OLDER-STYLE, NICELY FURNISHED RIVERSHIP HAS A WARM ATMOSPHERE.

Operator .... Newmarket Holidays	**Passenger beds** 102
Built 1984	**Sit outside (real) balcony** .... No
Registry .... Switzerland	**French (open-air) balcony** .... No
Identification number .... ENI 07001846	**Approximate cabin size (sq m)** 10–12
Length (m) 88.5	**Lift (elevator)** .... No
Number of decks (excluding sun deck) 2	**Rivers sailed** .... Rhine

BERLITZ'S RATINGS

	Possible	Achieved
Hardware	100	48
Accommodation	100	47
Cuisine	100	51
Service	100	50
Miscellaneous	100	52

OVERALL SCORE 248 points out of 500

POSEIDON ★★+
A SMALL, OLDER RIVERSHIP WITH DATED FACILITIES OFFERING NO-FRILLS CRUISING.

Operator .... Triton Reisen	**Passenger beds**..96
Built 1980	**Sit outside (real) balcony** .... No
Registry .... Netherlands	**French (open-air) balcony** .... No
Identification number ....ENI 02204965	**Approximate cabin size (sq m)** 8–10
Length (m) 78.0	**Lift (elevator)**.. No
Number of decks (excluding sun deck)......2	**Rivers sailed**...........Various European rivers

BERLITZ'S RATINGS		
	Possible	Achieved
Hardware	100	49
Accommodation	100	47
Cuisine	100	50
Service	100	51
Miscellaneous	100	50
OVERALL SCORE 247 points out of 500		

PREMICON QUEEN ★★★★
THIS DELIGHTFUL RIVERSHIP PROVIDES REALLY EXCELLENT CREATURE COMFORTS.

Operator .... Premicon Line	**Passenger beds**...104
Built 2007	**Sit outside (real) balcony** .... Yes
Registry ....Malta	**French (open-air) balcony** .... Yes
Identification number ....ENI 04806540	**Approximate cabin size (sq m)** 18–30
Length (m) 135.0	**Lift (elevator)**... Yes
Number of decks (excluding sun deck)......3	**Rivers sailed**............... Rhine, Main, Danube

BERLITZ'S RATINGS		
	Possible	Achieved
Hardware	100	82
Accommodation	100	82
Cuisine	100	70
Service	100	70
Miscellaneous	100	80
OVERALL SCORE 384 points out of 500		

PRIMADONNA ★★★
THIS DOUBLE-WIDE RIVERSHIP WITH AMPLE SPACE PROVIDES COMFORTABLE RIVER CRUISES.

Operator .... Euro Shipping Voyages
Built 1998
Registry .... Malta
Identification number .... ENI 09240010
Length (m) 113.4
Number of decks (excluding sun deck) 3

Passenger beds 152
Sit outside (real) balcony .... No
French (open-air) balcony .... Yes
Approximate cabin size (sq m) 11–16
Lift (elevator) .... Yes
Rivers sailed .... Danube

BERLITZ'S RATINGS		
	Possible	Achieved
Hardware	100	61
Accommodation	100	55
Cuisine	100	57
Service	100	58
Miscellaneous	100	60
OVERALL SCORE 291 points out of 500		

PRINCESS ★★+
A SMALL, DUMPY-LOOKING RIVERSHIP FOR BASIC, NO-FRILLS RIVER CRUISING.

Operator .... Swiss International Cruises
Built 1980
Registry .... Netherlands
Identification number .... ENI 02323525
Length (m) 80.0
Number of decks (excluding sun deck) 2

Passenger beds 102
Sit outside (real) balcony .... No
French (open-air) balcony .... No
Approximate cabin size (sq m) 10.5
Lift (elevator) .... No
Rivers sailed .... Elbe, Havel, Oder

BERLITZ'S RATINGS		
	Possible	Achieved
Hardware	100	48
Accommodation	100	47
Cuisine	100	50
Service	100	50
Miscellaneous	100	50
OVERALL SCORE 245 points out of 500		

PRINCESSE D'AQUITAINE ★★★

THIS SMART FRENCH RIVERSHIP DELIVERS A STANDARD, BUT GOOD-VALUE CRUISE.

Operator ....CroisiEurope	**Passenger beds**.. 138
Built 2001	**Sit outside (real) balcony** .... No
Registry ....France	**French (open-air) balcony** .... No
Identification number .... IMO 8919805	**Approximate cabin size (sq m)** 10–12
Length (m) 110.0	**Lift (elevator)**... No
Number of decks (excluding sun deck)...... 2	**Rivers sailed**......................Bordeaux region

BERLITZ'S RATINGS

	Possible	Achieved
Hardware	100	60
Accommodation	100	57
Cuisine	100	60
Service	100	57
Miscellaneous	100	61

OVERALL SCORE 295 points out of 500

PRINCESSE DE PROVENCE ★★★

AN ELEGANTLY DECORATED RIVERSHIP OFFERING DECENT HOSPITALITY.

Operator ....Konigstein River Cruises	**Passenger beds**.. 148
Built 1992	**Sit outside (real) balcony** .... No
Registry .... Switzerland	**French (open-air) balcony** .... No
Identification number .... IMO 8643353	**Approximate cabin size (sq m)** 11
Length (m) 110.7	**Lift (elevator)**... No
Number of decks (excluding sun deck)...... 2	**Rivers sailed**.......................... Rhône, Saône

BERLITZ'S RATINGS

	Possible	Achieved
Hardware	100	58
Accommodation	100	57
Cuisine	100	57
Service	100	58
Miscellaneous	100	60

OVERALL SCORE 290 points out of 500

PRINSES CHRISTINA ★★★+
THIS OLDER RIVERSHIP PROVIDES A NO-FRILLS CRUISE FOR TIGHT BUDGETS.

Operator .... Adelle Cruises	**Passenger beds** 107
Built 1969	**Sit outside (real) balcony** .... No
Registry .... Netherlands	**French (open-air) balcony** .... No
Identification number .... ENI 02326420	**Approximate cabin size (sq m)** 9
Length (m) 72.0	**Lift (elevator)** .... No
Number of decks (excluding sun deck) 2	**Rivers sailed** .... French rivers

BERLITZ'S RATINGS		
	Possible	Achieved
Hardware	100	41
Accommodation	100	39
Cuisine	100	43
Service	100	44
Miscellaneous	100	48
OVERALL SCORE 215 points out of 500		

PRINSES JULIANA ★★
A DATED, UNHANDSOME RIVERSHIP FOR BASIC NO-FRILLS CRUISING.

Operator .... Various tour operators	**Passenger beds** 132
Built 1960	**Sit outside (real) balcony** .... No
Registry .... Switzerland	**French (open-air) balcony** .... No
Identification number .... ENI 07001270	**Approximate cabin size (sq m)** 9
Length (m) 83.2	**Lift (elevator)** .... No
Number of decks (excluding sun deck) 1	**Rivers sailed** .... Mosel, Rhine

BERLITZ'S RATINGS		
	Possible	Achieved
Hardware	100	37
Accommodation	100	38
Cuisine	100	40
Service	100	40
Miscellaneous	100	40
OVERALL SCORE 195 points out of 500		

PRINZESSIN ISABELLA ★★★+
A VERY GOOD CHOICE FOR A WELL-ROUNDED RIVER CRUISE EXPERIENCE.

Operator .... Phoenix Cruises	**Passenger beds** 172
Built 2002	**Sit outside (real) balcony** .... No
Registry .... Malta	**French (open-air) balcony** .... Yes
Identification number .... ENI 04804660	**Approximate cabin size (sq m)** 14–21
Length (m) 125.5	**Lift (elevator)** .... Yes
Number of decks (excluding sun deck) 3	**Rivers sailed** .... Danube

BERLITZ'S RATINGS

	Possible	Achieved
Hardware	100	65
Accommodation	100	63
Cuisine	100	66
Service	100	59
Miscellaneous	100	63

OVERALL SCORE 316 points out of 500

PRINZESSIN KATHARINA ★★★
THIS DELIGHTFUL, GRAND HOTEL-STYLE RIVERSHIP DELIVERS CHARM AND GOOD CUISINE.

Operator .... SE Tours/KVS	**Passenger beds** 152
Built 1991	**Sit outside (real) balcony** .... No
Registry .... Malta	**French (open-air) balcony** .... Yes
Identification number .... ENI 09948003	**Approximate cabin size (sq m)** 11
Length (m) 110.0	**Lift (elevator)** .... No
Number of decks (excluding sun deck) 2	**Rivers sailed** .... Douro

BERLITZ'S RATINGS

	Possible	Achieved
Hardware	100	51
Accommodation	100	51
Cuisine	100	54
Service	100	55
Miscellaneous	100	60

OVERALL SCORE 271 points out of 500

PROVENCE ★★★
THIS CUTE LITTLE BARGE-LIKE VESSEL WILL PROVIDE AN ADEQUATE CRUISE.

Operator ....Grand Circle Cruise Line	**Passenger beds**..46
Built 2000	**Sit outside (real) balcony**....................... Yes
Registry ....France	**French (open-air) balcony** .... Yes
Identification number ....ENI 01830675	**Approximate cabin size (sq m)** 19–19.5
Length (m) 89.0	**Lift (elevator)**... No
Number of decks (excluding sun deck)......2	**Rivers sailed**........................... Rhône, Saône

BERLITZ'S RATINGS

	Possible	Achieved
Hardware	100	48
Accommodation	100	46
Cuisine	100	52
Service	100	60
Miscellaneous	100	60

OVERALL SCORE 266 points out of 500

QUEEN ISABEL ★★★★
THIS SMART-LOOKING RIVERSHIP PROVIDES A FINE DOURO CRUISE.

Operator .... Uniworld Grand	**Passenger beds**... 116
Built 2013	**Sit outside (real) balcony**....................... Yes
Registry ....Portugal	**French (open-air) balcony** .... Yes
Identification number ....N/A	**Approximate cabin size (sq m)** 15–30
Length (m) 79.0	**Lift (elevator)**.. Yes
Number of decks (excluding sun deck)......3	**Rivers sailed**......................................Douro

BERLITZ'S RATINGS

	Possible	Achieved
Hardware	100	80
Accommodation	100	80
Cuisine	100	75
Service	100	70
Miscellaneous	100	76

OVERALL SCORE 381 points out of 500

REGINA RHENI ★★★+

CHOOSE THIS SMART-LOOKING VESSEL FOR A HIGH-QUALITY CRUISE WITH GOOD FOOD.

Operator .... Rijfers River Cruises	**Passenger beds** 160
Built 2000	**Sit outside (real) balcony** .... No
Registry .... Netherlands	**French (open-air) balcony** .... No
Identification number ....ENI 02324591	**Approximate cabin size (sq m)** 11–14
Length (m) 110.0	**Lift (elevator)** .... No
Number of decks (excluding sun deck) 3	**Rivers sailed** .... Rhine, Danube, Main

BERLITZ'S RATINGS

	Possible	Achieved
Hardware	100	60
Accommodation	100	57
Cuisine	100	62
Service	100	62
Miscellaneous	100	67

OVERALL SCORE 311 points out of 500

REMBRANDT ★★★

A SMALL RIVERSHIP KNOWN FOR ITS REASONABLY DECENT CUISINE AND SERVICE.

Operator .... Various tour operators	**Passenger beds** 82
Built 2003	**Sit outside (real) balcony** .... No
Registry .... Switzerland	**French (open-air) balcony** .... No
Identification number ....ENI 07001819	**Approximate cabin size (sq m)** ....N/A
Length (m) 82.0	**Lift (elevator)** .... No
Number of decks (excluding sun deck) 2	**Rivers sailed** .... Rhône, Saône

BERLITZ'S RATINGS

	Possible	Achieved
Hardware	100	Yes
Accommodation	100	58
Cuisine	100	58
Service	100	60
Miscellaneous	100	61

OVERALL SCORE 297 points out of 500

REMBRANDT VON RIJN ★★★
THIS OLDER-STYLE RIVERSHIP OFFERS A BASIC, NO-FRILLS RIVER CRUISE.

Operator ....Feenstra Rhine Line
Built 1985
Registry .... Netherlands
Identification number ....ENI 07001818
Length (m) 110.0
Number of decks (excluding sun deck) 2

Passenger beds 106
Sit outside (real) balcony .... No
French (open-air) balcony .... No
Approximate cabin size (sq m) ....N/A
Lift (elevator) .... Yes
Rivers sailed .... Rhine, Main, Danube

BERLITZ'S RATINGS

	Possible	Achieved
Hardware	100	50
Accommodation	100	48
Cuisine	100	50
Service	100	51
Miscellaneous	100	53

OVERALL SCORE 252 points out of 500

RENOIR ★★★
THIS LITTLE FRENCH VESSEL OFFERS STANDARD CRUISING BUT LACKS PANACHE.

Operator ....CroisiEurope
Built 1999
Registry ....France
Identification number ....ENI 01822865
Length (m) 110.0
Number of decks (excluding sun deck) 2

Passenger beds 158
Sit outside (real) balcony .... No
French (open-air) balcony .... No
Approximate cabin size (sq m) 12
Lift (elevator) .... No
Rivers sailed ....Seine

BERLITZ'S RATINGS

	Possible	Achieved
Hardware	100	58
Accommodation	100	56
Cuisine	100	60
Service	100	56
Miscellaneous	100	62

OVERALL SCORE 292 points out of 500

REX RHENI ★★+
THIS SMALL, HIGH-DENSITY RIVERSHIP DELIVERS AN AVERAGE BASIC CRUISE EXPERIENCE.

Operator Saga Travel	**Passenger beds** 150
Built 1979	**Sit outside (real) balcony** No
Registry Netherlands	**French (open-air) balcony** No
Identification number ENI 02007993	**Approximate cabin size (sq m)** 11.25
Length (m) 90.5	**Lift (elevator)** No
Number of decks (excluding sun deck) 3	**Rivers sailed** Mosel, Rhine

BERLITZ'S RATINGS		
	Possible	Achieved
Hardware	100	48
Accommodation	100	46
Cuisine	100	45
Service	100	50
Miscellaneous	100	55
OVERALL SCORE 244 points out of 500		

RHEIN PRINZESSIN ★★★
THIS REBUILT, HIGH DENSITY VESSEL IS FOR LOW-BUDGET CRUISING.

Operator Phoenix Cruises	**Passenger beds** 140
Built 1999	**Sit outside (real) balcony** No
Registry Switzerland	**French (open-air) balcony** Yes
Identification number ENI 07001717	**Approximate cabin size (sq m)** 15
Length (m) 110.0	**Lift (elevator)** Yes
Number of decks (excluding sun deck) 2	**Rivers sailed** Rhine

BERLITZ'S RATINGS		
	Possible	Achieved
Hardware	100	56
Accommodation	100	53
Cuisine	100	54
Service	100	55
Miscellaneous	100	56
OVERALL SCORE 274 points out of 500		

RHINE PRINCESS ★★

AN OLDER RIVERSHIP SUITABLE FOR THOSE ON A REALLY TIGHT BUDGET.

Operator .... Various tour operators	**Passenger beds** 120
Built 1960	**Sit outside (real) balcony** .... No
Registry .... Switzerland	**French (open-air) balcony** .... No
Identification number .... ENI 07000661	**Approximate cabin size (sq m)** 15
Length (m) 83.2	**Lift (elevator)** .... No
Number of decks (excluding sun deck) 2	**Rivers sailed** .... Mosel, Rhine

BERLITZ'S RATINGS

	Possible	Achieved
Hardware	100	34
Accommodation	100	35
Cuisine	100	38
Service	100	40
Miscellaneous	100	37
OVERALL SCORE 184 points out of 500		

RIGOLETTO ★★★

THIS DATED RIVERSHIP OFFERS A STANDARD, NO-FRILLS CRUISE.

Operator .... SijFa Cruises	**Passenger beds** 120
Built 1987	**Sit outside (real) balcony** .... No
Registry .... Netherlands	**French (open-air) balcony** .... No
Identification number .... ENI 02325887	**Approximate cabin size (sq m)** .... N/A
Length (m) 105.0	**Lift (elevator)** .... No
Number of decks (excluding sun deck) 2	**Rivers sailed** .... Danube

BERLITZ'S RATINGS

	Possible	Achieved
Hardware	100	55
Accommodation	100	56
Cuisine	100	55
Service	100	56
Miscellaneous	100	60
OVERALL SCORE 282 points out of 500		

RIVER ADAGIO ★★★

A COMFORTABLE RIVERSHIP OFFERING A DECENT BUT DATED CRUISE EXPERIENCE.

Operator ....Grand Circle Cruise Line	**Passenger beds**.. 164
Built 2003	**Sit outside (real) balcony**........................ Yes
Registry ....Malta	**French (open-air) balcony** .... Yes
Identification number ....ENI 07001803	**Approximate cabin size (sq m)** 12–15
Length (m) 125.0	**Lift (elevator)**.. Yes
Number of decks (excluding sun deck)......2	**Rivers sailed**................Rhine, Main, Danube

BERLITZ'S RATINGS		
	Possible	Achieved
Hardware	100	57
Accommodation	100	61
Cuisine	100	57
Service	100	58
Miscellaneous	100	61
OVERALL SCORE 294 points out of 500		

RIVER ALLEGRO ★★★

A RIVERSHIP FOR THE ITINERARY AND DESTINATIONS, BUT NOT THE FOOD.

Operator ....Grand Circle Cruise Line	**Passenger beds**..90
Built 1991	**Sit outside (real) balcony** .... No
Registry ....Malta	**French (open-air) balcony** .... No
Identification number ....ENI 02315025	**Approximate cabin size (sq m)** 11
Length (m) 97.5	**Lift (elevator)**... No
Number of decks (excluding sun deck)......2	**Rivers sailed**......Elbe, Havel, Moldau, Vltava

BERLITZ'S RATINGS		
	Possible	Achieved
Hardware	100	54
Accommodation	100	56
Cuisine	100	57
Service	100	58
Miscellaneous	100	60
OVERALL SCORE 285 points out of 500		

RIVER AMBASSADOR ★★★

THIS RIVERSHIP HAS OODLES OF PANACHE AND DELIVERS AN 'INCLUSIVE' CRUISE.

Operator .... Uniworld Grand	Passenger beds... 128
Built 1993	Sit outside (real) balcony .... No
Registry .... Netherlands	French (open-air) balcony .... Yes
Identification number ....ENI 02320666	Approximate cabin size (sq m) 12–24
Length (m) 110.0	Lift (elevator)... No
Number of decks (excluding sun deck)...... 2	Rivers sailed .... Rhine, Main, Danube

BERLITZ'S RATINGS

	Possible	Achieved
Hardware	100	56
Accommodation	100	61
Cuisine	100	57
Service	100	59
Miscellaneous	100	60
OVERALL SCORE 293 points out of 500		

RIVER ARIA ★★★

THIS RIVERSHIP SHOULD PROVIDE YOU WITH A DECENT CRUISE EXPERIENCE.

Operator ....Grand Circle Cruise Line	Passenger beds... 164
Built 2001	Sit outside (real) balcony .... No
Registry ....Malta	French (open-air) balcony .... Yes
Identification number ....ENI 07001740	Approximate cabin size (sq m) 12–15
Length (m) 125.0	Lift (elevator)... Yes
Number of decks (excluding sun deck)...... 3	Rivers sailed .... Rhine, Main, Danube

BERLITZ'S RATINGS

	Possible	Achieved
Hardware	100	61
Accommodation	100	60
Cuisine	100	58
Service	100	57
Miscellaneous	100	62
OVERALL SCORE 298 points out of 500		

RIVER ART ★★★+

THIS MODERN VESSEL IS A GOOD CHOICE FOR A WELL-ROUNDED CRUISE.

Operator ....Konigstein River Cruises	**Passenger beds**.. 164
Built 2005	**Sit outside (real) balcony** .... No
Registry .... Switzerland	**French (open-air) balcony** .... Yes
Identification number ....ENI 07001812	**Approximate cabin size (sq m)** 13–20
Length (m) 109.9	**Lift (elevator)**.. No
Number of decks (excluding sun deck)...... 2	**Rivers sailed**....................................... Rhine

BERLITZ'S RATINGS

	Possible	Achieved
Hardware	100	67
Accommodation	100	64
Cuisine	100	62
Service	100	58
Miscellaneous	100	66
OVERALL SCORE 317 points out of 500		

RIVER BARONESS ★★★

THIS RIVERSHIP HAS CLUTTERED BUT GRAND HOTEL DECOR.

Operator .... Uniworld Grand	**Passenger beds**.. 132
Built 1995	**Sit outside (real) balcony** .... No
Registry .... Netherlands	**French (open-air) balcony** .... Yes
Identification number ....ENI 02320666	**Approximate cabin size (sq m)** 12–24
Length (m) 110.0	**Lift (elevator)**.. No
Number of decks (excluding sun deck)...... 2	**Rivers sailed**..Seine

BERLITZ'S RATINGS

	Possible	Achieved
Hardware	100	57
Accommodation	100	57
Cuisine	100	61
Service	100	58
Miscellaneous	100	61
OVERALL SCORE 294 points out of 500		

RIVER BEATRICE ★★★+

THIS BOUTIQUE RIVERSHIP OFFERS ELEGANT DECOR AND CHIC, QUALITY CRUISING.

Operator .... Uniworld Grand	**Passenger beds**... 160
Built 2007	**Sit outside (real) balcony**......................... No
Registry .... Netherlands	**French (open-air) balcony** .... Yes
Identification number ....ENI 02329007	**Approximate cabin size (sq m)** 14–28
Length (m) 125.0	**Lift (elevator)**... Yes
Number of decks (excluding sun deck)...... 3	**Rivers sailed**.................................. Danube

BERLITZ'S RATINGS

	Possible	Achieved
Hardware	100	67
Accommodation	100	70
Cuisine	100	66
Service	100	61
Miscellaneous	100	65

OVERALL SCORE 329 points out of 500

RIVER CHANSON ★★★+

PLEASING TRADITIONAL STYLE AND COMFORT WITHOUT ANY BLING.

Operator ....Grand Circle Cruise Line	**Passenger beds**... 88
Built 2001	**Sit outside (real) balcony**......................... No
Registry ....Malta	**French (open-air) balcony** .... No
Identification number ....ENI 04800450	**Approximate cabin size (sq m)** 11–14
Length (m) 103.0	**Lift (elevator)**... No
Number of decks (excluding sun deck)...... 2	**Rivers sailed**................................... Gironde

BERLITZ'S RATINGS

	Possible	Achieved
Hardware	100	62
Accommodation	100	64
Cuisine	100	60
Service	100	64
Miscellaneous	100	65

OVERALL SCORE 315 points out of 500

RIVER CONCERTO ★★★

THIS OLDER, WELL-PROPORTIONED RIVERSHIP WILL DELIVER A DECENT CRUISE EXPERIENCE.

Operator ....Grand Circle Cruise Line	**Passenger beds**.. 143
Built 2000	**Sit outside (real) balcony**......................... No
Registry ....Malta	**French (open-air) balcony** .... Yes
Identification number ....ENI 07001728	**Approximate cabin size (sq m)** 12–15
Length (m) 110.0	**Lift (elevator)**.. Yes
Number of decks (excluding sun deck)......3	**Rivers sailed**...............Rhine, Main, Danube

BERLITZ'S RATINGS

	Possible	Achieved
Hardware	100	59
Accommodation	100	61
Cuisine	100	58
Service	100	59
Miscellaneous	100	61
OVERALL SCORE 298 points out of 500		

RIVER COUNTESS ★★★+

CHOOSE THIS COMFORTABLE RIVERSHIP FOR ITS GOOD-QUALITY FURNISHINGS AND ITINERARY.

Operator .... Uniworld Grand	**Passenger beds**.. 134
Built 2003	**Sit outside (real) balcony**......................... No
Registry .... Switzerland	**French (open-air) balcony** .... No
Identification number ....ENI 07001802	**Approximate cabin size (sq m)** 14–21
Length (m) 110.0	**Lift (elevator)**.. Yes
Number of decks (excluding sun deck)......3	**Rivers sailed**......................Venetian Lagoon

BERLITZ'S RATINGS

	Possible	Achieved
Hardware	100	63
Accommodation	100	66
Cuisine	100	64
Service	100	59
Miscellaneous	100	63
OVERALL SCORE 315 points out of 500		

RIVER DISCOVERY II ★★★+
GOOD FACILITIES AND DECENT FOOD MAKE THIS RIVERSHIP A SOUND CHOICE.

Operator ....Vantage River Cruises	**Passenger beds**.. 176
Built 2013	**Sit outside (real) balcony**........................ No
Registry ....Germany	**French (open-air) balcony** .... Yes
Identification number ....ENI 02334834	**Approximate cabin size (sq m)** 11.5–33
Length (m) 135.0	**Lift (elevator)**... Yes
Number of decks (excluding sun deck)......3	**Rivers sailed**........................... Rhône, Saône

BERLITZ'S RATINGS		
	Possible	Achieved
Hardware	100	76
Accommodation	100	72
Cuisine	100	60
Service	100	60
Miscellaneous	100	65
OVERALL SCORE 333 points out of 500		

RIVER DUCHESS ★★★+
AN ELEGANT RIVERSHIP WITH ATTRACTIVE FEATURES FOR A DECENT CRUISE.

Operator .... Uniworld Grand	**Passenger beds**.. 134
Built 2003	**Sit outside (real) balcony**........................ No
Registry .... Switzerland	**French (open-air) balcony** .... Yes
Identification number ....ENI 08001805	**Approximate cabin size (sq m)** 14–21
Length (m) 110.0	**Lift (elevator)**... Yes
Number of decks (excluding sun deck)......3	**Rivers sailed**............... Rhine, Main, Danube

BERLITZ'S RATINGS		
	Possible	Achieved
Hardware	100	64
Accommodation	100	66
Cuisine	100	66
Service	100	59
Miscellaneous	100	65
OVERALL SCORE 320 points out of 500		

RIVER EMPRESS ★★★+
THIS MODERN RIVERSHIP MIGHT BE A GOOD CHOICE FOR A WELL-ROUNDED CRUISE.

Operator .... Uniworld Grand	Passenger beds.. 130
Built 2002	Sit outside (real) balcony .... No
Registry .... Switzerland	French (open-air) balcony .... Yes
Identification number ....ENI 08001740	Approximate cabin size (sq m) 14–21
Length (m) 110.0	Lift (elevator).. Yes
Number of decks (excluding sun deck)......3	Rivers sailed............... Rhine, Main, Danube

BERLITZ'S RATINGS

	Possible	Achieved
Hardware	100	62
Accommodation	100	64
Cuisine	100	64
Service	100	58
Miscellaneous	100	63
OVERALL SCORE 311 points out of 500		

RIVER EXPLORER II ᴺʸᴿ
CHOOSE THIS RIVERSHIP FOR A FINE OVERALL CRUISE EXPERIENCE.

Operator .... Vantage River Cruises	Passenger beds.. 176
Built 2016	Sit outside (real) balcony .... No
Registry .... Germany	French (open-air) balcony .... Yes
Identification number ....N/A	Approximate cabin size (sq m) 11.5–33
Length (m) 135.0	Lift (elevator).. Yes
Number of decks (excluding sun deck)......3	Rivers sailed............... Rhine, Main, Danube

BERLITZ'S RATINGS

	Possible	Achieved
Hardware	100	NYR
Accommodation	100	NYR
Cuisine	100	NYR
Service	100	NYR
Miscellaneous	100	NYR
OVERALL SCORE NYR points out of 500		

RIVER HARMONY ★★★
THIS SMALL RIVERSHIP IS DATED BUT HAS DECENT PRACTICAL FEATURES.

Operator ....Grand Circle Cruise Line
Built 1999
Registry ....Malta
Identification number ....ENI 07001721
Length (m) 110.0
Number of decks (excluding sun deck)......3

Passenger beds.. 143
Sit outside (real) balcony .... No
French (open-air) balcony .... Yes
Approximate cabin size (sq m) 12–15
Lift (elevator).. Yes
Rivers sailed................ Rhine, Main, Danube

BERLITZ'S RATINGS

	Possible	Achieved
Hardware	100	58
Accommodation	100	57
Cuisine	100	57
Service	100	57
Miscellaneous	100	61

OVERALL SCORE 290 points out of 500

RIVER MELODY ★★★
THIS DATED RIVERSHIP STILL PROVIDES A DECENT BACKDROP FOR A RIVER CRUISE.

Operator ....Grand Circle Cruise Line
Built 1999
Registry ....Malta
Identification number ....ENI 07001718
Length (m) 110.0
Number of decks (excluding sun deck)......3

Passenger beds.. 143
Sit outside (real) balcony .... No
French (open-air) balcony .... Yes
Approximate cabin size (sq m) 12–15
Lift (elevator).. Yes
Rivers sailed................ Rhine, Main, Danube

BERLITZ'S RATINGS

	Possible	Achieved
Hardware	100	58
Accommodation	100	57
Cuisine	100	57
Service	100	58
Miscellaneous	100	61

OVERALL SCORE 291 points out of 500

RIVER NAVIGATOR ★★★

THIS RIVERSHIP PROVIDES GOOD FACILITIES FOR A COMFORTABLE CRUISE EXPERIENCE.

Operator ....Vantage River Cruises	**Passenger beds**.. 142
Built 2002	**Sit outside (real) balcony** .... No
Registry ....Malta	**French (open-air) balcony** .... Yes
Identification number ....ENI 04804650	**Approximate cabin size (sq m)** 11.5–28
Length (m) 110.0	**Lift (elevator)**.. Yes
Number of decks (excluding sun deck)......3	**Rivers sailed**............... Rhine, Main, Danube

<table>
<tr><th colspan="3">BERLITZ'S RATINGS</th></tr>
<tr><th></th><th>Possible</th><th>Achieved</th></tr>
<tr><td>Hardware</td><td>100</td><td>62</td></tr>
<tr><td>Accommodation</td><td>100</td><td>56</td></tr>
<tr><td>Cuisine</td><td>100</td><td>58</td></tr>
<tr><td>Service</td><td>100</td><td>60</td></tr>
<tr><td>Miscellaneous</td><td>100</td><td>61</td></tr>
<tr><td colspan="3">OVERALL SCORE 297 points out of 500</td></tr>
</table>

RIVER PRINCESS ★★★+

THIS MODERN RIVERSHIP MIGHT BE A GOOD CHOICE FOR A WELL-ROUNDED CRUISE.

Operator .... Uniworld Grand	**Passenger beds**.. 130
Built 2001	**Sit outside (real) balcony** .... No
Registry .... Netherlands	**French (open-air) balcony** .... Yes
Identification number ....ENI 02325078	**Approximate cabin size (sq m)** 14–21
Length (m) 110.0	**Lift (elevator)**.. Yes
Number of decks (excluding sun deck)......3	**Rivers sailed**............... Rhine, Main, Danube

<table>
<tr><th colspan="3">BERLITZ'S RATINGS</th></tr>
<tr><th></th><th>Possible</th><th>Achieved</th></tr>
<tr><td>Hardware</td><td>100</td><td>61</td></tr>
<tr><td>Accommodation</td><td>100</td><td>62</td></tr>
<tr><td>Cuisine</td><td>100</td><td>61</td></tr>
<tr><td>Service</td><td>100</td><td>64</td></tr>
<tr><td>Miscellaneous</td><td>100</td><td>66</td></tr>
<tr><td colspan="3">OVERALL SCORE 314 points out of 500</td></tr>
</table>

RIVER QUEEN ★★★+

A RETRO-LOOK BOUTIQUE RIVERSHIP WITH TASTEFUL FEATURES AND BAGS OF STYLE.

Operator .... Uniworld Grand	**Passenger beds**.. 140
Built 1999	**Sit outside (real) balcony**......................... No
Registry .... Netherlands	**French (open-air) balcony** .... No
Identification number ....ENI 02323692	**Approximate cabin size (sq m)** 13–20
Length (m) 110.0	**Lift (elevator)**.. Yes
Number of decks (excluding sun deck)......3	**Rivers sailed**............... Rhine, Main, Danube

BERLITZ'S RATINGS

	Possible	Achieved
Hardware	100	61
Accommodation	100	61
Cuisine	100	62
Service	100	66
Miscellaneous	100	66

OVERALL SCORE 316 points out of 500

RIVER RHAPSODY ★★★

THIS SMALL, DATED RIVERSHIP HAS DECENT BASIC FEATURES AND IS GOOD VALUE.

Operator ....Grand Circle Cruise Line	**Passenger beds**.. 143
Built 1999	**Sit outside (real) balcony**......................... No
Registry ....Malta	**French (open-air) balcony** .... Yes
Identification number ....ENI 07001722	**Approximate cabin size (sq m)** 12–5
Length (m) 110.0	**Lift (elevator)**.. Yes
Number of decks (excluding sun deck)......3	**Rivers sailed**............... Rhine, Main, Danube

BERLITZ'S RATINGS

	Possible	Achieved
Hardware	100	57
Accommodation	100	57
Cuisine	100	58
Service	100	59
Miscellaneous	100	61

OVERALL SCORE 292 points out of 500

RIVER ROYALE ★★★+
THIS MODERN RIVERSHIP COULD BE A GOOD CHOICE FOR A WELL-ROUNDED CRUISE.

Operator .... Uniworld Grand	**Passenger beds**.. 143
Built 2006	**Sit outside (real) balcony**.......................... No
Registry .... Netherlands	**French (open-air) balcony** .... Yes
Identification number .... ENI 02327301	**Approximate cabin size (sq m)** 13–20
Length (m) 110.0	**Lift (elevator)**... Yes
Number of decks (excluding sun deck) 3	**Rivers sailed** .... Gironde

BERLITZ'S RATINGS		
	Possible	Achieved
Hardware	100	74
Accommodation	100	72
Cuisine	100	62
Service	100	60
Miscellaneous	100	65
OVERALL SCORE 333 points out of 500		

RIVER SPLENDOR ★★★+
WITH FINE FACILITIES AND FEATURES, THIS CONTEMPORARY RIVERSHIP IS A GOOD CHOICE.

Operator .... Vantage River Cruises	**Passenger beds**.. 176
Built 2013	**Sit outside (real) balcony**.......................... No
Registry .... Germany	**French (open-air) balcony** .... Yes
Identification number .... ENI 02334836	**Approximate cabin size (sq m)** 14–28
Length (m) 135.0	**Lift (elevator)**... Yes
Number of decks (excluding sun deck) 3	**Rivers sailed** .... Rhine, Main, Danube

BERLITZ'S RATINGS		
	Possible	Achieved
Hardware	100	76
Accommodation	100	72
Cuisine	100	60
Service	100	60
Miscellaneous	100	66
OVERALL SCORE 334 points out of 500		

RIVER VENTURE ★★★+

THIS CONTEMPORARY RIVERSHIP, WITH ITS EXCELLENT FACILITIES, MAKES A GOOD CHOICE.

Operator ....Vantage River Cruises	**Passenger beds**... 136
Built 2013	**Sit outside (real) balcony** .... No
Registry .... Germany	**French (open-air) balcony** .... Yes
Identification number ....ENI 02334835	**Approximate cabin size (sq m)** 11.5–23
Length (m) 110.0	**Lift (elevator)**... No
Number of decks (excluding sun deck)......3	**Rivers sailed**...Seine

BERLITZ'S RATINGS		
	Possible	Achieved
Hardware	100	75
Accommodation	100	75
Cuisine	100	60
Service	100	61
Miscellaneous	100	65
OVERALL SCORE 336 points out of 500		

RIVER VOYAGER NYR

A SMART RIVERSHIP THAT PROVIDES A HIGH-QUALITY, GOOD-VALUE CRUISE.

Operator ....Vantage River Cruises	**Passenger beds**... 176
Built 2016	**Sit outside (real) balcony** .... No
Registry .... Germany	**French (open-air) balcony** .... Yes
Identification number .... MMSI 269057538	**Approximate cabin size (sq m)** 11.5–33
Length (m) 135.0	**Lift (elevator)**.. Yes
Number of decks (excluding sun deck)......3	**Rivers sailed**...............Rhine, Main, Danube

NEW RIVERSHIP

BERLITZ'S RATINGS		
	Possible	Achieved
Hardware	100	NYR
Accommodation	100	NYR
Cuisine	100	NYR
Service	100	NYR
Miscellaneous	100	NYR
OVERALL SCORE NYR points out of 500		

ROSSINI ★★★
A DECENT RIVERSHIP FOR THE ITINERARY, NOT THE FOOD OR SPACE.

Operator ....Favorit Reisen	**Passenger beds**.................................. 180
Built 1983	**Sit outside (real) balcony**......................... No
Registry ....Germany	**French (open-air) balcony** .... No
Identification number ....ENI 05116760	**Approximate cabin size (sq m)** 11–14.5
Length (m) 111.0	**Lift (elevator)**.. No
Number of decks (excluding sun deck)...... 2	**Rivers sailed**.................................... Danube

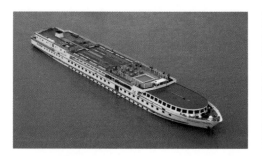

BERLITZ'S RATINGS		
	Possible	Achieved
Hardware	100	51
Accommodation	100	52
Cuisine	100	54
Service	100	54
Miscellaneous	100	58
OVERALL SCORE 269 points out of 500		

ROTTERDAM ★★
THIS SMALL, OLDER RIVERSHIP IS PASSABLE FOR A NO-FRILLS CRUISE EXPERIENCE.

Operator .... Shearings Holidays	**Passenger beds**.................................. 120
Built 1969	**Sit outside (real) balcony**......................... No
Registry .... Switzerland	**French (open-air) balcony** .... No
Identification number ....ENI 07001417	**Approximate cabin size (sq m)** 11–14
Length (m) 75.5	**Lift (elevator)**.. No
Number of decks (excluding sun deck)...... 2	**Rivers sailed**............... Rhine, Main, Danube

BERLITZ'S RATINGS		
	Possible	Achieved
Hardware	100	36
Accommodation	100	34
Cuisine	100	40
Service	100	44
Miscellaneous	100	44
OVERALL SCORE 198 points out of 500		

ROUSSE ★★+

THIS HIGH-DENSITY RIVERSHIP IS ADEQUATE FOR A BASIC NO-FRILLS EXPERIENCE.

Operator ....Various tour operators	**Passenger beds**...185
Built 1984	**Sit outside (real) balcony**.........................No
Registry ....Bulgaria	**French (open-air) balcony** ....No
Identification number ....ENI 47000014	**Approximate cabin size (sq m)** 9–17
Length (m) 113.5	**Lift (elevator)**..Yes
Number of decks (excluding sun deck)......2	**Rivers sailed**...................................Danube

BERLITZ'S RATINGS		
	Possible	Achieved
Hardware	100	46
Accommodation	100	46
Cuisine	100	49
Service	100	46
Miscellaneous	100	50
OVERALL SCORE 237 points out of 500		

ROUSSE PRESTIGE ★★★+

A CONSISTENT, GOOD-VALUE RIVER CRUISE ABOARD A MODERN RIVERSHIP.

Operator ....Phoenix Cruises	**Passenger beds**...156
Built 2004	**Sit outside (real) balcony**.........................No
Registry ....Bulgaria	**French (open-air) balcony** ....No
Identification number ....ENI 08923002	**Approximate cabin size (sq m)** 11–17
Length (m) 110.0	**Lift (elevator)**...No
Number of decks (excluding sun deck)......3	**Rivers sailed**...................................Danube

BERLITZ'S RATINGS		
	Possible	Achieved
Hardware	100	65
Accommodation	100	60
Cuisine	100	60
Service	100	66
Miscellaneous	100	65
OVERALL SCORE 316 points out of 500		

ROYAL CROWN ★★★+
THIS GRAND HOTEL-STYLE RIVERSHIP EVOKES THE PAST WITH FLAIR.

Operator .... Various tour operators	**Passenger beds** 90
Built 1994	**Sit outside (real) balcony** .... No
Registry .... Switzerland	**French (open-air) balcony** .... No
Identification number .... ENI 07001647	**Approximate cabin size (sq m)** 19
Length (m) 110.0	**Lift (elevator)** .... No
Number of decks (excluding sun deck) 2	**Rivers sailed** .... Rhine, Danube, Main

BERLITZ'S RATINGS

	Possible	Achieved
Hardware	100	67
Accommodation	100	62
Cuisine	100	62
Service	100	66
Miscellaneous	100	66

OVERALL SCORE 323 points out of 500

RUGEN ★★+
THIS SMALL, OLDER RIVERSHIP PROVIDES JUST THE BASICS FOR NO-FRILLS CRUISING.

Operator .... Various tour operators	**Passenger beds** 86
Built 1982	**Sit outside (real) balcony** .... No
Registry .... Poland	**French (open-air) balcony** .... No
Identification number .... ENI 04031590	**Approximate cabin size (sq m)** .... N/A
Length (m) 82.5	**Lift (elevator)** .... No
Number of decks (excluding sun deck) 2	**Rivers sailed** .... Vistula

BERLITZ'S RATINGS

	Possible	Achieved
Hardware	100	42
Accommodation	100	41
Cuisine	100	44
Service	100	45
Miscellaneous	100	47

OVERALL SCORE 219 points out of 500

SALVINIA ★★
THIS VINTAGE, HIGH-DENSITY RIVERSHIP OFFERS A BASIC, NO-FRILLS CRUISE.

Operator ....Feenstra Rhine Line	**Passenger beds**...130
Built 1939	**Sit outside (real) balcony**.........................No
Registry ....Netherlands	**French (open-air) balcony** ....No
Identification number ....ENI 02315334	**Approximate cabin size (sq m)** ....N/A
Length (m) 91.5	**Lift (elevator)**..Yes
Number of decks (excluding sun deck)......2	**Rivers sailed**..Rhine

BERLITZ'S RATINGS		
	Possible	Achieved
Hardware	100	35
Accommodation	100	35
Cuisine	100	38
Service	100	38
Miscellaneous	100	40
OVERALL SCORE 186 points out of 500		

SANS SOUCI ★★★
SPECIALLY DESIGNED FOR ELBE CRUISES, THIS RIVERSHIP IS A GOOD CHOICE.

Operator ....Various tour operators	**Passenger beds**...81
Built 2000	**Sit outside (real) balcony**.........................No
Registry ....Germany	**French (open-air) balcony** ....Yes
Identification number ....ENI 02324117	**Approximate cabin size (sq m)** 11
Length (m) 82.0	**Lift (elevator)**..Yes
Number of decks (excluding sun deck)......2	**Rivers sailed**............Elbe-Saal, Havel, Oder

BERLITZ'S RATINGS		
	Possible	Achieved
Hardware	100	60
Accommodation	100	60
Cuisine	100	60
Service	100	57
Miscellaneous	100	61
OVERALL SCORE 298 points out of 500		

SAVOR ★★★★
THIS RIVERSHIP HAS STATE-OF-THE-ART FEATURES, PLUS SPACIOUS CABINS.

Operator .... Tauck	**Passenger beds** 142
Built 2014	**Sit outside (real) balcony** .... No
Registry .... Switzerland	**French (open-air) balcony** .... Yes
Identification number ....ENI 07001997	**Approximate cabin size (sq m)** 14–28
Length (m) 135.0	**Lift (elevator)** .... Yes
Number of decks (excluding sun deck) 3	**Rivers sailed** .... Rhine, Main, Danube

BERLITZ'S RATINGS

	Possible	Achieved
Hardware	100	80
Accommodation	100	77
Cuisine	100	74
Service	100	76
Miscellaneous	100	77

OVERALL SCORE 384 points out of 500

SAXONIA ★★★
THIS SMALL RIVERSHIP HAS ELEGANT DECOR AND PROVIDES A DECENT CRUISE.

Operator .... Phoenix Cruises	**Passenger beds** 87
Built 2001	**Sit outside (real) balcony** .... No
Registry .... Switzerland	**French (open-air) balcony** .... No
Identification number ....ENI 07001736	**Approximate cabin size (sq m)** 11–12
Length (m) 82.0	**Lift (elevator)** .... No
Number of decks (excluding sun deck) 2	**Rivers sailed** .... Elbe-Saal, Havel, Oder

BERLITZ'S RATINGS

	Possible	Achieved
Hardware	100	60
Accommodation	100	54
Cuisine	100	55
Service	100	56
Miscellaneous	100	57

OVERALL SCORE 282 points out of 500

SCENIC AMBER NYR

THIS EXCELLENT VESSEL PROVIDES A WELL-PROGRAMMED CRUISE EXPERIENCE.

Operator .... Scenic	**Passenger beds** 169
Built 2016	**Sit outside (real) balcony** .... No
Registry .... Malta	**French (open-air) balcony** .... Yes
Identification number .... N/A	**Approximate cabin size (sq m)** 19–44
Length (m) 135.0	**Lift (elevator)** .... Yes
Number of decks (excluding sun deck) 3	**Rivers sailed** .... Rhine, Main, Danube

BERLITZ'S RATINGS

	Possible	Achieved
Hardware	100	NYR
Accommodation	100	NYR
Cuisine	100	NYR
Service	100	NYR
Miscellaneous	100	NYR

OVERALL SCORE NYR points out of 500

SCENIC AZURE NYR

CHOOSE THIS VERY COMFORTABLE VESSEL FOR A STYLISH DOURO CRUISE.

Operator .... Scenic	**Passenger beds** 96
Built 2016	**Sit outside (real) balcony** .... No
Registry .... Portugal	**French (open-air) balcony** .... No
Identification number .... N/A	**Approximate cabin size (sq m)** 16–39
Length (m) 80.0	**Lift (elevator)** .... No
Number of decks (excluding sun deck) 3	**Rivers sailed** .... Douro

BERLITZ'S RATINGS

	Possible	Achieved
Hardware	100	NYR
Accommodation	100	NYR
Cuisine	100	NYR
Service	100	NYR
Miscellaneous	100	NYR

OVERALL SCORE NYR points out of 500

SCENIC CRYSTAL ★★★★

THIS RIVERSHIP IS JUST THE TICKET FOR A REALLY FINE CRUISE EXPERIENCE.

Operator	Scenic	**Passenger beds**	171
Built	2012	**Sit outside (real) balcony**	No
Registry	Malta	**French (open-air) balcony**	Yes
Identification number	ENI 02334159	**Approximate cabin size (sq m)**	19–30
Length (m)	135.0	**Lift (elevator)**	Yes
Number of decks (excluding sun deck)	3	**Rivers sailed**	Danube, Rhine, Main

BERLITZ'S RATINGS

	Possible	Achieved
Hardware	100	80
Accommodation	100	79
Cuisine	100	78
Service	100	76
Miscellaneous	100	80
OVERALL SCORE 393 points out of 500		

SCENIC DIAMOND ★★★★

THIS RIVERSHIP IS A GOOD CHOICE FOR A WELL-PROGRAMMED CRUISE EXPERIENCE.

Operator	Scenic	**Passenger beds**	167
Built	2009	**Sit outside (real) balcony**	No
Registry	Malta	**French (open-air) balcony**	Yes
Identification number	ENI 07001905	**Approximate cabin size (sq m)**	15–30
Length (m)	135.0	**Lift (elevator)**	Yes
Number of decks (excluding sun deck)	3	**Rivers sailed**	Bordeaux region

BERLITZ'S RATINGS

	Possible	Achieved
Hardware	100	77
Accommodation	100	76
Cuisine	100	78
Service	100	73
Miscellaneous	100	76
OVERALL SCORE 380 points out of 500		

SCENIC EMERALD ★★★★

THIS RIVERSHIP IS A FINE CHOICE FOR A WELL-ORGANISED CRUISE EXPERIENCE.

Operator .... Scenic	**Passenger beds**...................................... 171
Built 2008	**Sit outside (real) balcony** .... No
Registry ....Malta	**French (open-air) balcony** .... Yes
Identification number ....ENI 07001869	**Approximate cabin size (sq m)** 15–30
Length (m) 134.9	**Lift (elevator)**... Yes
Number of decks (excluding sun deck)......3	**Rivers sailed** .... Rhône, Saône

BERLITZ'S RATINGS

	Possible	Achieved
Hardware	100	73
Accommodation	100	76
Cuisine	100	78
Service	100	73
Miscellaneous	100	77
OVERALL SCORE 377 points out of 500		

SCENIC GEM ★★★★+

THIS IS A GOOD CHOICE FOR A WELL-ORGANISED CRUISE.

Operator .... Scenic	**Passenger beds**...................................... 128
Built 2014	**Sit outside (real) balcony** .... No
Registry ....Malta	**French (open-air) balcony** .... Yes
Identification number ....ENI 02335900	**Approximate cabin size (sq m)** 15–42
Length (m) 110.0	**Lift (elevator)**... Yes
Number of decks (excluding sun deck)......3	**Rivers sailed** ....Seine

BERLITZ'S RATINGS

	Possible	Achieved
Hardware	100	80
Accommodation	100	80
Cuisine	100	82
Service	100	78
Miscellaneous	100	82
OVERALL SCORE 402 points out of 500		

SCENIC JADE ★★★★+
CHOOSE THIS RIVERSHIP FOR A WELL-ORGANISED CRUISE.

Operator	Scenic	**Passenger beds**	171
Built	2014	**Sit outside (real) balcony**	No
Registry	Malta	**French (open-air) balcony**	Yes
Identification number	ENI 02335641	**Approximate cabin size (sq m)**	19–30
Length (m)	135.0	**Lift (elevator)**	Yes
Number of decks (excluding sun deck)	3	**Rivers sailed**	Rhine, Main, Danube

BERLITZ'S RATINGS		
	Possible	Achieved
Hardware	100	81
Accommodation	100	80
Cuisine	100	82
Service	100	78
Miscellaneous	100	82
OVERALL SCORE 403 points out of 500		

SCENIC JASPER ★★★★+
THIS EXTREMELY COMFORTABLE RIVERSHIP PROVIDES A HIGH-QUALITY INCLUSIVE EXPERIENCE.

Operator	Scenic	**Passenger beds**	171
Built	2015	**Sit outside (real) balcony**	No
Registry	Malta	**French (open-air) balcony**	Yes
Identification number	ENI 02335907	**Approximate cabin size (sq m)**	15–44
Length (m)	135.0	**Lift (elevator)**	Yes
Number of decks (excluding sun deck)	3	**Rivers sailed**	Rhine, Main, Danube

BERLITZ'S RATINGS		
	Possible	Achieved
Hardware	100	83
Accommodation	100	82
Cuisine	100	82
Service	100	81
Miscellaneous	100	84
OVERALL SCORE 412 points out of 500		

SCENIC JEWEL ★★★★+

THIS RIVERSHIP IS JUST THE TICKET FOR A REALLY FINE CRUISE EXPERIENCE.

Operator Scenic	**Passenger beds** 171
Built 2013	**Sit outside (real) balcony** No
Registry Malta	**French (open-air) balcony** Yes
Identification number ENI 07001906	**Approximate cabin size (sq m)** 15–30
Length (m) 135.0	**Lift (elevator)** Yes
Number of decks (excluding sun deck) 3	**Rivers sailed** Rhine, Main, Danube

BERLITZ'S RATINGS

	Possible	Achieved
Hardware	100	81
Accommodation	100	78
Cuisine	100	82
Service	100	80
Miscellaneous	100	81
OVERALL SCORE 402 points out of 500		

SCENIC OPAL ★★★★+

THIS WELL-DESIGNED RIVERSHIP PROVIDES AN EXCELLENT INCLUSIVE CRUISE EXPERIENCE.

Operator Scenic	**Passenger beds** 171
Built 2015	**Sit outside (real) balcony** No
Registry Malta	**French (open-air) balcony** Yes
Identification number ENI 02335984	**Approximate cabin size (sq m)** 15–44
Length (m) 135.0	**Lift (elevator)** Yes
Number of decks (excluding sun deck) 3	**Rivers sailed** Rhine

BERLITZ'S RATINGS

	Possible	Achieved
Hardware	100	83
Accommodation	100	82
Cuisine	100	83
Service	100	81
Miscellaneous	100	84
OVERALL SCORE 413 points out of 500		

SCENIC PEARL ★★★★

A STYLISH RIVERSHIP OFFERING A WELL-PROGRAMMED CRUISE.

Operator .... Scenic	**Passenger beds** 171
Built 2011	**Sit outside (real) balcony** .... No
Registry .... Malta	**French (open-air) balcony** .... Yes
Identification number .... ENI 65000002	**Approximate cabin size (sq m)** 15–30
Length (m) 135.0	**Lift (elevator)** .... Yes
Number of decks (excluding sun deck) 2	**Rivers sailed** .... Rhine, Main, Danube

BERLITZ'S RATINGS

	Possible	Achieved
Hardware	100	77
Accommodation	100	77
Cuisine	100	78
Service	100	74
Miscellaneous	100	80

OVERALL SCORE 386 points out of 500

SCENIC RUBY ★★★★

CHOOSE THIS STYLISH RIVERSHIP FOR A GOOD-QUALITY RIVER CRUISE EXPERIENCE.

Operator .... Scenic	**Passenger beds** 171
Built 2009	**Sit outside (real) balcony** .... No
Registry .... Malta	**French (open-air) balcony** .... Yes
Identification number .... ENI 07001907	**Approximate cabin size (sq m)** 15–30
Length (m) 135.0	**Lift (elevator)** .... Yes
Number of decks (excluding sun deck) 3	**Rivers sailed** .... Rhine, Main, Danube

BERLITZ'S RATINGS

	Possible	Achieved
Hardware	100	75
Accommodation	100	77
Cuisine	100	78
Service	100	74
Miscellaneous	100	76

OVERALL SCORE 380 points out of 500

SCENIC SAPPHIRE ★★★★
THIS SOUND RIVERSHIP OFFERS A WELL-PROGRAMMED CRUISE EXPERIENCE.

Operator .... Scenic	Passenger beds.. 171
Built 2008	Sit outside (real) balcony......................... No
Registry ....Malta	French (open-air) balcony .... Yes
Identification number ....ENI 07001865	Approximate cabin size (sq m) 15–30
Length (m) 135.0	Lift (elevator)... Yes
Number of decks (excluding sun deck)......3	Rivers sailed............... Rhine, Main, Danube

BERLITZ'S RATINGS

	Possible	Achieved
Hardware	100	74
Accommodation	100	75
Cuisine	100	78
Service	100	74
Miscellaneous	100	76

OVERALL SCORE 377 points out of 500

SEINE PRINCESS ★★★+
THIS OLDER VESSEL PROVIDES UNFUSSY LOW-COST FRENCH CHIC.

Operator ....CroisiEurope	Passenger beds.. 138
Built 2002	Sit outside (real) balcony......................... No
Registry ....France	French (open-air) balcony .... No
Identification number ....ENI 01823132	Approximate cabin size (sq m) 13
Length (m) 110.0	Lift (elevator)... No
Number of decks (excluding sun deck)......2	Rivers sailed..Seine

BERLITZ'S RATINGS

	Possible	Achieved
Hardware	100	61
Accommodation	100	61
Cuisine	100	64
Service	100	60
Miscellaneous	100	62

OVERALL SCORE 308 points out of 500

SELECT EXPLORER ★★★+
THIS SMART-LOOKING VESSEL HAS GOOD FEATURES, BUT SMALL CABINS.

Operator .... Various tour operators	**Passenger beds**.. 170
Built 2001	**Sit outside (real) balcony**.......................... No
Registry .... Netherlands	**French (open-air) balcony** .... Yes
Identification number .... MMSI 249102000	**Approximate cabin size (sq m)** 14–28
Length (m) 125.5	**Lift (elevator)**.. No
Number of decks (excluding sun deck)......3	**Rivers sailed**............... Rhine, Main, Danube

BERLITZ'S RATINGS

	Possible	Achieved
Hardware	100	62
Accommodation	100	56
Cuisine	100	64
Service	100	64
Miscellaneous	100	65
OVERALL SCORE 311 points out of 500		

SERENADE I ★★★+
A MODESTLY COMFORTABLE VESSEL THAT DELIVERS A DECENT CRUISE EXPERIENCE.

Operator ....Travelsphere	**Passenger beds**.. 130
Built 2005	**Sit outside (real) balcony** .... No
Registry .... Netherlands	**French (open-air) balcony** .... Yes
Identification number ....ENI 02326953	**Approximate cabin size (sq m)** 16
Length (m) 110.0	**Lift (elevator)**... Yes
Number of decks (excluding sun deck)......3	**Rivers sailed**............... Rhine, Main, Danube

BERLITZ'S RATINGS

	Possible	Achieved
Hardware	100	66
Accommodation	100	65
Cuisine	100	61
Service	100	64
Miscellaneous	100	66
OVERALL SCORE 322 points out of 500		

SERENADE 2 ★★★+
THIS IS A COMFORTABLE RIVERSHIP FOR JAPANESE-SPEAKING TRAVELLERS.

Operator ....Nikko Travel	**Passenger beds**.......................137
Built 2007	**Sit outside (real) balcony**.......... No
Registry .... Netherlands	**French (open-air) balcony** .... Yes
Identification number ....ENI 02328761	**Approximate cabin size (sq m)** 16
Length (m) 110.0	**Lift (elevator)**............................. Yes
Number of decks (excluding sun deck)......3	**Rivers sailed**...............Danube, Rhine, Main

BERLITZ'S RATINGS

	Possible	Achieved
Hardware	100	67
Accommodation	100	70
Cuisine	100	65
Service	100	66
Miscellaneous	100	68

OVERALL SCORE 336 points out of 500

SERENITY ★★★+
A HIGH-DENSITY MODERN RIVERSHIP NOTABLE FOR ITS DISTINCTIVE BOLD EXTERIOR.

Operator ....Various tour operators	**Passenger beds**.......................180
Built 2006	**Sit outside (real) balcony**.......... No
Registry .... Netherlands	**French (open-air) balcony** .... Yes
Identification number ....ENI 07001831	**Approximate cabin size (sq m)** 12–12.5
Length (m) 110.0	**Lift (elevator)**............................. Yes
Number of decks (excluding sun deck)......2	**Rivers sailed**...............Danube, Rhine, Main

BERLITZ'S RATINGS

	Possible	Achieved
Hardware	100	72
Accommodation	100	67
Cuisine	100	65
Service	100	66
Miscellaneous	100	68

OVERALL SCORE 338 points out of 500

SONATA ★★★+
THIS RIVERSHIP SHOULD PROVIDE YOU WITH A REALLY FINE CRUISE EXPERIENCE.

Operator .... Various tour operators	**Passenger beds**... 188
Built 2010	**Sit outside (real) balcony** .... No
Registry .... Germany	**French (open-air) balcony** .... Yes
Identification number ....ENI 65000001	**Approximate cabin size (sq m)** 12–15
Length (m) 135.0	**Lift (elevator)**... No
Number of decks (excluding sun deck)......3	**Rivers sailed** .... Rhine, Main, Danube

BERLITZ'S RATINGS		
	Possible	Achieved
Hardware	100	75
Accommodation	100	68
Cuisine	100	63
Service	100	65
Miscellaneous	100	71
OVERALL SCORE 342 points out of 500		

SOUND OF MUSIC ★★★+
ONE FOR THE ITINERARY AND PRICE RATHER THAN THE FOOD.

Operator .... Various tour operators	**Passenger beds**... 132
Built 2006	**Sit outside (real) balcony** .... No
Registry .... Netherlands	**French (open-air) balcony** .... Yes
Identification number ....ENI 02327687	**Approximate cabin size (sq m)** 11.5–18
Length (m) 110.0	**Lift (elevator)**... No
Number of decks (excluding sun deck)......3	**Rivers sailed** .... Rhine, Main, Danube

BERLITZ'S RATINGS		
	Possible	Achieved
Hardware	100	71
Accommodation	100	66
Cuisine	100	66
Service	100	66
Miscellaneous	100	71
OVERALL SCORE 340 points out of 500		

SPIRIT OF CHARTWELL ★★★+
CHOOSE THIS REGAL RIVERSHIP FOR A FINE DOURO CRUISE EXPERIENCE.

Operator .... Various tour operators	**Passenger beds** 30
Built 1997	**Sit outside (real) balcony** .... No
Registry .... Portugal	**French (open-air) balcony** .... No
Identification number .... ENI 07001842	**Approximate cabin size (sq m)** .... N/A
Length (m) 53.8	**Lift (elevator)** .... No
Number of decks (excluding sun deck) 2	**Rivers sailed** .... Douro

BERLITZ'S RATINGS

	Possible	Achieved
Hardware	100	75
Accommodation	100	65
Cuisine	100	66
Service	100	67
Miscellaneous	100	71

OVERALL SCORE 347 points out of 500

S.S. ANTOINETTE ★★★★
THIS UPPER-RANGE VESSEL IS WELL DESIGNED AS A GRAND HOTEL.

Operator .... Uniworld Grand	**Passenger beds** 164
Built 2011	**Sit outside (real) balcony** .... Yes
Registry .... Netherlands	**French (open-air) balcony** .... Yes
Identification number .... ENI 07001935	**Approximate cabin size (sq m)** 15–36
Length (m) 135.0	**Lift (elevator)** .... Yes
Number of decks (excluding sun deck) 3	**Rivers sailed** .... Rhine, Main, Danube

BERLITZ'S RATINGS

	Possible	Achieved
Hardware	100	81
Accommodation	100	81
Cuisine	100	74
Service	100	71
Miscellaneous	100	76

OVERALL SCORE 383 points out of 500

S.S. CATHERINE ★★★★
CHOOSE THIS STYLISH RIVERSHIP FOR A HIGH-QUALITY RIVER CRUISE EXPERIENCE.

Operator .... Uniworld Grand	**Passenger beds** 164
Built 2014	**Sit outside (real) balcony** .... Yes
Registry .... Netherlands	**French (open-air) balcony** .... Yes
Identification number ....ENI 02335392	**Approximate cabin size (sq m)** 11–38
Length (m) 135.0	**Lift (elevator)** .... Yes
Number of decks (excluding sun deck) 3	**Rivers sailed** .... Rhône, Saône

BERLITZ'S RATINGS		
	Possible	Achieved
Hardware	100	82
Accommodation	100	81
Cuisine	100	74
Service	100	74
Miscellaneous	100	76
OVERALL SCORE 387 points out of 500		

S.S. JOSEPHINE NYR
A VESSEL WITH OPULENT, BLING-RICH DECOR.

Operator .... Uniworld Grand	**Passenger beds** 160
Built 2016	**Sit outside (real) balcony** .... Yes
Registry .... Netherlands	**French (open-air) balcony** .... Yes
Identification number ....N/A	**Approximate cabin size (sq m)** 15–38
Length (m) 135.0	**Lift (elevator)** .... Yes
Number of decks (excluding sun deck) 3	**Rivers sailed** .... Rhine, Main, Danube

NEW RIVERSHIP

BERLITZ'S RATINGS		
	Possible	Achieved
Hardware	100	NYR
Accommodation	100	NYR
Cuisine	100	NYR
Service	100	NYR
Miscellaneous	100	NYR
OVERALL SCORE NYR points out of 500		

S.S. MARIA THERESA ★★★★
COMBINES OPULENT DECOR WITH MODERATE FOOD AND SERVICE.

Operator .... Uniworld Grand	**Passenger beds**.. 160
Built 2015	**Sit outside (real) balcony** .... Yes
Registry .... Netherlands	**French (open-air) balcony** .... Yes
Identification number .... MMSI 244830865	**Approximate cabin size (sq m)** 15–38
Length (m) 135.0	**Lift (elevator)**.. Yes
Number of decks (excluding sun deck) 3	**Rivers sailed** .... Rhine, Main, Danube

BERLITZ'S RATINGS		
	Possible	Achieved
Hardware	100	82
Accommodation	100	81
Cuisine	100	74
Service	100	75
Miscellaneous	100	76
OVERALL SCORE 388 points out of 500		

SWISS CORONA ★★★+
THIS VERY COMFORTABLE VESSEL OFFERS A GOOD-QUALITY CRUISE EXPERIENCE.

Operator .... Riviera Travel UK	**Passenger beds**.. 154
Built 2004	**Sit outside (real) balcony** .... No
Registry .... Switzerland	**French (open-air) balcony** .... Yes
Identification number .... ENI 07001807	**Approximate cabin size (sq m)** 15–18
Length (m) 110.0	**Lift (elevator)**.. Yes
Number of decks (excluding sun deck) 3	**Rivers sailed**...................................... Rhône

BERLITZ'S RATINGS		
	Possible	Achieved
Hardware	100	70
Accommodation	100	70
Cuisine	100	63
Service	100	66
Miscellaneous	100	71
OVERALL SCORE 334 points out of 500		

SWISS CROWN ★★★+

THIS MODERN RIVERSHIP WILL PROVIDE YOU WITH A WELL-ROUNDED CRUISE.

Operator ....Scylla		**Passenger beds**.......................................156	
Built 2000		**Sit outside (real) balcony** .... No	
Registry .... Switzerland		**French (open-air) balcony** .... Yes	
Identification number ....ENI 07001725		**Approximate cabin size (sq m)** 13–16	
Length (m) 110.0		**Lift (elevator)**... Yes	
Number of decks (excluding sun deck)......3		**Rivers sailed**............... Danube, Rhine, Main	

BERLITZ'S RATINGS

	Possible	Achieved
Hardware	100	66
Accommodation	100	66
Cuisine	100	64
Service	100	68
Miscellaneous	100	70

OVERALL SCORE 334 points out of 500

SWISS CRYSTAL ★★★+

THIS RIVERSHIP IS A GOOD CHOICE FOR A WELL-ORGANISED CRUISE.

Operator ....Scylla		**Passenger beds**.......................................125	
Built 1995		**Sit outside (real) balcony** .... No	
Registry .... Switzerland		**French (open-air) balcony** .... No	
Identification number ....ENI 07001643		**Approximate cabin size (sq m)** ....N/A	
Length (m) 101.3		**Lift (elevator)**... No	
Number of decks (excluding sun deck)......2		**Rivers sailed**............... Main, Danube, Rhine	

BERLITZ'S RATINGS

	Possible	Achieved
Hardware	100	61
Accommodation	100	58
Cuisine	100	64
Service	100	66
Miscellaneous	100	68

OVERALL SCORE 317 points out of 500

SWISS DIAMOND ★★★+

A SIMPLY DESIGNED RIVERSHIP OFFERING A WELL-ROUNDED RIVER CRUISE.

Operator .... Various tour operators	**Passenger beds** 123
Built 1996	**Sit outside (real) balcony** .... No
Registry .... Switzerland	**French (open-air) balcony** .... No
Identification number .... ENI 07001646	**Approximate cabin size (sq m)** 12
Length (m) 101.3	**Lift (elevator)** .... No
Number of decks (excluding sun deck) 2	**Rivers sailed** .... Main, Danube, Rhine

BERLITZ'S RATINGS		
	Possible	Achieved
Hardware	100	63
Accommodation	100	61
Cuisine	100	64
Service	100	67
Miscellaneous	100	68
OVERALL SCORE 323 points out of 500		

SWISS EMERALD ★★★+

A WELL-RUN RIVERSHIP OFFERING VERY COMFORTABLE CRUISING AND GREAT CUISINE.

Operator .... Tauck	**Passenger beds** 124
Built 2006	**Sit outside (real) balcony** .... No
Registry .... Switzerland	**French (open-air) balcony** .... Yes
Identification number .... ENI 07001825	**Approximate cabin size (sq m)** .... N/A
Length (m) 110.0	**Lift (elevator)** .... Yes
Number of decks (excluding sun deck) 3	**Rivers sailed** .... Rhône, Saône

BERLITZ'S RATINGS		
	Possible	Achieved
Hardware	100	68
Accommodation	100	65
Cuisine	100	65
Service	100	68
Miscellaneous	100	74
OVERALL SCORE 340 points out of 500		

SWISS GLORIA ★★★+
THIS VERY COMFORTABLE VESSEL PROVIDES A WELL-ROUNDED CRUISE.

Operator	Phoenix Cruises	**Passenger beds**	153
Built	2005	**Sit outside (real) balcony**	No
Registry	Switzerland	**French (open-air) balcony**	Yes
Identification number	ENI 07001814	**Approximate cabin size (sq m)**	14–17
Length (m)	110.0	**Lift (elevator)**	Yes
Number of decks (excluding sun deck)	3	**Rivers sailed**	Danube, Main, Rhine

BERLITZ'S RATINGS		
	Possible	Achieved
Hardware	100	70
Accommodation	100	65
Cuisine	100	62
Service	100	64
Miscellaneous	100	71
OVERALL SCORE 332 points out of 500		

SWISS JEWEL ★★★+
CHOOSE THIS STYLISH RIVERSHIP FOR AN EXCELLENT, WELL-ORGANISED RIVER CRUISE.

Operator	Tauck	**Passenger beds**	124
Built	2009	**Sit outside (real) balcony**	No
Registry	Switzerland	**French (open-air) balcony**	Yes
Identification number	ENI 07001906	**Approximate cabin size (sq m)**	15–30
Length (m)	110.0	**Lift (elevator)**	Yes
Number of decks (excluding sun deck)	3	**Rivers sailed**	Danube, Main, Rhine

BERLITZ'S RATINGS		
	Possible	Achieved
Hardware	100	72
Accommodation	100	66
Cuisine	100	64
Service	100	68
Miscellaneous	100	73
OVERALL SCORE 343 points out of 500		

SWISS PEARL ★★★+

AN OLDER RIVERSHIP THAT STILL DELIVERS A GOOD-VALUE CRUISE EXPERIENCE.

Operator .... Various tour operators	Passenger beds.. 123
Built 1993	Sit outside (real) balcony .... No
Registry .... Switzerland	French (open-air) balcony .... No
Identification number ....ENI 08001632	Approximate cabin size (sq m) ....N/A
Length (m) 110.0	Lift (elevator)... No
Number of decks (excluding sun deck)......2	Rivers sailed.......................... Rhône, Saône

BERLITZ'S RATINGS

	Possible	Achieved
Hardware	100	57
Accommodation	100	56
Cuisine	100	61
Service	100	64
Miscellaneous	100	63
OVERALL SCORE 301 points out of 500		

SWISS RUBY ★★★+

CHOOSE THIS SMALL RIVERSHIP FOR A DECENT-QUALITY RIVER CRUISE EXPERIENCE.

Operator .... Rivage Cruises	Passenger beds.. 88
Built 2002	Sit outside (real) balcony .... No
Registry .... Switzerland	French (open-air) balcony .... Yes
Identification number ....ENI 07001742	Approximate cabin size (sq m) ....N/A
Length (m) 85.0	Lift (elevator)... No
Number of decks (excluding sun deck)......2	Rivers sailed.......................... French rivers

BERLITZ'S RATINGS

	Possible	Achieved
Hardware	100	64
Accommodation	100	64
Cuisine	100	65
Service	100	66
Miscellaneous	100	70
OVERALL SCORE 329 points out of 500		

SWISS SAPPHIRE ★★★+

THIS WINNER FROM TAUCK OFFERS AN EXCELLENT UPMARKET ALL-ROUND CRUISE.

Operator .... Tauck	Passenger beds.................................... 124
Built 2008	Sit outside (real) balcony .... No
Registry .... Switzerland	French (open-air) balcony .... Yes
Identification number ....ENI 07001858	Approximate cabin size (sq m) 15–30
Length (m) 110.0	Lift (elevator).. Yes
Number of decks (excluding sun deck)......3	Rivers sailed..Seine

BERLITZ'S RATINGS		
	Possible	Achieved
Hardware	100	70
Accommodation	100	66
Cuisine	100	65
Service	100	66
Miscellaneous	100	73
OVERALL SCORE 340 points out of 500		

SWISS TIARA ★★★+

THIS MODERN VESSEL IS A GOOD CHOICE FOR A DECENT-QUALITY CRUISE.

Operator .... Plantours Cruises	Passenger beds....................................... 153
Built 2006	Sit outside (real) balcony .... No
Registry .... Switzerland	French (open-air) balcony .... Yes
Identification number ....ENI 07001832	Approximate cabin size (sq m) 14–18
Length (m) 110.0	Lift (elevator).. Yes
Number of decks (excluding sun deck)......3	Rivers sailed............... Danube, Rhine, Main

BERLITZ'S RATINGS		
	Possible	Achieved
Hardware	100	67
Accommodation	100	65
Cuisine	100	66
Service	100	66
Miscellaneous	100	70
OVERALL SCORE 334 points out of 500		

SWITZERLAND II ★★★
THIS DATED BUT MODESTLY COMFORTABLE VESSEL HAS GOOD STYLE.

Operator .... Various tour operators	Passenger beds.. 108
Built 1991	Sit outside (real) balcony .... No
Registry .... Switzerland	French (open-air) balcony .... No
Identification number .... ENI 02329015	Approximate cabin size (sq m) 12.5–25
Length (m) 100.0	Lift (elevator)... No
Number of decks (excluding sun deck) 2	Rivers sailed .... Danube, Rhine, Main

BERLITZ'S RATINGS

	Possible	Achieved
Hardware	100	55
Accommodation	100	56
Cuisine	100	65
Service	100	62
Miscellaneous	100	60
OVERALL SCORE 298 points out of 500		

SYMPHONIE ★★★
A FRENCH RIVERSHIP FOR A STRAIGHTFORWARD BUT RELIABLE CRUISE.

Operator .... CroisiEurope	Passenger beds.. 160
Built 1997	Sit outside (real) balcony .... No
Registry .... France	French (open-air) balcony .... No
Identification number .... ENI 01822862	Approximate cabin size (sq m) 10–12
Length (m) 110.0	Lift (elevator)... No
Number of decks (excluding sun deck) 2	Rivers sailed .... Danube, Rhine, Main

BERLITZ'S RATINGS

	Possible	Achieved
Hardware	100	60
Accommodation	100	56
Cuisine	100	58
Service	100	58
Miscellaneous	100	62
OVERALL SCORE 294 points out of 500		

THEODOR KÖRNER ★★
THIS VINTAGE RIVERSHIP IS FOR BICYCLE TOUR PARTICIPANTS ON A TIGHT BUDGET.

Operator ....Rad + Reisen	**Passenger beds**...135
Built 1965	**Sit outside (real) balcony** .... No
Registry ....Germany	**French (open-air) balcony** .... No
Identification number .... MMSI 203999376	**Approximate cabin size (sq m)** 9–10
Length (m) 87.0	**Lift (elevator)**.. No
Number of decks (excluding sun deck)...... 2	**Rivers sailed**.................................... Danube

BERLITZ'S RATINGS		
	Possible	Achieved
Hardware	100	38
Accommodation	100	34
Cuisine	100	40
Service	100	40
Miscellaneous	100	41
OVERALL SCORE 193 points out of 500		

TRAVELMARVEL DIAMOND ★★★+
A STYLISH RIVERSHIP WITH GOOD FACILITIES FOR A DECENT-STANDARD CRUISE.

Operator .... Travel Marvel (APT)	**Passenger beds**...170
Built 2007	**Sit outside (real) balcony** .... No
Registry ....Malta	**French (open-air) balcony** .... Yes
Identification number ....ENI 09948014	**Approximate cabin size (sq m)** 16–24
Length (m) 135.0	**Lift (elevator)**.. No
Number of decks (excluding sun deck)...... 3	**Rivers sailed**.................................... Danube

BERLITZ'S RATINGS		
	Possible	Achieved
Hardware	100	71
Accommodation	100	61
Cuisine	100	67
Service	100	65
Miscellaneous	100	67
OVERALL SCORE 331 points out of 500		

TRAVELMARVEL JEWEL ★★★+
THIS GLASS-FRONTED, MODERN VESSEL DELIVERS A DECENT CRUISE.

Operator .... Travel Marvel (APT)	**Passenger beds**.. 170
Built 2007	**Sit outside (real) balcony**........................ No
Registry ....Malta	**French (open-air) balcony** .... Yes
Identification number ....ENI 09948015	**Approximate cabin size (sq m)** 16–24
Length (m) 135.0	**Lift (elevator)**.. No
Number of decks (excluding sun deck)......3	**Rivers sailed**................................... Danube

BERLITZ'S RATINGS		
	Possible	Achieved
Hardware	100	71
Accommodation	100	61
Cuisine	100	67
Service	100	65
Miscellaneous	100	67
OVERALL SCORE 331 points out of 500		

TRAVELMARVEL SAPPHIRE ★★★+
A MODERATELY PRICED RIVERSHIP FOR ACTIVE, YOUTHFUL TYPES.

Operator .... Travelmarket (APT)	**Passenger beds**.. 164
Built 2006	**Sit outside (real) balcony**........................ No
Registry ....Malta	**French (open-air) balcony** .... Yes
Identification number ....ENI 09948012	**Approximate cabin size (sq m)** 15–22
Length (m) 135.0	**Lift (elevator)**.. No
Number of decks (excluding sun deck)......3	**Rivers sailed**................................... Danube

BERLITZ'S RATINGS		
	Possible	Achieved
Hardware	100	70
Accommodation	100	61
Cuisine	100	67
Service	100	65
Miscellaneous	100	67
OVERALL SCORE 330 points out of 500		

TREASURES ★★★★
THIS COMFORTABLE, MODERN RIVERSHIP OFFERS A WELL-ROUNDED RIVER CRUISE.

Operator .... Tauck	**Passenger beds** 124
Built 2011	**Sit outside (real) balcony** .... No
Registry .... Switzerland	**French (open-air) balcony** .... Yes
Identification number .... ENI 07001943	**Approximate cabin size (sq m)** 15–30
Length (m) 110.0	**Lift (elevator)** .... Yes
Number of decks (excluding sun deck) 3	**Rivers sailed** .... Rhine, Main, Danube

BERLITZ'S RATINGS

	Possible	Achieved
Hardware	100	77
Accommodation	100	77
Cuisine	100	68
Service	100	71
Miscellaneous	100	73
OVERALL SCORE 366 points out of 500		

VAN GOGH ★★★
A STANDARD OLDER VESSEL GOOD FOR FRENCH AMBIENCE AND FOOD.

Operator .... CroisiEurope	**Passenger beds** 160
Built 1999	**Sit outside (real) balcony** .... No
Registry .... France	**French (open-air) balcony** .... No
Identification number .... ENI 02205451	**Approximate cabin size (sq m)** 12
Length (m) 110.0	**Lift (elevator)** .... No
Number of decks (excluding sun deck) 2	**Rivers sailed** .... Rhône, Saône

BERLITZ'S RATINGS

	Possible	Achieved
Hardware	100	56
Accommodation	100	56
Cuisine	100	60
Service	100	56
Miscellaneous	100	58
OVERALL SCORE 286 points out of 500		

VASCO DA GAMA ★★★
THIS STANDARD RIVERSHIP WITHOUT BALCONIES PROVIDES COMFORTABLE TRANSPORT.

Operator ....CroisiEurope	**Passenger beds**....................................... 142
Built 2002	**Sit outside (real) balcony** .... No
Registry ....Portugal	**French (open-air) balcony** .... No
Identification number ...... MMSI 263022000	**Approximate cabin size (sq m)** 10–12
Length (m) 75.0	**Lift (elevator)**... Yes
Number of decks (excluding sun deck)...... 2	**Rivers sailed**......................................Douro

BERLITZ'S RATINGS		
	Possible	Achieved
Hardware	100	60
Accommodation	100	57
Cuisine	100	60
Service	100	56
Miscellaneous	100	60
OVERALL SCORE 293 points out of 500		

VERDI ★★★
GO FOR THE LOW-PRICE AND ITINERARY RATHER THAN THE COMFORT.

Operator .... SijFa Cruises	**Passenger beds**....................................... 150
Built 1995	**Sit outside (real) balcony** .... No
Registry .... Switzerland	**French (open-air) balcony** .... No
Identification number .... MMSI 269057088	**Approximate cabin size (sq m)** ....N/A
Length (m) 101.5	**Lift (elevator)**.. No
Number of decks (excluding sun deck)...... 2	**Rivers sailed**...................................... Rhine

BERLITZ'S RATINGS		
	Possible	Achieved
Hardware	100	54
Accommodation	100	52
Cuisine	100	60
Service	100	60
Miscellaneous	100	62
OVERALL SCORE 288 points out of 500		

VICTOR HUGO ★★★

A STANDARD CRUISE THAT IS NOTHING SPECIAL, BUT COMES WITH FRENCH CHARM.

Operator ....CroisiEurope	**Passenger beds**..100
Built 2000	**Sit outside (real) balcony** ....No
Registry ....France	**French (open-air) balcony** ....No
Identification number ....ENI 01823025	**Approximate cabin size (sq m)** 10–12
Length (m) 82.5	**Lift (elevator)**...No
Number of decks (excluding sun deck)......2	**Rivers sailed**................Danube, Rhine, Main

BERLITZ'S RATINGS		
	Possible	Achieved
Hardware	100	58
Accommodation	100	58
Cuisine	100	62
Service	100	58
Miscellaneous	100	60
OVERALL SCORE 296 points out of 500		

VIKING AEGIR ★★★★

CHOOSE THIS RIVERSHIP FOR A WELL-ORGANISED, HIGH-QUALITY CRUISE EXPERIENCE.

Operator ....Viking River Cruises	**Passenger beds**..190
Built 2012	**Sit outside (real) balcony** ....Yes
Registry .... Switzerland	**French (open-air) balcony** ....Yes
Identification number ....ENI 07001957	**Approximate cabin size (sq m)** 12.5–41
Length (m) 135.0	**Lift (elevator)**...Yes
Number of decks (excluding sun deck)......3	**Rivers sailed**................Danube, Rhine, Main

BERLITZ'S RATINGS		
	Possible	Achieved
Hardware	100	84
Accommodation	100	84
Cuisine	100	75
Service	100	75
Miscellaneous	100	76
OVERALL SCORE 394 points out of 500		

VIKING ALRUNA NYR
ONE OF A SERIES OF VIKING 'LONGSHIPS', EACH NAMED AFTER A NORSE GOD.

Operator ....Viking River Cruises	**Passenger beds**..190
Built 2016	**Sit outside (real) balcony**........................ Yes
Registry .... Switzerland	**French (open-air) balcony** .... Yes
Identification number ....N/A	**Approximate cabin size (sq m)** 12.5–41
Length (m) 135.0	**Lift (elevator)**... Yes
Number of decks (excluding sun deck)......3	**Rivers sailed**....................................... Rhine

BERLITZ'S RATINGS		
	Possible	Achieved
Hardware	100	NYR
Accommodation	100	NYR
Cuisine	100	NYR
Service	100	NYR
Miscellaneous	100	NYR
OVERALL SCORE NYR points out of 500		

VIKING ALSVIN ★★★★
THIS STYLISH, SPACIOUS VESSEL PROVIDES A WELL-ORGANISED CRUISE.

Operator ....Viking River Cruises	**Passenger beds**..190
Built 2014	**Sit outside (real) balcony**........................ Yes
Registry .... Switzerland	**French (open-air) balcony** .... Yes
Identification number ....ENI 07001989	**Approximate cabin size (sq m)** 12.5–41
Length (m) 135.0	**Lift (elevator)**... Yes
Number of decks (excluding sun deck)......3	**Rivers sailed**...............Danube, Rhine, Main

BERLITZ'S RATINGS		
	Possible	Achieved
Hardware	100	84
Accommodation	100	84
Cuisine	100	75
Service	100	76
Miscellaneous	100	77
OVERALL SCORE 396 points out of 500		

VIKING ASTRILD ★★★★
ONE OF A SERIES OF VIKING 'LONGSHIPS', EACH NAMED AFTER A NORSE GOD.

Operator .... Viking River Cruises	**Passenger beds**.. 98
Built 2015	**Sit outside (real) balcony**....................... Yes
Registry .... Switzerland	**French (open-air) balcony** .... Yes
Identification number .... MMSI 269057521	**Approximate cabin size (sq m)** 13–23
Length (m) 110.0	**Lift (elevator)**.. No
Number of decks (excluding sun deck)......3	**Rivers sailed**..Elbe

BERLITZ'S RATINGS

	Possible	Achieved
Hardware	100	84
Accommodation	100	84
Cuisine	100	75
Service	100	75
Miscellaneous	100	76
OVERALL SCORE 394 points out of 500		

VIKING ATLA ★★★★
A GOOD CHOICE FOR A STYLISH, FIRST-RATE RIVER CRUISE.

Operator .... Viking River Cruises	**Passenger beds**.. 190
Built 2013	**Sit outside (real) balcony**....................... Yes
Registry .... Switzerland	**French (open-air) balcony** .... Yes
Identification number ....ENI 07001968	**Approximate cabin size (sq m)** 12.5–41
Length (m) 135.0	**Lift (elevator)**... Yes
Number of decks (excluding sun deck)......3	**Rivers sailed**....................................... Rhine

BERLITZ'S RATINGS

	Possible	Achieved
Hardware	100	83
Accommodation	100	83
Cuisine	100	75
Service	100	75
Miscellaneous	100	76
OVERALL SCORE 392 points out of 500		

VIKING BALDUR ★★★★

A GOOD CHOICE FOR A WELL-PROGRAMMED, STYLISH, FIRST-RATE RIVER CRUISE.

Operator ....Viking River Cruises	**Passenger beds**..190
Built 2014	**Sit outside (real) balcony**........................Yes
Registry ....Switzerland	**French (open-air) balcony**.....................Yes
Identification number ....ENI 07001969	**Approximate cabin size (sq m)** 12.5–41
Length (m) 135.0	**Lift (elevator)**..Yes
Number of decks (excluding sun deck)......3	**Rivers sailed**...............Danube, Rhine, Main

BERLITZ'S RATINGS

	Possible	Achieved
Hardware	100	84
Accommodation	100	84
Cuisine	100	75
Service	100	76
Miscellaneous	100	76
OVERALL SCORE 395 points out of 500		

VIKING BESTLA ★★★★

THIS STYLISH VESSEL IS GREAT FOR A WELL-ORGANISED CRUISE.

Operator ....Viking River Cruises	**Passenger beds**..190
Built 2014	**Sit outside (real) balcony**........................Yes
Registry ....Switzerland	**French (open-air) balcony**.....................Yes
Identification number ....ENI 07001988	**Approximate cabin size (sq m)** 12.5–41
Length (m) 135.0	**Lift (elevator)**..Yes
Number of decks (excluding sun deck)......3	**Rivers sailed**...............Danube, Rhine, Main

BERLITZ'S RATINGS

	Possible	Achieved
Hardware	100	84
Accommodation	100	84
Cuisine	100	75
Service	100	76
Miscellaneous	100	77
OVERALL SCORE 396 points out of 500		

VIKING BEYLA ★★★★

ONE OF A SERIES OF VIKING 'LONGSHIPS', EACH NAMED AFTER A NORSE GOD.

Operator .... Viking River Cruises	**Passenger beds**...98
Built 2015	**Sit outside (real) balcony** .... Yes
Registry .... Switzerland	**French (open-air) balcony** .... Yes
Identification number .... IMO 8053068	**Approximate cabin size (sq m)** 13–23
Length (m) 110.0	**Lift (elevator)**.. No
Number of decks (excluding sun deck) 3	**Rivers sailed**...Elbe

BERLITZ'S RATINGS		
	Possible	Achieved
Hardware	100	84
Accommodation	100	84
Cuisine	100	75
Service	100	76
Miscellaneous	100	76
OVERALL SCORE 395 points out of 500		

VIKING BRAGI ★★★★

A STYLISH CHOICE FOR A WELL-PROGRAMMED, FIRST-RATE RIVER CRUISE.

Operator .... Viking River Cruises	**Passenger beds**...190
Built 2012	**Sit outside (real) balcony** .... Yes
Registry .... Switzerland	**French (open-air) balcony** .... Yes
Identification number .... ENI 07001961	**Approximate cabin size (sq m)** 12.5–41
Length (m) 135.0	**Lift (elevator)**.. Yes
Number of decks (excluding sun deck) 3	**Rivers sailed**............... Rhine, Main, Danube

BERLITZ'S RATINGS		
	Possible	Achieved
Hardware	100	84
Accommodation	100	84
Cuisine	100	75
Service	100	76
Miscellaneous	100	76
OVERALL SCORE 395 points out of 500		

VIKING BURI ★★★★
CHOOSE THIS STYLISH VESSEL FOR A WELL-ORGANISED CRUISE.

Operator ....Viking River Cruises	**Passenger beds**...190
Built 2014	**Sit outside (real) balcony**.........................No
Registry ....Switzerland	**French (open-air) balcony**.....................Yes
Identification number ....ENI 07001978	**Approximate cabin size (sq m)** 12.5–41
Length (m) 135.0	**Lift (elevator)**...Yes
Number of decks (excluding sun deck)......3	**Rivers sailed**...........................Rhône, Saône

BERLITZ'S RATINGS

	Possible	Achieved
Hardware	100	84
Accommodation	100	84
Cuisine	100	75
Service	100	76
Miscellaneous	100	76

OVERALL SCORE 395 points out of 500

VIKING DELLING ★★★★
THIS IS A GOOD CHOICE FOR A FIRST-RATE RIVER CRUISE ON A STYLISH VESSEL.

Operator ....Viking River Cruises	**Passenger beds**...84
Built 2014	**Sit outside (real) balcony**.......................Yes
Registry ....Switzerland	**French (open-air) balcony**.....................Yes
Identification number ....ENI 07001982	**Approximate cabin size (sq m)** 12.5–41
Length (m) 135.0	**Lift (elevator)**...Yes
Number of decks (excluding sun deck)......3	**Rivers sailed**...........................Rhône, Saône

BERLITZ'S RATINGS

	Possible	Achieved
Hardware	100	84
Accommodation	100	84
Cuisine	100	75
Service	100	77
Miscellaneous	100	76

OVERALL SCORE 396 points out of 500

VIKING DOURO ★★★★
CHOOSE THIS STYLISH RIVERSHIP FOR A GOOD-QUALITY DOURO RIVER CRUISE.

Operator ....Viking River Cruises	**Passenger beds**...124
Built 2011	**Sit outside (real) balcony** .... No
Registry .... Switzerland	**French (open-air) balcony** .... Yes
Identification number ....n/a	**Approximate cabin size (sq m)** 14–28
Length (m) 79.5	**Lift (elevator)**....................................... Yes
Number of decks (excluding sun deck)......3	**Rivers sailed**......................................Douro

BERLITZ'S RATINGS		
	Possible	Achieved
Hardware	100	77
Accommodation	100	73
Cuisine	100	73
Service	100	73
Miscellaneous	100	76
OVERALL SCORE 372 points out of 500		

VIKING EGIL ᴺʸᴿ
ONE OF A SERIES OF VIKING 'LONGSHIPS', EACH NAMED AFTER A NORSE GOD.

Operator ....Viking River Cruises	**Passenger beds**...190
Built 2016	**Sit outside (real) balcony** .... Yes
Registry .... Switzerland	**French (open-air) balcony** .... Yes
Identification number ....N/A	**Approximate cabin size (sq m)** 12.5–41
Length (m) 135.0	**Lift (elevator)**....................................... Yes
Number of decks (excluding sun deck)......3	**Rivers sailed**...............Rhine, Main, Danube

BERLITZ'S RATINGS		
	Possible	Achieved
Hardware	100	NYR
Accommodation	100	NYR
Cuisine	100	NYR
Service	100	NYR
Miscellaneous	100	NYR
OVERALL SCORE NYR points out of 500		

VIKING EIR ★★★★
ONE OF A SERIES OF VIKING 'LONGSHIPS', EACH NAMED AFTER A NORSE GOD.

Operator ....Viking River Cruises	**Passenger beds**..190
Built 2015	**Sit outside (real) balcony**.......................Yes
Registry ....Switzerland	**French (open-air) balcony** ....Yes
Identification number ....ENI 07002021	**Approximate cabin size (sq m)** 12.5–41
Length (m) 135.0	**Lift (elevator)**...Yes
Number of decks (excluding sun deck)......3	**Rivers sailed**.......................................Rhine

BERLITZ'S RATINGS

	Possible	Achieved
Hardware	100	84
Accommodation	100	84
Cuisine	100	75
Service	100	76
Miscellaneous	100	77

OVERALL SCORE 396 points out of 500

VIKING EISTLA ★★★★
A STYLISH, CONTEMPORARY RIVERSHIP FOR A REALLY WELL-ORGANISED CRUISE.

Operator ....Viking River Cruises	**Passenger beds**..190
Built 2014	**Sit outside (real) balcony**.......................Yes
Registry ....Switzerland	**French (open-air) balcony** ....Yes
Identification number ....ENI 07001987	**Approximate cabin size (sq m)** 12.5–41
Length (m) 135.0	**Lift (elevator)**...Yes
Number of decks (excluding sun deck)......3	**Rivers sailed**...............Rhine, Main, Danube

BERLITZ'S RATINGS

	Possible	Achieved
Hardware	100	84
Accommodation	100	84
Cuisine	100	75
Service	100	86
Miscellaneous	100	77

OVERALL SCORE 396 points out of 500

VIKING EMBLA ★★★★
THIS STYLISH VESSEL IS EXCELLENT FOR A WELL-ORGANISED CRUISE.

Operator ....Viking River Cruises	**Passenger beds**...190
Built 2012	**Sit outside (real) balcony** ....Yes
Registry ....Switzerland	**French (open-air) balcony** ....Yes
Identification number ....ENI 07001957	**Approximate cabin size (sq m)** 12.5–41
Length (m) 135.0	**Lift (elevator)**..Yes
Number of decks (excluding sun deck)......3	**Rivers sailed**...............Danube, Rhine, Main

BERLITZ'S RATINGS

	Possible	Achieved
Hardware	100	84
Accommodation	100	84
Cuisine	100	75
Service	100	75
Miscellaneous	100	77

OVERALL SCORE 395 points out of 500

VIKING FORSETI ★★★★
THIS RIVERSHIP HAS STATE-OF-THE-ART FEATURES AND GOOD FOOD AND SERVICE.

Operator ....Viking River Cruises	**Passenger beds**...190
Built 2013	**Sit outside (real) balcony** ....Yes
Registry ....Switzerland	**French (open-air) balcony** ....Yes
Identification number ....ENI 07001965	**Approximate cabin size (sq m)** 12.5–41
Length (m) 135.0	**Lift (elevator)**..Yes
Number of decks (excluding sun deck)......3	**Rivers sailed**...................................Gironde

BERLITZ'S RATINGS

	Possible	Achieved
Hardware	100	84
Accommodation	100	84
Cuisine	100	75
Service	100	74
Miscellaneous	100	76

OVERALL SCORE 393 points out of 500

VIKING FREYA ★★★★

THIS HIGH-TECH, STYLISH VESSEL OFFERS A WELL-ORGANISED CRUISE.

Operator ....Viking River Cruises	**Passenger beds**... 190
Built 2012	**Sit outside (real) balcony**........................ Yes
Registry .... Switzerland	**French (open-air) balcony** .... Yes
Identification number ....ENI 07001954	**Approximate cabin size (sq m)** 12.5–41
Length (m) 135.0	**Lift (elevator)**... Yes
Number of decks (excluding sun deck)......3	**Rivers sailed** .... Danube

BERLITZ'S RATINGS		
	Possible	Achieved
Hardware	100	83
Accommodation	100	81
Cuisine	100	75
Service	100	76
Miscellaneous	100	77
OVERALL SCORE 392 points out of 500		

VIKING GEFJON ★★★★

ONE OF A SERIES OF VIKING 'LONGSHIPS', EACH NAMED AFTER A NORSE GOD.

Operator ....Viking River Cruises	**Passenger beds**... 190
Built 2015	**Sit outside (real) balcony**........................ Yes
Registry .... Switzerland	**French (open-air) balcony** .... Yes
Identification number ....ENI 07002016	**Approximate cabin size (sq m)** 12.5–41
Length (m) 135.0	**Lift (elevator)**... Yes
Number of decks (excluding sun deck)......3	**Rivers sailed** ....Rhine, Main, Danube

BERLITZ'S RATINGS		
	Possible	Achieved
Hardware	100	84
Accommodation	100	84
Cuisine	100	75
Service	100	76
Miscellaneous	100	76
OVERALL SCORE 395 points out of 500		

VIKING GULLVEIG ★★★★
CHOOSE THIS STYLISH CONTEMPORARY RIVERSHIP FOR A WELL-ORGANISED CRUISE.

Operator .... Viking River Cruises	**Passenger beds**.. 190
Built 2014	**Sit outside (real) balcony**........................ Yes
Registry .... Switzerland	**French (open-air) balcony** .... Yes
Identification number ....ENI 07001984	**Approximate cabin size (sq m)** 12.5–41
Length (m) 135.0	**Lift (elevator)**... Yes
Number of decks (excluding sun deck)......3	**Rivers sailed**...................................... Rhine

BERLITZ'S RATINGS		
	Possible	Achieved
Hardware	100	84
Accommodation	100	84
Cuisine	100	75
Service	100	76
Miscellaneous	100	76
OVERALL SCORE 395 points out of 500		

VIKING HEIMDAL ★★★★
THIS AIRY, SPACIOUS VESSEL OFFERS A STYLISH, WELL-ORGANISED CRUISE EXPERIENCE.

Operator .... Viking River Cruises	**Passenger beds**.. 190
Built 2014	**Sit outside (real) balcony**........................ Yes
Registry .... Switzerland	**French (open-air) balcony** .... Yes
Identification number ....ENI 07001979	**Approximate cabin size (sq m)** 12.5–41
Length (m) 135.0	**Lift (elevator)**... Yes
Number of decks (excluding sun deck)......3	**Rivers sailed**.......................... Rhône, Saône

BERLITZ'S RATINGS		
	Possible	Achieved
Hardware	100	84
Accommodation	100	84
Cuisine	100	76
Service	100	76
Miscellaneous	100	77
OVERALL SCORE 396 points out of 500		

VIKING HEMMING ★★★★
A STYLISH, CONTEMPORARY RIVERSHIP FOR A REALLY WELL-ORGANISED CRUISE.

Operator Viking River Cruises	**Passenger beds** 106
Built 2014	**Sit outside (real) balcony** No
Registry Switzerland	**French (open-air) balcony** Yes
Identification number N/A	**Approximate cabin size (sq m)** 14–28
Length (m) 135.0	**Lift (elevator)** Yes
Number of decks (excluding sun deck) 3	**Rivers sailed** Douro

BERLITZ'S RATINGS		
	Possible	Achieved
Hardware	100	76
Accommodation	100	76
Cuisine	100	72
Service	100	73
Miscellaneous	100	74
OVERALL SCORE 371 points out of 500		

VIKING HERMOD ★★★★
CHOOSE THIS STYLISH, CONTEMPORARY RIVERSHIP FOR A REALLY WELL-ORGANISED CRUISE.

Operator Viking River Cruises	**Passenger beds** 190
Built 2014	**Sit outside (real) balcony** Yes
Registry Switzerland	**French (open-air) balcony** Yes
Identification number ENI 07001977	**Approximate cabin size (sq m)** 12.5–41
Length (m) 135.0	**Lift (elevator)** Yes
Number of decks (excluding sun deck) 3	**Rivers sailed** Rhône

BERLITZ'S RATINGS		
	Possible	Achieved
Hardware	100	84
Accommodation	100	84
Cuisine	100	75
Service	100	76
Miscellaneous	100	77
OVERALL SCORE 396 points out of 500		

VIKING HLIN ★★★★
ONE OF A SERIES OF VIKING 'LONGSHIPS', EACH NAMED AFTER A NORSE GOD.

Operator ....Viking River Cruises
Built 2014
Registry .... Switzerland
Identification number ....ENI 07002001
Length (m) 135.0
Number of decks (excluding sun deck) 3

Passenger beds 190
Sit outside (real) balcony .... Yes
French (open-air) balcony .... Yes
Approximate cabin size (sq m) 12.5–41
Lift (elevator) .... Yes
Rivers sailed .... Rhine, Main, Danube

BERLITZ'S RATINGS		
	Possible	Achieved
Hardware	100	84
Accommodation	100	84
Cuisine	100	75
Service	100	76
Miscellaneous	100	77
OVERALL SCORE 396 points out of 500		

VIKING IDI ★★★★
CHOOSE THIS STYLISH CONTEMPORARY RIVERSHIP FOR A VERY WELL-ROUNDED CRUISE.

Operator ....Viking River Cruises
Built 2014
Registry .... Switzerland
Identification number ....ENI 07001992
Length (m) 135.0
Number of decks (excluding sun deck) 3

Passenger beds 190
Sit outside (real) balcony .... Yes
French (open-air) balcony .... Yes
Approximate cabin size (sq m) 12.5–41
Lift (elevator) .... Yes
Rivers sailed .... Danube, Rhine, Main

BERLITZ'S RATINGS		
	Possible	Achieved
Hardware	100	84
Accommodation	100	84
Cuisine	100	75
Service	100	76
Miscellaneous	100	77
OVERALL SCORE 396 points out of 500		

VIKING IDUN ★★★★

THIS STYLISH VESSEL IS GREAT FOR A WELL-ORGANISED CRUISE.

Operator .... Viking River Cruises	**Passenger beds** 190
Built 2012	**Sit outside (real) balcony** .... Yes
Registry .... Switzerland	**French (open-air) balcony** .... Yes
Identification number .... ENI 07001951	**Approximate cabin size (sq m)** 12.5–41
Length (m) 135.0	**Lift (elevator)** .... Yes
Number of decks (excluding sun deck) 3	**Rivers sailed** .... Danube

BERLITZ'S RATINGS

	Possible	Achieved
Hardware	100	84
Accommodation	100	81
Cuisine	100	75
Service	100	76
Miscellaneous	100	77

OVERALL SCORE 393 points out of 500

VIKING INGVI ★★★★

THIS STYLISH RIVERSHIP WILL LAUNCH YOU ON A WELL-ORGANISED CRUISE.

Operator .... Viking River Cruises	**Passenger beds** 190
Built 2014	**Sit outside (real) balcony** .... Yes
Registry .... Switzerland	**French (open-air) balcony** .... Yes
Identification number .... MMSI 269057465	**Approximate cabin size (sq m)** 12.5–41
Length (m) 135.0	**Lift (elevator)** .... Yes
Number of decks (excluding sun deck) 3	**Rivers sailed** .... Rhine

BERLITZ'S RATINGS

	Possible	Achieved
Hardware	100	84
Accommodation	100	84
Cuisine	100	75
Service	100	75
Miscellaneous	100	77

OVERALL SCORE 395 points out of 500

VIKING JARL ★★★★

GOOD CHOICE FOR A WELL-PROGRAMMED, FIRST-RATE RIVER CRUISE ON A STYLISH VESSEL.

Operator .... Viking River Cruises	Passenger beds 190
Built 2013	Sit outside (real) balcony .... Yes
Registry .... Switzerland	French (open-air) balcony .... Yes
Identification number .... ENI 07001970	Approximate cabin size (sq m) 12.5–41
Length (m) 135.0	Lift (elevator) .... Yes
Number of decks (excluding sun deck) 3	Rivers sailed .... Rhine, Main, Danube

BERLITZ'S RATINGS		
	Possible	Achieved
Hardware	100	84
Accommodation	100	84
Cuisine	100	76
Service	100	76
Miscellaneous	100	77
OVERALL SCORE 396 points out of 500		

VIKING KADLIN NYR

ONE OF A SERIES OF VIKING 'LONGSHIPS', EACH NAMED AFTER A NORSE GOD.

Operator .... Viking River Cruises	Passenger beds 190
Built 2016	Sit outside (real) balcony .... Yes
Registry .... Switzerland	French (open-air) balcony .... Yes
Identification number .... MMSI 211686470	Approximate cabin size (sq m) 12.5–41
Length (m) 135.0	Lift (elevator) .... Yes
Number of decks (excluding sun deck) 3	Rivers sailed .... Seine

BERLITZ'S RATINGS		
	Possible	Achieved
Hardware	100	NYR
Accommodation	100	NYR
Cuisine	100	NYR
Service	100	NYR
Miscellaneous	100	NYR
OVERALL SCORE NYR points out of 500		

VIKING KARA NYR

ONE OF A SERIES OF VIKING 'LONGSHIPS', EACH NAMED AFTER A NORSE GOD.

Operator ....Viking River Cruises	Passenger beds.. 190
Built 2016	Sit outside (real) balcony......................... Yes
Registry .... Switzerland	French (open-air) balcony .... Yes
Identification number .... MMSI 269057477	Approximate cabin size (sq m) 12.5–41
Length (m) 135.0	Lift (elevator)... Yes
Number of decks (excluding sun deck).....3	Rivers sailed................ Rhine, Main, Danube

BERLITZ'S RATINGS

	Possible	Achieved
Hardware	100	NYR
Accommodation	100	NYR
Cuisine	100	NYR
Service	100	NYR
Miscellaneous	100	NYR
OVERALL SCORE NYR points out of 500		

VIKING KVASIR ★★★★

THIS SUPERBLY DESIGNED, COMFORTABLE, CONTEMPORARY SHIP IS A WINNER.

Operator ....Viking River Cruises	Passenger beds.. 190
Built 2014	Sit outside (real) balcony......................... Yes
Registry .... Switzerland	French (open-air) balcony .... Yes
Identification number ....ENI 07001981	Approximate cabin size (sq m) 12.5–41
Length (m) 135.0	Lift (elevator)... Yes
Number of decks (excluding sun deck)......3	Rivers sailed................ Rhine, Main, Danube

BERLITZ'S RATINGS

	Possible	Achieved
Hardware	100	83
Accommodation	100	83
Cuisine	100	75
Service	100	76
Miscellaneous	100	77
OVERALL SCORE 394 points out of 500		

VIKING LEGEND ★★★★

THIS RIVERSHIP IS AN EXCELLENT CHOICE FOR A GOOD-QUALITY CRUISE.

Operator .... Viking River Cruises	**Passenger beds** 190
Built 2009	**Sit outside (real) balcony** .... No
Registry .... Switzerland	**French (open-air) balcony** .... Yes
Identification number .... ENI 07001911	**Approximate cabin size (sq m)** 14–15.5
Length (m) 135.0	**Lift (elevator)** .... Yes
Number of decks (excluding sun deck) 3	**Rivers sailed** .... Danube

BERLITZ'S RATINGS

	Possible	Achieved
Hardware	100	75
Accommodation	100	68
Cuisine	100	73
Service	100	74
Miscellaneous	100	74

OVERALL SCORE 364 points out of 500

VIKING LIF ★★★★

CHOOSE THIS STYLISH CONTEMPORARY RIVERSHIP FOR AN EXCELLENTLY ORGANISED CRUISE.

Operator .... Viking River Cruises	**Passenger beds** 190
Built 2013	**Sit outside (real) balcony** .... Yes
Registry .... Switzerland	**French (open-air) balcony** .... Yes
Identification number .... ENI 07001983	**Approximate cabin size (sq m)** 12.5–41
Length (m) 135.0	**Lift (elevator)** .... Yes
Number of decks (excluding sun deck) 3	**Rivers sailed** .... Rhine, Main, Danube

BERLITZ'S RATINGS

	Possible	Achieved
Hardware	100	84
Accommodation	100	83
Cuisine	100	75
Service	100	76
Miscellaneous	100	77

OVERALL SCORE 395 points out of 500

VIKING LOFN ★★★★

ONE OF A SERIES OF VIKING 'LONGSHIPS', EACH NAMED AFTER A NORSE GOD.

Operator ....Viking River Cruises	**Passenger beds**..190
Built 2015	**Sit outside (real) balcony**.......................Yes
Registry ....Switzerland	**French (open-air) balcony** ....Yes
Identification number ....IMO 1342177	**Approximate cabin size (sq m)** 12.5–41
Length (m) 135.0	**Lift (elevator)**..Yes
Number of decks (excluding sun deck)......3	**Rivers sailed**...............Rhine, Main, Danube

BERLITZ'S RATINGS

	Possible	Achieved
Hardware	100	84
Accommodation	100	84
Cuisine	100	75
Service	100	76
Miscellaneous	100	77

OVERALL SCORE 396 points out of 500

VIKING MAGNI ★★★★

THIS IS A GREAT CHOICE FOR A STYLISH, CONTEMPORARY CRUISE.

Operator ....Viking River Cruises	**Passenger beds**..190
Built 2013	**Sit outside (real) balcony**.......................Yes
Registry ....Switzerland	**French (open-air) balcony** ....Yes
Identification number ....ENI 07001972	**Approximate cabin size (sq m)** 12.5–41
Length (m) 135.0	**Lift (elevator)**..Yes
Number of decks (excluding sun deck)......3	**Rivers sailed**...............Rhine, Main, Danube

BERLITZ'S RATINGS

	Possible	Achieved
Hardware	100	84
Accommodation	100	84
Cuisine	100	75
Service	100	76
Miscellaneous	100	77

OVERALL SCORE 395 points out of 500

VIKING MANI ★★★★

ONE OF A SERIES OF VIKING 'LONGSHIPS', EACH NAMED AFTER A NORSE GOD.

Operator	Viking River Cruises	Passenger beds	190
Built	2015	Sit outside (real) balcony	Yes
Registry	Switzerland	French (open-air) balcony	Yes
Identification number	ENI 07002003	Approximate cabin size (sq m)	12.5–41
Length (m)	135.0	Lift (elevator)	Yes
Number of decks (excluding sun deck)	3	Rivers sailed	Rhine

BERLITZ'S RATINGS

	Possible	Achieved
Hardware	100	84
Accommodation	100	84
Cuisine	100	75
Service	100	76
Miscellaneous	100	77

OVERALL SCORE 396 points out of 500

VIKING MIMIR ★★★★

ONE OF A SERIES OF VIKING 'LONGSHIPS', EACH NAMED AFTER A NORSE GOD.

Operator	Viking River Cruises	Passenger beds	190
Built	2015	Sit outside (real) balcony	Yes
Registry	Switzerland	French (open-air) balcony	Yes
Identification number	MMSI 269057518	Approximate cabin size (sq m)	12.5–41
Length (m)	135.0	Lift (elevator)	Yes
Number of decks (excluding sun deck)	3	Rivers sailed	Rhine, Main, Danube

BERLITZ'S RATINGS

	Possible	Achieved
Hardware	100	84
Accommodation	100	84
Cuisine	100	75
Service	100	76
Miscellaneous	100	77

OVERALL SCORE 396 points out of 500

VIKING MODI ★★★★
ONE OF A SERIES OF VIKING 'LONGSHIPS', EACH NAMED AFTER A NORSE GOD.

Operator ....Viking River Cruises	**Passenger beds**.......................................190
Built 2015	**Sit outside (real) balcony**.......................Yes
Registry ....Switzerland	**French (open-air) balcony** ....Yes
Identification number ....IMO 171008	**Approximate cabin size (sq m)** 12.5–41
Length (m) 135.0	**Lift (elevator)**..Yes
Number of decks (excluding sun deck)......3	**Rivers sailed**...............Rhine, Main, Danube

BERLITZ'S RATINGS

	Possible	Achieved
Hardware	100	84
Accommodation	100	84
Cuisine	100	75
Service	100	76
Miscellaneous	100	77

OVERALL SCORE 396 points out of 500

VIKING NERTHUS ★★★★
ONE OF A SERIES OF VIKING 'LONGSHIPS', EACH NAMED AFTER A NORSE GOD.

Operator ....Viking River Cruises	**Passenger beds**.......................................190
Built 2015	**Sit outside (real) balcony**.......................Yes
Registry ....Switzerland	**French (open-air) balcony** ....Yes
Identification number ....N/A	**Approximate cabin size (sq m)** 12.5–41
Length (m) 135.0	**Lift (elevator)**..Yes
Number of decks (excluding sun deck)......3	**Rivers sailed**..........Various European rivers

BERLITZ'S RATINGS

	Possible	Achieved
Hardware	100	84
Accommodation	100	84
Cuisine	100	75
Service	100	76
Miscellaneous	100	77

OVERALL SCORE 396 points out of 500

VIKING NJORD ★★★★

THIS STYLISH VESSEL IS A GOOD CHOICE FOR A WELL-ORGANISED CRUISE EXPERIENCE.

Operator ....Viking River Cruises	**Passenger beds**.. 208
Built 2012	**Sit outside (real) balcony** .... Yes
Registry .... Switzerland	**French (open-air) balcony** .... Yes
Identification number ....ENI 07001955	**Approximate cabin size (sq m)** 12.5–41
Length (m) 135.0	**Lift (elevator)**.. Yes
Number of decks (excluding sun deck)......3	**Rivers sailed**.................................... Danube

BERLITZ'S RATINGS

	Possible	Achieved
Hardware	100	83
Accommodation	100	81
Cuisine	100	75
Service	100	76
Miscellaneous	100	77

OVERALL SCORE 392 points out of 500

VIKING ODIN ★★★★

A STYLISH CHOICE FOR A WELL-PROGRAMMED, FIRST-RATE RIVER CRUISE.

Operator ....Viking River Cruises	**Passenger beds**.. 208
Built 2012	**Sit outside (real) balcony** .... Yes
Registry .... Switzerland	**French (open-air) balcony** .... Yes
Identification number ....ENI 07001950	**Approximate cabin size (sq m)** 12.5–41
Length (m) 135.0	**Lift (elevator)**.. Yes
Number of decks (excluding sun deck)......3	**Rivers sailed**.... Danube, Rhine, Main, Mosel

BERLITZ'S RATINGS

	Possible	Achieved
Hardware	100	84
Accommodation	100	81
Cuisine	100	75
Service	100	75
Miscellaneous	100	77

OVERALL SCORE 392 points out of 500

VIKING OSFRID NYR

ONE OF A SERIES OF VIKING 'LONGSHIPS', EACH NAMED AFTER A NORSE GOD.

Operator .... Viking River Cruises	**Passenger beds** 106
Built 2016	**Sit outside (real) balcony** .... Yes
Registry .... Portugal	**French (open-air) balcony** .... Yes
Identification number .... N/A	**Approximate cabin size (sq m)** 14–28
Length (m) 80.0	**Lift (elevator)** .... Yes
Number of decks (excluding sun deck) 3	**Rivers sailed** .... Douro

BERLITZ'S RATINGS		
	Possible	Achieved
Hardware	100	NYR
Accommodation	100	NYR
Cuisine	100	NYR
Service	100	NYR
Miscellaneous	100	NYR
OVERALL SCORE NYR points out of 500		

VIKING PRESTIGE ★★★★

CHOOSE THIS RIVERSHIP FOR A FINE-QUALITY, WELL-ORGANISED CRUISE EXPERIENCE.

Operator .... Viking River Cruises	**Passenger beds** 184
Built 2011	**Sit outside (real) balcony** .... No
Registry .... Switzerland	**French (open-air) balcony** .... No
Identification number .... ENI 07001942	**Approximate cabin size (sq m)** 14–15.5
Length (m) 135.0	**Lift (elevator)** .... Yes
Number of decks (excluding sun deck) 3	**Rivers sailed** .... Danube, Rhine, Main

BERLITZ'S RATINGS		
	Possible	Achieved
Hardware	100	76
Accommodation	100	66
Cuisine	100	74
Service	100	75
Miscellaneous	100	73
OVERALL SCORE 364 points out of 500		

VIKING RINDA ★★★★
CHOOSE THIS STYLISH, CONTEMPORARY RIVERSHIP FOR A WELL-PROGRAMMED CRUISE.

Operator ....Viking River Cruises	**Passenger beds**...190
Built 2013	**Sit outside (real) balcony**........................ Yes
Registry .... Switzerland	**French (open-air) balcony** .... Yes
Identification number ....ENI 07001966	**Approximate cabin size (sq m)** 12.5–41
Length (m) 135.0	**Lift (elevator)**... Yes
Number of decks (excluding sun deck)......3	**Rivers sailed**...Seine

BERLITZ'S RATINGS

	Possible	Achieved
Hardware	100	84
Accommodation	100	84
Cuisine	100	75
Service	100	76
Miscellaneous	100	77
OVERALL SCORE 396 points out of 500		

VIKING ROLF ★★★★
ONE OF A SERIES OF VIKING 'LONGSHIPS', EACH NAMED AFTER A NORSE GOD.

Operator .... Switzerland	**Passenger beds**...190
Built 2015	**Sit outside (real) balcony**........................ Yes
Registry .... Switzerland	**French (open-air) balcony** .... Yes
Identification number .... MMSI 211686460	**Approximate cabin size (sq m)** 12.5–41
Length (m) 135.0	**Lift (elevator)**... Yes
Number of decks (excluding sun deck)......3	**Rivers sailed**...Seine

BERLITZ'S RATINGS

	Possible	Achieved
Hardware	100	84
Accommodation	100	84
Cuisine	100	75
Service	100	77
Miscellaneous	100	77
OVERALL SCORE 397 points out of 500		

VIKING SKADI ★★★★

THIS STYLISH VESSEL PROVIDES A COMFORTABLE, WELL-ORGANISED CRUISE.

Operator .... Viking River Cruises	**Passenger beds** 190
Built 2013	**Sit outside (real) balcony** .... Yes
Registry .... Switzerland	**French (open-air) balcony** .... Yes
Identification number .... ENI 07001960	**Approximate cabin size (sq m)** 12.5–41
Length (m) 135.0	**Lift (elevator)** .... Yes
Number of decks (excluding sun deck) 3	**Rivers sailed** .... Rhine, Main, Danube

BERLITZ'S RATINGS

	Possible	Achieved
Hardware	100	84
Accommodation	100	84
Cuisine	100	75
Service	100	77
Miscellaneous	100	77

OVERALL SCORE 397 points out of 500

VIKING SKIRMIR ★★★★

ONE OF A SERIES OF VIKING 'LONGSHIPS', EACH NAMED AFTER A NORSE GOD.

Operator .... Viking River Cruises	**Passenger beds** 190
Built 2015	**Sit outside (real) balcony** .... Yes
Registry .... Switzerland	**French (open-air) balcony** .... Yes
Identification number .... ENI 07002018	**Approximate cabin size (sq m)** 12.5–41
Length (m) 135.0	**Lift (elevator)** .... Yes
Number of decks (excluding sun deck) 3	**Rivers sailed** .... Rhine, Main, Danube

BERLITZ'S RATINGS

	Possible	Achieved
Hardware	100	84
Accommodation	100	84
Cuisine	100	75
Service	100	77
Miscellaneous	100	77

OVERALL SCORE 397 points out of 500

VIKING TIALFI NYR

ONE OF A SERIES OF VIKING 'LONGSHIPS', EACH NAMED AFTER A NORSE GOD.

Operator ....Viking River Cruises	**Passenger beds**..190
Built 2016	**Sit outside (real) balcony**........................Yes
Registry ....Switzerland	**French (open-air) balcony** ....Yes
Identification number ....MMSI 211686440	**Approximate cabin size (sq m)** 12.5–41
Length (m) 135.0	**Lift (elevator)**...Yes
Number of decks (excluding sun deck)......3	**Rivers sailed**..Rhine

NEW RIVERSHIP

BERLITZ'S RATINGS

	Possible	Achieved
Hardware	100	NYR
Accommodation	100	NYR
Cuisine	100	NYR
Service	100	NYR
Miscellaneous	100	NYR

OVERALL SCORE NYR points out of 500

VIKING TOR ★★★★

A SUPERBLY DESIGNED, VERY COMFORTABLE CONTEMPORARY SHIP FOR GREAT CRUISING.

Operator ....Viking River Cruises	**Passenger beds**..190
Built 2013	**Sit outside (real) balcony**........................Yes
Registry ....Switzerland	**French (open-air) balcony** ....Yes
Identification number ....ENI 07001962	**Approximate cabin size (sq m)** 12.5–41
Length (m) 135.0	**Lift (elevator)**...Yes
Number of decks (excluding sun deck)......3	**Rivers sailed**...............Danube, Rhine, Main

BERLITZ'S RATINGS

	Possible	Achieved
Hardware	100	84
Accommodation	100	84
Cuisine	100	75
Service	100	76
Miscellaneous	100	77

OVERALL SCORE 396 points out of 500

VIKING TORGIL ★★★★
THIS STYLISH RIVERSHIP WILL LAUNCH YOU ON A WELL-ROUNDED CRUISE.

Operator	Viking River Cruises	Passenger beds	106
Built	2014	Sit outside (real) balcony	Yes
Registry	Switzerland	French (open-air) balcony	Yes
Identification number	N/A	Approximate cabin size (sq m)	14–28
Length (m)	135.0	Lift (elevator)	Yes
Number of decks (excluding sun deck)	3	Rivers sailed	Douro

BERLITZ'S RATINGS		
	Possible	Achieved
Hardware	100	76
Accommodation	100	76
Cuisine	100	72
Service	100	73
Miscellaneous	100	74
OVERALL SCORE 371 points out of 500		

VIKING VAR ★★★★
THIS STYLISH VESSEL IS A GOOD CHOICE FOR A WELL-ORGANISED CRUISE.

Operator	Viking River Cruises	Passenger beds	190
Built	2013	Sit outside (real) balcony	Yes
Registry	Switzerland	French (open-air) balcony	Yes
Identification number	ENI 07001963	Approximate cabin size (sq m)	12.5–41
Length (m)	135.0	Lift (elevator)	Yes
Number of decks (excluding sun deck)	3	Rivers sailed	Danube, Rhine, Main

BERLITZ'S RATINGS		
	Possible	Achieved
Hardware	100	84
Accommodation	100	84
Cuisine	100	75
Service	100	76
Miscellaneous	100	77
OVERALL SCORE 396 points out of 500		

VIKING VE ★★★★

ONE OF A SERIES OF VIKING 'LONGSHIPS', EACH NAMED AFTER A NORSE GOD.

Operator .... Viking River Cruises	**Passenger beds** 190
Built 2015	**Sit outside (real) balcony** .... Yes
Registry .... Switzerland	**French (open-air) balcony** .... Yes
Identification number .... ENI 07002015	**Approximate cabin size (sq m)** 12.5–41
Length (m) 135.0	**Lift (elevator)** .... Yes
Number of decks (excluding sun deck) 3	**Rivers sailed** .... Rhine, Main, Danube

BERLITZ'S RATINGS

	Possible	Achieved
Hardware	100	84
Accommodation	100	84
Cuisine	100	75
Service	100	76
Miscellaneous	100	77

OVERALL SCORE 396 points out of 500

VIKING VIDAR ★★★★

ONE OF A SERIES OF VIKING 'LONGSHIPS', EACH NAMED AFTER A NORSE GOD.

Operator .... Viking River Cruises	**Passenger beds** 190
Built 2015	**Sit outside (real) balcony** .... Yes
Registry .... Switzerland	**French (open-air) balcony** .... Yes
Identification number .... ENI 07002019	**Approximate cabin size (sq m)** 12.5–41
Length (m) 135.0	**Lift (elevator)** .... Yes
Number of decks (excluding sun deck) 3	**Rivers sailed** .... Rhine, Main, Danube

BERLITZ'S RATINGS

	Possible	Achieved
Hardware	100	84
Accommodation	100	84
Cuisine	100	75
Service	100	76
Miscellaneous	100	77

OVERALL SCORE 396 points out of 500

VIKING VILI ★★★★
ONE OF A SERIES OF VIKING 'LONGSHIPS', EACH NAMED AFTER A NORSE GOD.

Operator .... Viking River Cruises	**Passenger beds**.. 190
Built 2015	**Sit outside (real) balcony**........................ Yes
Registry .... Switzerland	**French (open-air) balcony** .... Yes
Identification number .... MMSI 269057519	**Approximate cabin size (sq m)** 12.5–41
Length (m) 135.0	**Lift (elevator)**.. Yes
Number of decks (excluding sun deck)......3	**Rivers sailed**............... Rhine, Main, Danube

BERLITZ'S RATINGS		
	Possible	Achieved
Hardware	100	84
Accommodation	100	84
Cuisine	100	75
Service	100	76
Miscellaneous	100	77
OVERALL SCORE 396 points out of 500		

VIKTORIA ★★★+
A WELL-DESIGNED VESSEL WITH SOME ATTRACTIVE FEATURES.

Operator .... Various tour operators	**Passenger beds**.. 180
Built 2004	**Sit outside (real) balcony**......................... No
Registry .... Germany	**French (open-air) balcony** .... Yes
Identification number ....ENI 09948008	**Approximate cabin size (sq m)** 16
Length (m) 126.7	**Lift (elevator)**... No
Number of decks (excluding sun deck)......3	**Rivers sailed**............... Danube, Main, Rhine

BERLITZ'S RATINGS		
	Possible	Achieved
Hardware	100	73
Accommodation	100	74
Cuisine	100	61
Service	100	61
Miscellaneous	100	71
OVERALL SCORE 340 points out of 500		

VIRGINIA ★★

THIS OLDER, VERY SMALL RIVERSHIP DELIVERS A BASIC, LOW-COST CRUISE.

Operator .... Shearings Holidays	**Passenger beds**.................................... 106
Built 1965	**Sit outside (real) balcony** .... No
Registry .... Netherlands	**French (open-air) balcony** .... No
Identification number .... ENI 6000051	**Approximate cabin size (sq m)** ....N/A
Length (m) 67.5	**Lift (elevator)**... No
Number of decks (excluding sun deck)......3	**Rivers sailed**............................Rhine, Mosel

BERLITZ'S RATINGS		
	Possible	Achieved
Hardware	100	36
Accommodation	100	36
Cuisine	100	40
Service	100	42
Miscellaneous	100	44
OVERALL SCORE 198 points out of 500		

VISTA FIDELIO ★★★+

GO FOR THE LOW-PRICE AND ITINERARY RATHER THAN THE FOOD.

Operator .... 1AVista Travel	**Passenger beds**.................................... 148
Built 1995	**Sit outside (real) balcony** .... No
Registry .... Switzerland	**French (open-air) balcony** .... No
Identification number ....ENI 04801210	**Approximate cabin size (sq m)** 14
Length (m) 110.0	**Lift (elevator)**... No
Number of decks (excluding sun deck)......3	**Rivers sailed**............... Rhine, Main, Danube

BERLITZ'S RATINGS		
	Possible	Achieved
Hardware	100	47
Accommodation	100	44
Cuisine	100	51
Service	100	51
Miscellaneous	100	53
OVERALL SCORE 246 points out of 500		

VIVALDI ★★★

THIS STANDARD, FRENCH-STYLE RIVERSHIP PROVIDES A GOOD-VALUE CRUISE.

Operator	CroisiEurope	**Passenger beds**	176
Built	2009	**Sit outside (real) balcony**	No
Registry	France	**French (open-air) balcony**	No
Identification number	ENI 01823464	**Approximate cabin size (sq m)**	12
Length (m)	110.0	**Lift (elevator)**	Yes
Number of decks (excluding sun deck)	3	**Rivers sailed**	Danube, Rhine, Main

BERLITZ'S RATINGS		
	Possible	Achieved
Hardware	100	65
Accommodation	100	58
Cuisine	100	58
Service	100	57
Miscellaneous	100	60
OVERALL SCORE 298 points out of 500		

WILLIAM SHAKESPEARE ★★★★

EXUDES BRITISH-STYLE WITH BOTH CONTEMPORARY AND TRADITIONAL FEATURES.

Operator	Riviera Travel	**Passenger beds**	140
Built	2014	**Sit outside (real) balcony**	Yes
Registry	Switzerland	**French (open-air) balcony**	Yes
Identification number	ENI 02335914	**Approximate cabin size (sq m)**	14–22
Length (m)	110.0	**Lift (elevator)**	Yes
Number of decks (excluding sun deck)	3	**Rivers sailed**	Rhine, Main, Danube

BERLITZ'S RATINGS		
	Possible	Achieved
Hardware	100	81
Accommodation	100	77
Cuisine	100	75
Service	100	75
Miscellaneous	100	77
OVERALL SCORE 385 points out of 500		

Credits

Photo Credits

Cover Credits

Berlitz/Insight Guide Credits

Distribution

UK
Dorling Kindersley Ltd
A Penguin Group company
80 The Strand, London, WC2R 0RL
sales@uk.dk.com

United States
Ingram Publisher Services
1 Ingram Boulevard, PO Box 3006
La Vergne, TN 37086-1986
ips@ingramcontent.com

Australia and New Zealand
Woodslane
14 Apollo St, Warriewood
NSW 2102 Australia
info@woodslane.com.au

Worldwide
Apa Publications (Singapore) Pte
7030 Ang Mo Kio Avenue 5
08-65 Northstar @ AMK
Singapore 569880
apasin@signet.com.sg

© 2016 Apa Publications (UK) Ltd/
Douglas Ward
All Rights Reserved

Printed by CTPS-China

First Edition 2014
Second Edition 2016

www.berlitzpublishing.com

Written by
Douglas Ward

Edited by
Sarah Clark and Clare Peel

Picture edit by
Tom Smyth

Production by
Rebeka Davies

TELL US YOUR THOUGHTS

Dear Cruiser,

I hope you have found this edition
of Berlitz River Cruising in Europe
enjoyable, informative and useful. If
you have any comments or queries, or
experiences of cruising that you would
like to pass on, or perhaps some ideas
for subjects that could be included
in the future, I would be delighted to
read them.

The world of cruising is evolving
fast and certain facts and figures may
have changed since this guide went to
print, so if you have found any outdated
information in these pages, please do
let me know and I will make sure it is
corrected as soon as possible.

You can write to me by email at:
bertliz@apaguide.co.uk

Or by post to:
Berlitz Publishing
PO Box 7910
London SE1 1WE
United Kingdom

Thank you,
Douglas Ward

Index